Kicking and Screaming

Kicking and Screaming

a memoir of madness
and martial arts

MELANIE D. GIBSON

SHE WRITES PRESS

Published 2020
Printed in the United States of America
Print ISBN: 978-1-64742-028-4
E-ISBN: 978-1-64742-029-1
Library of Congress Control Number: 2020910155

For information, address:
She Writes Press
1569 Solano Ave #546
Berkeley, CA 94707

Interior design by Tabitha Lahr

She Writes Press is a division of SparkPoint Studio, LLC.

For Margaret Blakely, AJ Wall IV, and Meredith Oney. Thanks for bringing out the best in me and occasionally putting up with the worst.

Contents

PROLOGUE   Fear of Flying Kicks xi

PART ONE: WHITE BELT

CHAPTER 1   Obligatory Rock Bottom. 3

CHAPTER 2   Kicking Up Dust in Snyder, Texas 8

CHAPTER 3   Child of Darkness 16

CHAPTER 4   Coming Out of the Crazy Closet. 22

CHAPTER 5   Out of My Head, into the Dojang 29

PART TWO: YELLOW BELT (Sort Of)

CHAPTER 6   New Ventures 41

CHAPTER 7   Brunch and a Boyfriend. 49

CHAPTER 8   Green Belt Test. 57

PART THREE: GREEN BELT AND GREEN BELT / BLUE TIP

CHAPTER 9   Splats and Sparring 65

CHAPTER 10   Didn't You Know the First Six Months
                        Don't Count?. 73

CHAPTER 11   Blue Tip Test. 80

CHAPTER 12   The Click. 84

CHAPTER 13   Goodbye . . . Just Kidding! 90

CHAPTER 14   Blue Belt Test 96

PART FOUR: BLUE BELT AND BLUE BELT / RED TIP

CHAPTER 15   The Amazing Walking Uterus 103

CHAPTER 16   Home Life. 109

CHAPTER 17   Getting Fat Shamed as a Size Four 113

PART FIVE: RED BELT AND RED BELT / BLACK TIP

CHAPTER 18   Welcome to Red Belt Class 125

CHAPTER 19   Obligatory Nervous Breakdown. 130

CHAPTER 20   Will This Be on the Test?. 138

CHAPTER 21   Frustration and Resignation. 145

CHAPTER 22   Conversations in the Jewelry Box. 151

CHAPTER 23   Down but Not Out for the Count 157

CHAPTER 24   New Year's Reservations 163

CHAPTER 25   Sparring with Demons. 169

CHAPTER 26   Adult Class 173

CHAPTER 27   Vices 178

CHAPTER 28   Black Belt Candidate. 183

PART SIX: BO DAN TO BLACK BELT

CHAPTER 29   Sucker Punched. 193

CHAPTER 30   Aftermath 199

CHAPTER 31   I Hate Taekwondo . . . for a Day or So 203

CHAPTER 32   And Then We Had Cake 208

CHAPTER 33   Don't Let It Escalate 212

CHAPTER 34   Pain in the Ass 218

CHAPTER 35   Baby Got Piriformis 223

CHAPTER 36   Growth Spurt 229

CHAPTER 37   Exorcism 236

CHAPTER 38   Final Exam 243

EPILOGUE   The Beginning. 251

PROLOGUE

Fear of Flying Kicks

"Um . . . no, I'll break a hip," I said, raising an eyebrow and tilting my head.

The imposing, baritone-voiced master teaching the taekwondo class sighed. Rather than leaping over the stack of pads the master had set up for flying side kick practice, I'd hopped daintily to the left of it. Ah, flying side kick, the bane of my existence, the barometer of my physical strength and grace . . . or lack thereof. I was eight months into my taekwondo training, long having graduated from the white belt class to the more advanced color belt class but still wondering what I'd gotten myself into.

"It's okay. I know you're scared, but you need to try again," the master said.

Wait a minute, hold up, *what*? I didn't want to own up to it, but maybe I *was* scared. I was scared of being less than perfect. I was scared of being exposed as a fraud and failing at the one thing that had finally stuck and saved me from the hellish mental mess I'd created for myself.

Why couldn't I just jump?

How often do we stop short of taking a leap? How often do we let the fear of failure derail us before we even get one foot off the ground? I've faced larger challenges than jumping over a pile of soft kicking pads: I've done two successful stints in grad school, bought a home with my own hard-earned money, and survived the pain of disappointment and heartbreak time and again. I've learned to be my own white knight. I was doing what women fought for the right to do for generations and was living a life that seemed problem-free, at least from an outsider's perspective. So why couldn't I do what comes so easily to children? Why couldn't I take that leap?

The weight of the world gets heavier as the years click by: the obligations, the regrets, the triumphs and mishaps. Worry and logic perch on opposite shoulders and make their seductive arguments. My ability to trust myself had diminished to the point where my heels were metaphorically and physically dug into the ground.

Perhaps this was my chance to redeem myself. I'd spent most of my life wallowing in self-loathing and self-pitying anger, and that mindset had held me back from taking chances and creating a fulfilling life for myself. All right, let's do this.

My classmates and I trotted back to the front of the training room, panting and shuffling our feet. It was my turn to try the flying side kick again. The master gave me an encouraging nod. I crouched, glared at the pile of pads in front of me, took a running start, and leapt. . . .

I wrote a memoir because I am a bad liar. Reality begs to be recorded, and it's often much more interesting than fiction. My story threads began to weave themselves together in my brain when I realized with horror I'd woken up as the heroine of a romantic comedy.

The thing is, I *hate* romantic comedies. Not only are they tiresomely predictable, rife with bad acting and sappy clichés, but they always made me feel really damn bad about being single. And yet here I was, juggling rudimentary pieces of the equation:

1. I was a perpetually single and lonely overachiever.
2. I was a career girl in a metropolitan area.
3. My pursuits of education and work were much more successful than my disastrous dating life.
4. I bought a cute home in the trendy part of town.
5. I fell for a smooth talker with a motorcycle and bad credit shortly after I started taekwondo.
6. I was at a very low emotional point when I found my salvation in taekwondo. Cue the montage of me doing knuckle push-ups, doubling over trying not to throw up while my heart is going all Keith Moon in my chest, crying at home alone in my condo, being meticulously corrected by my instructors, yelling and kicking at focus pads and preteens, gazing in the mirror at new abdominal muscles, and zoning out in an Epsom salt bath (with bubbles and a glass of wine, of course).

Crap. It was the perfect storm.

No! No! *No*! When I imagine my life in celluloid, it's full of long witty conversations and quick camera zooms, and narrated with wry voiceovers set against ominously cheery Motown music, classic rock, and gangster rap. My dream directors would be Wes Anderson for the saturated colors, Martin Scorsese for his choice of soundtrack and delicious depictions of violence, the Coen brothers for quirky characters, or some cool independent director who most definitely does *not* have a romantic comedy on his or her résumé.

I don't even look like a romantic comedy heroine: I'm short with the face of a Soviet Bloc mail-order bride and the bulky shoulders of a swimmer. I live in a spacious condo in Fort Worth, Texas, rather than some tiny walk-up in Manhattan. I don't have a job at a fancy magazine or a public-relations firm. My aforementioned condo is painted in bright Mexican-inspired colors with Day of the Dead skulls and Greek evil-eye charms decorating the rooms. Not an Audrey Hepburn poster in sight. I'm not aching for a baby, and at this point in my life, I'd rather spend whatever money I'd blow on a wedding on an over-the-top trip to Hawaii . . . alone.

Have I made my point?

Although my story doesn't fit neatly into the romantic comedy genre, I don't think I've quite hit the murder-and-cocaine quota required for a Scorsese film. I'll have to work on that.

Look, I'm not going to sugarcoat this. I don't portray myself as the poor innocent victim or the saintly selfless heroine. Most of my problems have stemmed not from external forces but rather from the depths of the crossed wires in my own chemically imbalanced brain. To be frank: I'm crazy, and my biggest challenges have stemmed from what being crazy makes me do. I'm a shifty, mistrusting loner with addictions and demons to spare. I have spent years alternately isolating myself or clinging to abusive, dysfunctional relationships. I don't have a tight network of friends whom I could count on to take me to the airport early in the morning or pick me up from the hospital late at night. I'm the antiheroine and sometimes the villain, but I'm no cautionary tale. There is a happy ending.

I wrote this memoir because my story would no longer let me ignore it. The life-changing lessons I learned from taekwondo were too profound to be kept a secret. For most of my life, I had unsuccessfully sought ways to quiet my troubled mind and undo the damage it had created. I looked to taekwondo as a salve for my wounds. What I found was a path to inner peace and a mode for my real self to emerge. This is a story of passion and pursuit, grief and triumph, and love and discovery. I sincerely hope I will make you laugh, reflect, and sign up for taekwondo classes. Most of all, I hope my story prompts you to ask yourself if you're happy with your life's path, and I hope your answer is yes.

PART ONE:

WHITE BELT

CHAPTER 1

Obligatory Rock Bottom

I'm no sommelier, but experience has taught me a thing or two about wine pairing. Along with wine, I also appreciate a nice, biting glass of whiskey. In March of 2013, my favorite thing to pair with Jack Daniel's was the antianxiety drug Klonopin. I was thirty-three years old and had developed a nightly ritual of drinking whiskey for dinner and sobbing incoherently into the phone to my worried parents. I was lonely, inconsolably sad for reasons I'd half forgotten, and trapped inside self-destructive thinking cultivated by a lifetime of fear, doubt, and self-loathing. I was constantly promising my parents I wouldn't kill myself but secretly wishing I could. I would end my evening by gulping down a Klonopin to knock myself out and shut down my reeling mind. I couldn't even enjoy the smooth burn and sweet-and-sour flavor of the whiskey anymore.

Klonopin is a sneaky drug. I was prescribed it for general anxiety disorder and was instructed to take it "as needed." The trouble was I was anxious every damned day and therefore needed my drug just as frequently. Take the drug sparingly, and it's like hitting a reset button on a computer—your system powers down, you hibernate, and then you can go about the next day feeling refreshed, albeit a bit forgetful. Take it too late in the evening, and you wake up with blurry vision, and you're falling asleep on the freeway while driving to work. Take it too often, and you develop an addiction that reveals itself in crippling insomnia when you try to stop taking it. The days began to blur together, and I dreaded the sleepless nights that would follow if I tried to go without my magic pill.

I'm a little embarrassed to admit now that this near total loss of my mind was triggered by a failed relationship, at least on a superficial level. It was so short-lived that I don't think it could even be classified as a true relationship. At the beginning of 2013, I had been on a few dates with a handsome restaurateur with a lilting Spanish accent and a sweet smile. This was early into my second round of online dating, brought on by an enraged reaction to being dumped via text message by another guy I wasn't even that attracted to and had just dated because I was lonely. When I met this new fellow, my heart was fluttering, and my hopes were high that he could solve my problems and cure me of my crushing sadness and loneliness.

Things seemed to be promising at the beginning of this new "relationship." My first date with Salad Guy (he owned a salad and sandwich shop) was at a romantic, candlelit restaurant and was filled with silly grins and conversations about our favorite books. We giggled over the menu and spooned portions of our entrees onto each other's plates so we could taste everything. We couldn't decide between two of the desserts, so he flipped a dime, and we ordered chocolate cookies and ice cream. I pocketed the dime and treasured it like a talisman. We finally parted ways that night when we were too tired to continue our lingering conversation. I was infatuated immediately. In hindsight I know I certainly didn't love him, but I clung tightly to the idea of him as a means to escape my feelings of worthlessness.

A few weeks after my first date with Salad Guy, one of the most humiliating nights of my life led me to the best decision I've ever made.

"I don't want any drama!" Salad Guy snapped as I gasped and pleaded and wrung my hands in apologetic fervor. Oh no! My perfect plan to have a perfect relationship with the perfect guy was crumbling before me!

Sigh. . . .

Here's what happened: He had been a little distant for the past few days, blaming his mood on the demands of his work schedule and the pressure of opening a new restaurant. He had even canceled our plans for Valentine's Day. I had decided to confront him at his workplace, because that *always* works out well.

Of course, I wasn't going to confront him directly. I was just going to look pretty and innocent until he broke down and apologized for ignoring me. It was a flawless plan!

He didn't seem very happy to see me when I pranced into the shop. As we walked down opposite sides of the salad bar, he made a sandwich for me and suddenly blurted out that he might have to move thirty-five miles away to Dallas for his job.

Great, another man leaving me because he's "busy with work." Not again! Not on my watch! I was *not* going to be passed over again and let a man value me less (at least in my troubled mind) than his job. When he announced his plans, I left the sandwich on the counter, turned on my heel, and stormed out. I stumbled onto the bustling streets of downtown Fort Worth as my eyes were blinded with tears and the glare of the city lights. I immediately regretted what I'd done and scurried back into the restaurant to be greeted by his *I-don't-want-any-drama* declaration.

I never saw him again.

How could I have let this coveted specimen get away? I *had* to find a way to get back into his good graces again. I spent the next few weeks ruminating over that night, making shaky wishes, whispering desperate prayers, and berating myself for being so impulsive and stupid to walk out instead of simply listening to him. When I wasn't mired in guilt, I blamed him and fumed with self-righteous indignation that he, Mr. Intolerant and Not Listening to Reason, had rejected poor innocent *me*. I scoured the internet for stories of people who had gone through breakups and had experienced the miracle of reconciliation, drugging myself with false hope (along with Klonopin) that if I changed myself inside and out, that if I just closed my eyes and wished hard enough, if I prayed the right magical prayer, he would show up at my door with arms full of flowers and forgiveness. *Maybe* I would take him back.

I was batshit crazy.

I lost over ten pounds in two weeks and was eventually cornered privately by several people at work who'd noticed my sunken eyes, sallow skin, and baggy pants. I lied when asked if I was sick and brushed off their concern with the claim that I had merely given up junk food. I felt a constant burning sensation on the right side of my clenching jaw, and my stomach reacted violently to any food.

And that's how I found myself downing Klonopin with whiskey and crying to my parents about how much I hated my life but promising them (regretfully) that I wouldn't end it.

I finally became so exhausted from torturing myself that I stopped longing for a reconciliation with Salad Guy and decided to focus on healing and improving my life. I was tired of bouncing from one failed relationship to the next and tired of hating myself for acting so needy and desperate. Therapy and medication were keeping me from completely going over the edge, but *something* was still missing.

One lonely night, I remembered a conversation I'd had with my mother a few weeks earlier, back when I was happily obsessed with my new catch.

"If it doesn't work out with this new guy I just met," I'd said on the phone to her, "I'm going to start taekwondo again."

I had taken taekwondo lessons as a child in my hometown of Snyder, a small Texas town about 250 miles west of the Dallas–Fort

Worth Metroplex. I had always liked it and told myself that one day when the time was right, I would take it up again. During one of my nightly drunken rages in my self-imposed isolation, the thought popped into my mind again: Why not start now?

Through a few clicks on my computer, I discovered what could only be attributed to fate, the law of attraction, or as we say in Texas, "a God thing."

My childhood grandmaster, who had overseen the branch school where I'd studied taekwondo in Snyder, operated his main taekwondo school five miles from my home in Fort Worth.

CHAPTER 2

Kicking Up Dust in Snyder, Texas

Growing up in the stark moonscape of West Texas allows an inordinate amount of time for contemplation, especially for the introverted child I was. West Texas reflects silence and space, an enormous sky swabbed with orange-and-pink sunsets, and dusty cotton fields baked in the blinding sun. In the vast depths of the western horizon are adventures created from nothing but imagination and blue-eyed aching dreams. It was in the lonely little West Texas town of Snyder where I first fell in love with taekwondo.

In the clichéd-romantic-comedy-movie version of this story, I have a tobacco-chewing, football-watching father I call "Daddy" and a doughy, loud, bottle-blonde, Bible-quoting mother I call "Mama." "Daddy" wipes the oil field dust off his boots at the end of the day, and "Mama" washes his jeans that have the telltale outline of a can of snuff on the back pocket. We subsist on a steady diet of sweet tea, giant dill pickles, and chicken spaghetti casserole, which is . . . well, don't ask. We never miss a high school football game, and all of our "kin" live just a few blocks away. The rest of this story would be peppered with quaint sayings and sage advice from my country-fried parents juxtaposed against my big-city problems. You couldn't help but read our dialogue with the ridiculous Foghorn Leghorn Civil War accent only heard in bad Hollywood impersonations of Texans.

That's not how it happened at all.

I only say "y'all" when I'm being silly. I didn't buy cowboy boots until I was thirty years old. I talked my way into a college scholarship with a tongue-in-cheek essay about being an atypical West Texan. Although I'm always one beer away from a more pronounced Texas drawl, I still tend to sound less like a native and more like a foreign actor who's lived in the United States for so long that the accent has become a weird, unrecognizable hybrid.

Dad was a mercurial art instructor at the local community college, and he only watched football when his alma mater, the University of Oklahoma, was playing. Mom was small, dark, and angular, a dry-witted product of the East Coast who was more comfortable with sarcasm than with sentiment. The only "chicken spaghetti" we ever ate was my half-Italian mother's homemade chicken cacciatore. Like their siblings, my parents had scattered across the United States before settling in Texas, where they had me and my brother, their babies who eventually turned them into die-hard Texans (still without the accents).

For most of my childhood, I was content holing up in my room with books and drawing paper until my parents decided to make good on one of my requests.

"Mom and I signed you up for taekwondo lessons," Dad said one night as we sat at our yellow Formica kitchen table eating meatloaf and baked potatoes under the dying glow of a Texas sunset. I was ten years old and perfectly happy in my self-imposed exile of reading and drawing. "We're all going to take lessons as a family. Doesn't that sound fun? You said you wanted to learn karate."

For a moment I panicked. True, I *had* mentioned in passing that I wanted to learn karate (as a kid, karate was the only martial art I'd ever heard of), but I never thought my parents would follow through on it. Even today my childhood desire to learn a martial art still befuddles me. I don't know how that thought originated. I was a painfully shy child who preferred to be alone rather than play with other children, whom I didn't like very much anyway. I was never bullied, at least not physically, so I had no need to learn how to defend myself. I was never what I'd consider a tomboy either, but I had a hidden tough streak and an athleticism that had so far remained dormant in my dreaded elementary school PE classes. I had a fight in me waiting to happen, and perhaps it manifested itself in that desire to learn a martial art.

But back to my dinnertime internal turmoil. I wasn't so much frightened of doing taekwondo as I was annoyed that my parents had made this decision without my express consent, a pet peeve that has followed me into the buttoned-up corporate world. As a younger child, I had been signed up against my will for soccer and basketball, and I was abysmal at both. I *do* remember being excited about the turquoise-blue Converse sneakers my mom bought me for basketball, which was the one thing I enjoyed as I miserably loped back and forth across the echoing court well behind the kids who actually had talent.

Well, "against my will" might be a bit dramatic. I don't remember being asked whether I wanted to do sports, but I also don't remember saying no. In hindsight, I figure my mom wanted to put me in an activity that would keep me active and healthy. Or maybe she wanted me to have some social interaction with other kids, which I certainly wasn't pursuing on my own. Maybe this time with this new thing called taekwondo, things would be different. I calmly considered my fate and agreed to watch a class the next night.

The taekwondo school, or *dojang*, was wedged in with businesses and law offices on the quaint Snyder town square. Inside was one large, long room with a small changing room and restroom in the back. The front of the dojang was bulging with trophies and photographs, and the rest of the space was covered in thin dark carpet with mirrors and a ballet barre on opposing walls. My family and I perched on a raised platform near the door and held our breaths as students of all belt ranks were ordered to line up facing the mirrors, above which the United States and South Korean flags loomed regally.

After bowing to the flags and to the instructors, the students began warming up, loudly counting in Korean as they did push-ups and stretches. Everyone was "Mr. This" and "Miss That" and answered their instructors with "Yes, sir!" and "Yes, ma'am!" The discipline and formality instantly appealed to my organized, studious brain. The students then moved on to kicks, with the instructors and older black belts holding pads for targets. The forceful yells and slaps of feet against the pads punctuated the clear night air. The students ended the night with self-defense techniques, during which one partner would move in with a kick or punch while the other partner defended with blocks, strikes, and takedowns. By the end of the class, I was staring with glee at the sweating students. This looked like a lot more fun than soccer or basketball!

When we returned home, my dad and I danced around on the beige carpet of our living room. "They did this!" we shouted, waving slow-motion knife-hands at each other. "And then they did this!" I kicked at my dad as he pretended to block. We fell over laughing while my mom and brother looked on worriedly, wondering if they actually had to go through with it. I couldn't wait to begin training, although I did face a minor setback when I mentioned my new hobby to a friend at school.

"My mom says that's a waste of time and money!" my fifth-grade friend Sarah snarled at me. The day before, I had excitedly told her my family was going to start taekwondo lessons, and I was surprised and confused when she began relentlessly harassing me about it. I pictured her parents gossiping about me over the dinner table and felt betrayed. How was it any of her mother's business what we did with our money? My "friend" acted as if she were trying to save me from some terrible fate.

"They'll punch you and kick you!" she shouted, her voice echoing across the cool taupe-colored bricks of the elementary school hallway. "Don't come crying to me when you have a broken leg!"

"That's not going to happen! They're really nice!" I protested, baffled at her hostility and refusal to reason with me.

Sarah was the type of persuasive, persistent, possessive bully I would later repeatedly attract in the forms of female friends and boyfriends, with a few exceptions. She became angry when I befriended a girl she didn't like. She bragged about wanting to run away from home, pestering me on several occasions to help her write the notes we were going to leave for our parents. I would roll my eyes and mutter an excuse about having to finish my homework before I finally escaped her house to trudge into the sanctity of my bedroom, feeling exhausted and henpecked. I wasn't disappointed about the prospect of spending my evenings without her company.

Interestingly enough, after I'd started taekwondo lessons, Sarah would prance around the boys at school shouting, "I can kick higher than your head!" and slinging her leg into the air like a Radio City Music Hall Rockette. I ignored her and looked forward to my evening classes. It amused and saddened me to realize she might have actually been jealous. After that experience, I vowed not to let my excitement show too much lest someone I trusted ridicule me for it.

Sarah and I wordlessly cut ties in junior high and maintained a pleasant but cool friendliness whenever we saw each other over the years. I never understood why she would latch on to my interests (taekwondo, band, theater) with an odd mix of fascination and sneering hatred. She was attractive, athletic, and very smart. She was from one of the wealthiest families in town. Why was she so hostile and always trying to act tough? Why couldn't she be happy with her own life without having to stomp all over my choices? We were both proof that storms often lurk below a smooth surface.

Okay, so Sarah did get a few things right. My childhood instructors never laid a hand on me, but as an adult I've become much more rough-and-tumble. My arms and legs are bruised on a weekly basis, I've been thrown to the ground so hard I've seen stars (don't worry, I've returned the favor many times), and I actually high-fived one of my sparring partners the first time he kicked me in the head, but I swear, there's a lot of love behind our smackdowns.

As a child I *loved* taekwondo. I loved the discipline and the slow, meticulous metronome of progress. The brief meditation we did at the beginning of class was magical. I kept my eyes straight ahead at all times, answering my teachers with militant precision. I excelled at forms (also known as *poomsae* in Korean), which are patterns of kicks, blocks, and hand strikes designed to simulate self-defense and hone technique. The lyrical beauty of the movement, the expressive focus, and the mind-body connection of taekwondo seeped into the marrow of my bones and would later guide me through college dance training and decades of yoga.

My instructors were Dave and Maria Weber, a married couple with a daughter around my age, a cotton farm, and a strong devotion to their Christian faith. They were gentle and always smiling, even when they ordered us to do knuckle push-ups when we were late to class. Our dojang was considered a branch school under the leadership of Grandmaster Kim, an ominous force who would sweep into town for our monthly belt testing and yearly tournament.

Grandmaster Kim operated his large school in Fort Worth, Texas, but he made the time to oversee our tests in Snyder, as he did with his other branch schools. (I never knew his home base was in Fort Worth until I sought out taekwondo training as an adult.) He sat austerely behind the table set up for the testing judges, glaring at us until we looked away. Behind Grandmaster's austerity was a mischievous twinkle in his eye and a dry sense of humor that I could only appreciate later as an adult. I was in awe of him and a little bit afraid of him. Come to think of it, I still am.

The only thing about taekwondo I hated with sheer choking dread was free sparring. Free sparring, more commonly just called "sparring," is free-form fighting. There are rules to follow (no punches to the face or kicks below the belt, for example), but it is not prescribed self-defense with a clear attacker and defender like one-step sparring (I'll explain that later). You just put on pads—or not—and go for it.

Most of my childhood sparring matches were spent standing frozen in place and praying for it to be over as my opponent repeatedly kicked my chest protector. The gracefulness I exhibited in forms and the precision I used during kicking or self-defense practice went out the window. I couldn't think of what to do next after an attack, and that sent me into a tailspin of panic. My clockwork, lockstep brain simply refused to improvise on the spot. Sparring brought to light everything I was terrified people would find out about me: weakness, inability to think cleverly, *imperfection*. My loathing of sparring began to overshadow everything else I loved about taekwondo, so much so that by the time my family stopped going altogether, I felt a sense of relief.

These days as an adult taekwondo practitioner, I actually look forward to the raw brutality and delicate art of sparring, especially after a long day of wearing my prim corporate persona. The mix of endorphins and exhaustion is intoxicating. Sparring is a perfect vehicle for practicing the art of being present. I simply can't over-think. The threat of being kicked in the head is a good motivator to stay alert.

Sparring is not so much improvisation as it is using intuition. I usually have some preplanned strategies, but I also have to be able to read my partner and adjust to them in the moment. All of these nuances were, of course, lost on me when I was a child. It turned out I didn't have much time to discover the more enjoyable parts of sparring. The year I turned twelve and had earned the red tip for my blue belt, just over the halfway mark toward black belt, my sparring days came to an end.

In September of 1991, three significant things happened. My dad got a promotion and was suddenly required to spend much more time at work. Shortly afterward, his beloved older sister died of a brain aneurysm at age forty, which sent our entire family reeling. I also started junior high, where I became quickly engulfed in the frenzy of friends and extracurricular activities. I don't remember a collective decision being made as a family to stop going. We just . . . stopped going.

There was no longer a place for taekwondo in our lives. I didn't think too much about it. I was at a new school and in a new phase of my life. I preferred to spend my time drawing cartoons, obsessing over my parents' Beatles records, and hanging out with the band and theater kids. Until I started taekwondo again in my thirties, I didn't recognize the giant void that had been inside me for so long.

When I left taekwondo, I lost myself for the next twenty-two years.

CHAPTER 3

Child of Darkness

Coincidentally, my mental state started slowly unraveling after my family stopped going to taekwondo and as I entered adolescence, but the seeds of self-destruction had been planted much earlier. The irony isn't lost on me that the name Melanie means "darkness." For as long as I can remember, I've had a dark sensibility about me. As a young child I was anxious, quick to anger, and painfully sensitive to perceived injustices. I would feel sad for no apparent reason, and I didn't know how to express to my family what I was feeling. I turned inward, preferring to read and draw rather than play with other children.

Early on I learned to be ashamed of myself. While we were a loving family, cruel teasing was a common blood sport among us all. I'm not sure why it took such a hold of us, and I can't say whether this was a direct cause of my dangerous perfectionism or just coincided with it. I was in on it too and now regret the callous things I said to my parents and brother. It was a hard habit to break as I got older. I think my parents did the best they could with the resources and knowledge they had. I know they never meant to purposefully hurt me. . . . That being said, whether it was nature or nurture, I was an easily embarrassed and wounded child, so teasing and humiliation didn't bode well for me.

If I expressed my anger at my parents' taunts, I was ridiculed even further or banished to my room. I was chastised for being "moody" and "melodramatic." Every embarrassing story or mockery sent me further into my shell. Sometimes I would sit at the small desk in my room and sink my teeth into my forearm to release my overwhelming frustration and anger. I would chomp down hard and fast, feeling my saliva coating my skin and experiencing a deep sense of relief with the rush of pain. The more emotionally wounded and ashamed I felt, the harder I bit. Then I would look at the pink indentation of my teeth with a mix of shock and amusement. Shame and frustration took on different forms as I got older.

Childhood anxiety gave way to the depression that hit full force when I was a teenager. I began to hate myself more and more for not being what I deemed "good enough," although on the surface I looked like an accomplished kid: I got good grades, I was attractive, and I participated in several activities. Yet I couldn't shake the inexplicable waves of sadness and frustration. I didn't even feel I was worthy of being sad. I was in good health and had a loving family, teasing notwithstanding. How dare I feel sad! My parents tried to be supportive, but they simply didn't know how to deal with the demon dwelling in their child. A sadness lacking an obvious cause is a slippery beast to catch. Mental illness is an elusive fiend that does not discriminate among its casualties.

As a teen I began to exhibit what could be classified as the volatile characteristics of bipolar disorder, or possibly borderline personality disorder, although the suicidal thoughts didn't erupt until college. I struggled with regulating my emotional outbursts—namely desperate crying jags and fits of rage—and my relationships came unglued as I lost my sense of identity and any remaining confidence. I was never officially diagnosed with borderline personality disorder as I was with bipolar disorder, but when my therapist suggested it as a possibility at age thirty-two, things finally started to make sense. It seemed to manifest itself most poisonously in my relationships with people.

As antisocial and quiet as I was, I desperately craved that golden egg of attention. Attention represented the love I was incapable of providing myself. My achievements meant nothing if I didn't have the approval of others. Although I latched on to people in hopes they would provide me with some validation, I was a master of self-sabotage. I sulked when I was ignored by friends or romantic interests, but I wasn't interested in putting forth the effort to make myself approachable and enjoyable to be around. Although no one ever said it to my face, I know I developed a reputation for being an overly emotional, clingy weirdo.

At the beginning of my freshman year in high school, my sadness and self-loathing were directed squarely at my body. I've always been small and never weighed more than about 110 pounds as a teenager, but sometime during the summer between eighth and ninth grade, I had convinced myself I was unacceptably fat. I've always had a little bit of a belly, a thin spare tire around the lower abdomen while the rest of my body was (and still is) toned and fit. Everything that was wrong in my life stemmed from that little piece of chub. If only I could have a flat stomach, I believed I would finally be happy. I wanted to slice that piece of chub off with a chainsaw.

A few years later, a full-blown eating disorder snuck up on me while I was minding my own business being depressed. I had gone through a breakup with a slightly older boy who decided the best way to end things was to simply stop taking my phone calls. I was devastated, which was my usual reaction to rejection. We only went out a few times, but, as I had with Salad Guy at the beginning of this story (flip back to Chapter One if you don't remember), I latched my hopes of identity, accomplishment, and acceptance on the whims of this poor guy and made him responsible for my feelings of self-worth.

I channeled my disappointment about being unceremoniously dumped into perfecting my body through hours of exercise.
I'd already built a solid foundation of body hatred by my junior year
of high school, so fueling all my rage and loneliness into what I
hated the most made perfect sense. Each day during that summer
before my senior year, I would swim, run, lift weights, and skate
for hours on Rollerblades around the Snyder elementary school
and junior high. (It was the late nineties, and Rollerblading was
still cool back then, so shut up.) My period stopped for about three
months, and dark circles were permanently etched under my eyes.
But damn it, that little piece of chub around my stomach was still
there, and that boy certainly wasn't calling me.

For most of the summer, I stuck to a highly regimented diet
of lean protein, fruit, and vegetables. I was coasting along with my
exercise addiction when binge eating came calling. One night after
two hours of skating, I plopped down at the kitchen table and ate
a bowl of cereal . . . and then another . . . and then I wolfed down
a peanut butter and jelly sandwich so quickly I couldn't taste it.
The rush of the secret high was alluring. I'd found another way to
numb my pain. I still maintained my exercise routine, but I began
shoveling in food late at night, even sneaking down to the base-
ment to swipe snacks from the freezer.

The more I binged, the more I exercised, and throughout this
cycle I became angrier that while the rest of my body was becoming
more lean and muscular, my flabby little stomach wouldn't flatten
out. Late at night in my room (either before or after a binge), I
would yank my shirt up to my chin and scowl at my body in disgust. Having moved on from biting my forearm, as I had when I
was upset as a child, I would rake my nails across my white flesh
or sometimes beat my pudgy little stomach with my fist, leaving
red marks on my skin. I felt horrified and scared, but I knew I
deserved my punishment.

My secret eating disorder followed me closely throughout
the rest of senior year, peaked in college, and began to slow down

into my twenties. Once I hit my thirties, I no longer felt the urge to binge to soothe myself, at least not the way I had when I was younger. I still get a rush from overindulging and, on the other end of the spectrum, still haven't quite kicked the latent urge to restrict food when I'm stressed, but the desperation for numbness eventually dissipated.

Meanwhile my emotional hang-ups, demons, and doubts from high school clung tightly to my side like wayward guardian angels as I entered college. While I never did drugs, I binge drank long before I turned twenty-one. I would stay out until three or four in the morning partying and then drag myself to my eight o'clock classes. I had drinking buddies, but few friendships have survived from those years. No one knew how much pain I was in, and I didn't think to tell anyone. I was lonely, self-loathing, and very much lost. I spent many days alone in my dorm room, perched on the thick windowsill (thankfully behind reinforced sealed glass) and looking down onto the street, wondering why I was so damned lonely and completely inept at making friends and, of course, hating myself for being fat and ugly. The thought of suicide became warm, tangible, and constant.

As a college sophomore, I had no idea what was wrong with me and didn't know how to ask for help. I tried going to the university counseling center, which was manned by inexperienced graduate counseling students, and at the time, I felt like I was being pushed away because I didn't have anything substantial to justify my sadness. I'd never experienced horrific abuse, nor was I in imminent danger of killing myself, at least not during those few minutes I spent talking to a counselor. All I did was beat my stomach and scream in my car and daydream about suicide once or twice a week, so I guess that didn't count. The clinic called me three months later to ask how their service was. I hung up on them. I couldn't even get being crazy right.

Killing myself would be an escape from the crying jags and inconsolable despair I still couldn't explain. It would mean I could escape the fact that I really wasn't that talented at anything other than changing my major after each grand-scale emotional meltdown (five times as an undergrad, twice as a grad student). Killing myself would mean that I could escape the fact that I had neither close friends nor romantic partners and lacked the social skills to acquire new ones.

Killing myself would also mean I could finally escape the fact that my fucking stomach would never be flat, and that I couldn't stop stuffing my face during secret, shameful binges. Death would mean the little voice in my head—the one that was becoming louder and louder as it reminded me I was ugly, fat, worthless, and incapable of being loved—might finally get its wish.

CHAPTER 4

Coming Out of the Crazy Closet

I'd been living in the Crazy Closet for years. Since I never did get around to killing myself in college, I figured I'd stay in the Crazy Closet for a while longer and keep up the façade of achievement. During my many mood swings and crying jags, I would angrily brush aside delicate suggestions by my parents to seek therapy. Although I never expressed my full anger or sadness in front of anyone—other than sobbing over the phone to my mom and dad—I threw frequent fits of rage when the frustration of daily loneliness and self-doubt became too oppressive. I punched many pillows in private and thought that weekly bouts of screaming and crying and banging the steering wheel of my car and cursing God as I drove down the highway were perfectly normal.

Still, I maintained a face of accomplishment to the outside world. I had earned a bachelor's degree in English and a master's degree in library science by the time I was twenty-four. I went on to establish a solid career and returned to school for an MBA at age thirty. I bought a home when I was thirty-two. Meanwhile, outside of school and work, my mental state was deteriorating faster and faster, especially when it came to matters of the heart.

One of my biggest triggers for suicidal thoughts was rejection by men. Although by age sixteen I'd already experienced the pain and shame of a boy rejecting me, that particular breakup—the one that triggered my summertime exercise addiction and binge eating—cemented the way I would respond to relationship disappointments for the next twenty years. I lost my self-respect and hung all my worth on the opinions of other people, especially romantic interests. My personality was an odd mix of vulnerability and manipulative volatility. My naiveté led my trusting heart to be crushed on numerous occasions, although that didn't make me an innocent victim. If someone failed to worship me as I saw fit, I would respond with a murderous temper tantrum.

I *hated* being ignored. In relationships I would quickly fall into a pattern of infatuation, whirlwind romance, and then feelings of fury and betrayal when the men, like clockwork (well, according to my Crazy Cuckoo Clock), stopped calling. I was "that girl," the one who would leave notes on cars, drive by houses, and send long nonsensical e-mails. The self-hatred and self-blame would remain until I could lure another man into my needy, sticky clutches. I devalued friendships and overloaded my stock in romantic relationships. Friends meant nothing because they couldn't make me happy the way I thought a boyfriend could.

After graduate school, I grew more and more isolated. While I never dabbled in drugs, other than my accidental addiction to Klonopin, I often looked to alcohol and occasionally restricting or bingeing food in order to dull the pain of being a failure at relationships. No man would ever want to date me, and I couldn't even conceive of a man wanting to marry me. At my lowest points, I actually resented having a family who loved me, because I couldn't take my own life without destroying theirs. Still, I refused to seek counseling. Just like school and work, I figured I could handle my problems on my own . . . until I couldn't.

At the end of 2010, when I was thirty-one, an epic, desperate, sob-filled breakdown finally pushed me to take action. Tension and pain had been building for months, and as usual, a stupid trivial event over a romantic interest set off the explosion. I had met up for drinks with a man I'd been pursuing off and on for years but never dated. I'd gotten completely smashed and sloppily poured out my declarations of attraction and desire to have a relationship with him. While he was typically gruff and abrasive, in this instance he looked into my drunken, glassy eyes with pity as he gently but firmly told me it wasn't going to happen. He made sure I got home safely and suggested we shouldn't spend any more time together. I melted into tears when I was alone in my bedroom, leaving a black stain of runny mascara that has never fully washed out of the particular set of white sheets that were on my bed at the time. I still think about that moment every time I use those sheets. I wasn't so much upset about letting that particular man slip through my fingers as I was drowning in deeply rooted feelings of worthlessness and despair.

As I lay on my bed twisting and crying after he left, I heard a disembodied, gravelly voice in my head snap, "Kill yourself! Do it now!" Great, not only was I a pathetic crazy loser incapable of being loved, but now I was possessed by some asshole demon who had nothing better to do on a Sunday evening than crawl into my head and stir up trouble. Spooked into sobriety, I sat up immediately and wiped away my tears. This was it. This was the night I could die if I let the demon take over. I'd been playing a game of suicidal chicken with myself for years, but I'd never taken it this seriously before. I grabbed my phone and called a crisis hotline. The gentle voice on the other end asked me if I was in danger of hurting myself.

"No," I answered. "I'm okay now." And for the first time, I believed it. The nice person on the phone put me in touch with a therapist named Ramona, a sweet woman with curly white hair, an endearing smile, and an adorable little dog named Charlie who would sleep at her feet during our sessions. She was kind and curious and, when necessary, called me on my crap. She became a dear confidante, coach, and cheerleader for the next seven years. I shared with her my deepest pain and greatest desires, and I worked very hard to harness my thoughts and emotions and make better choices. I'd been hiding for so long I'd forgotten who I was. But before that happened, I still had that pesky matter of suicidal thinking to deal with.

Despite the strides I'd made with dealing with my depression and anxiety through counseling, the urge to kill myself didn't go away. About six months after I began seeing Ramona, she referred me to a psychiatrist named Dr. Kapoor. He was a thin, soft-spoken Indian man who would gaze at me over his glasses with grand-fatherly reproach. He listened patiently as I rambled about my sadness and mood swings and presented me with a diagnosis of depression, bipolar disorder, and general anxiety disorder.

At first, I wanted to hide my diagnoses under Dr. Kapoor's pile of messy file folders. If they remained unknown, perhaps they would fade into the ether. I figured I had depression, but I was in denial of anything beyond that. Dr. Kapoor prescribed me Wellbutrin for the depression, Geodon as a mood stabilizer, and Klonopin to soften the anxiety. The medications did not com-pletely stop my periods of sadness or bubbling mania (or the meltdown I had after Salad Guy dumped me for bringing the "drama"), but they kept me from going over the edge into the madness of violent crying jags and fantasies of suicide, and that was a new and welcome change.

I still didn't want to admit any of this was happening, though, especially the fact that I'd been prescribed a mood stabilizer, also known as an antipsychotic. Antidepressants are almost fashionable now, but an anti*psychotic*? That's . . . well, that's for crazy people. That's not me. It can't be me.

Is that me?

Wait, isn't this supposed to be the climax of this story? Isn't this the part where I narrowly survive a suicide attempt and spend the next chapters describing the quirky friends I meet at the mental hospital? Is this too boring? Am I a failure at being mentally ill? Do I have to turn in my crazy card??

Nope. I didn't give you stereotypical Texans, and I'm not going to give you stereotypical crazy. I have no judgment or condemnation for how people individually address their mental conditions. I just handled my mental illness differently from other people and certainly unlike the stereotype that is fed to us through media and pop culture. I always pushed down the crazy in order to keep up appearances. The need for financial stability and job security outweighed the temptation to act out the violence in my head, let myself be engulfed by depression, or gulp down a cocktail of pills. Rent had to be paid, and laundry had to be folded.

Still, I had many early mornings of lying in a puddle on the floor, wearing nothing but a bath towel and tasting the fibers of the carpet as I drooled and cried. I hated myself profusely and, in those moments, often wondered aloud, "Should I drive myself to the emergency room or clean myself up and go to work?" I *always* chose to go to work. There was simply no alternative. No one could know about my darkest moments.

I was all I had. If I crumbled, who would catch me? Taking extended time off from work or school to focus solely on healing would probably have done me a world of good, but who would pay the bills? Who would put gas in the car? Who would buy groceries? Falling apart was not an option. I read stories about people with my same diagnoses, and their lives were cautionary tales of destroyed families, rehab, and financial ruin. That didn't happen to me, mostly due to my own sheer stubbornness.

Relative to other people with mental illnesses, I was quite blessed, although rest assured, being crazy still sucks. I was fortunate to have access to and the finances for mental health resources that are desperately needed by and unfortunately unavailable to far too many people in this country. I was connected with a great counselor, an experienced psychiatrist, and effective medication on the very first shot, not to mention I had health insurance that would help subsidize the aforementioned counselor, doctor, and meds. I held a steady job and was even able to make a successful career change shortly after I started going to therapy and taking medication. I'm one of the lucky ones. I got out alive.

I've been passing as sane for years. I'm *high-functioning* crazy. We get shit done.

The fact that one is capable of having suicidal thoughts disturbs people in a way I can't quite understand. Despite all the melodrama I pulled in relationships, I *never* threatened to kill myself as a ploy to scare someone or get an ex-boyfriend to take me back. I've kept those feelings secret from most people in my life. I've grown accustomed to rolling them around in my mouth and swatting them aside without a thought the way I swipe at mosquitoes on a hot summer night. I'm a little surprised when people gasp with horror and say they'd never dream of even exploring the idea of committing suicide. That's when I shrug, act just as baffled as they are, and distract them with a joke while I change the subject.

Slowly, with my therapist's guidance and the good doctor's drugs, my mental state began to stabilize in my early thirties, and the despair-filled days, rapid-fire disjointed thoughts, and surging feelings of anger or anxiety became less and less frequent. On the very rare occasion suicide has crossed my mind, it's usually brought on by sheer laziness and a desire to get out of doing things I don't want to do, or occasionally just feeling sorry for myself and letting my anxious or depressed thoughts take the wheel. Bill Burr, one of my favorite comedians, once said he wanted to kill himself to get out of making a pumpkin pie for Thanksgiving. My suicidal thoughts are kind of like that.

A terrible thought occurred to me once, long into my recovery: No one would ever see it coming. My suicide, I mean. Never. I would keep up the responsible, funny, polite front until the very end, and there's nothing anyone could do to predict or prevent it. That gives me a strange sense of power and an awful sense of responsibility. The list of people I would hurt is endless, and that burden weighs me down in the safety of reality.

Let's address something: I realize my use of the word "crazy" in reference to my mental illness will offend some people. Mental illness is not something I take lightly. There is a dangerous and pervasive societal stigma against people with mental illness, and far too many sufferers go without proper treatment, which leads to tragic results. I've accepted my diagnoses as an inextricable part of who I am, although I've been very hesitant to share them with anyone but a trusted few. People are quick to judge and slow to understand, which makes traversing the territory of mental illness a lonely endeavor.

Putting my truth in writing rings a bell that cannot be unrung.

I've finally learned to channel my mental illnesses into creative endeavors and can, at least most of the time, sit observantly with them when I know they're rubbing my emotions raw or dragging me back into despair. Sometimes I welcome the waves of depression as a chance to slow down. The mania comes in shorter spurts and feels like a distant static radio voice jabbering in my head, feeding me with insights and ideas. The anxiety is more troublesome, although I've developed ways to handle it over time. It's not all bad. Breakdowns and breakups always seemed to lead to breakthroughs for me. Okay, so many of these major changes were punctuated by hysterical sobbing and dark nights of the soul, but I always came out on top with new opportunities, such as the idea to return to taekwondo.

I've suffered, but I'm not defeated.

I'm a warrior.

CHAPTER 5

Out of My Head, into the Dojang

"A re you interested in lessons for yourself or for your children?" the Korean-accented voice over the phone asked. It was late March 2013. I was still starving myself and having Jack Daniel's and Klonopin dinners after the ill-fated, short-lived relationship with Salad Guy, but I was determined to make a major positive change in my life. By sheer fate (and the internet), I had discovered that Grandmaster Kim—my childhood teachers' grandmaster, who oversaw our branch school in rural Snyder—operated his dojang a little over five miles from my home in Fort Worth. I had been living in the Dallas–Fort Worth Metroplex since 1997 and Fort Worth itself since 2005, but I never knew a remnant of my childhood had always been just down the road.

I couldn't believe I was talking to *the* Grandmaster Kim, a legend in the taekwondo world and a representative of something that had made a huge impact on me as a child. Huddling in a hallway at work and clutching my cell phone to my chest, I snickered silently at the idea of someone actually thinking I was a mother.

"I want lessons for myself," I said breathlessly. "I studied as a child with the Webers in Snyder! I, uh, I remember you from my tests. I want to start again as a white belt!" I didn't remember much other than a few basics from my childhood training, so I figured a figurative and literal fresh start was just what I needed.

Just as when I was ten, I was invited to watch a class before I made my final decision. After I hung up, I rested my hands on a counter in the hallway as I trembled and smiled. This was really happening! I hadn't felt this happy or relieved in years.

The following Monday I drove past a cluster of auto repair shops and an orange-and-white Whataburger, the iconic Texas fast-food joint, to a strip mall on the west side of Fort Worth. The long building was anchored by a tattoo parlor on one end and a rundown sports bar on the other, and the little dojang peeked out from the middle. The neon lights of a greasy spoon diner beckoned from across the parking lot.

The afternoon sun was shining into the small lobby of the dojang. Heart pounding, I poked my head into the side office and did a stiff little bow before I shook Grandmaster Kim's hand. While he now had gray hair and glasses, he still had the commanding expression he'd worn during those childhood belt tests. We made stilted, shy chitchat until we warmed up to each other, reveling in the fact we could both share memories about Snyder taekwondo. I never did watch that class. We ended up talking for two straight hours, jumping from one subject to the next until our voices went dry. He was cheerful, chatty, and had a razor-sharp wit.

"Every morning I wake up, I thank God," Grandmaster said as our conversation slowed down, pointing toward the ceiling and smiling broadly as he turned his face upward.

I blushed with shame as I thought about how I had been slinking around the house, pouting and crying for weeks over yet another guy I'd run off because of my own foolishness. (I'm still talking about Salad Guy from Chapter One—remember him? Yeah, I barely do either.) Grandmaster Kim, meanwhile, had escaped the poverty and terror of North Korea as a child, come to the United States with nothing but a suitcase and a dream, and successfully run his dojang for decades, and not once had he complained or asked for pity. That night I promised myself I would always work hard for him, even when I didn't want to work hard for myself.

"You're nice to talk to. I think you'll make a good black belt," Grandmaster declared as I got up from his office chair to leave. He stood and promptly handed me a stiff white *dobok* (uniform) and a thick white belt, both shrink-wrapped in plastic. Black belt? It hadn't even occurred to me that I would train for a black belt. All I knew at the time was that if I didn't get into the dojang and out of my addled, dangerous mind, I might end up dead. Therapy and medications weren't cutting it anymore. This was my last resort to save my life and my sanity. Black belt? Just let me get past white belt first. Grandmaster gathered some papers and began walking toward the door of his office.

"Wait, I don't know how to tie the belt!" I said anxiously as I clawed at the soft, crinkly package. I still worried about looking stupid, and taekwondo was no exception. With a sigh and a grumble, he expertly wrapped the belt around my waist, yanking the ends and tightening the knot like an exclamation point before he gently shoved me out of his office. I still had to watch videos online to learn how to tie my belt. I wanted everything to be perfect for my first class.

I officially returned from my twenty-two year taekwondo hiatus on the auspicious date of April 1, 2013, April Fools' Day. Perhaps that was fitting, because I'd been playing a hapless fool for years, and now I was making the choice to grow up rather than give up. All day at work I was antsy and distracted as I anticipated my first white belt class. I squirmed during meetings and stared dreamily out the window until my watch ticked to five o'clock. I raced home and paced excitedly around my condo, for once not being lulled into depression by the looming shadows and quiet rooms.

Shaking with excitement, I stripped off my shift dress and four-inch heels; tucked my Gucci purse in the closet as I snatched my wallet; and changed into stretch pants, a sports bra, and a T-shirt. I stuffed my new white belt and dobok into my gym bag and tossed the bag into my car, checking one more time to make sure I hadn't left anything before I slammed down the lid of the trunk. I drove to the dojang, all the while squinting into the hot setting sun and hoping that the school hadn't somehow disappeared from the address I had memorized.

With a bow and a grin, I greeted Grandmaster Kim, bowed again to the United States and South Korean flags as I entered the training room, and practically ran across the green and orange rubber mats to the women's bathroom to change into my dobok, which was still heavily creased from the packaging. My heart raced as my fingers fumbled with the drawstring of the white pants. I caught my eye in the mirror above the small sink and made a silly face at myself. Here we go!

I padded barefoot onto the soft mats and gazed at the photos on the wall. There was a black-and-white poster-sized photo of Grandmaster as a young man, slamming his foot into a hanging bag with an impossibly high flying side kick. There was a young female black belt frozen in a dramatic pose like a tiny fierce goddess as she performed a form at a tournament. There was my childhood instructor, Master Weber from Snyder, just as I remembered him with his glasses and wide smile, winking at me from the long line of photographs of masters and instructors from Grandmaster's school and various branch schools.

"Line up!" Grandmaster barked quietly but forcefully.

"Yes, sir!" I shouted and scrambled into a line with the rest of my classmates. Our small class consisted of a goofy preteen boy with spiky hair; a quiet father and his tiny rambunctious son; a bespectacled middle school boy; and me, a nervous, giddy, thirty-three-year-old female cubicle dweller who was already sweating under the lights and the stiff, thick material of my dobok. We snapped to attention, bowed to the flags, sat down and quietly meditated for a few seconds, and then popped up and bowed to Grandmaster.

After some jumping jacks and stretches to warm up, Grandmaster explained that we would be working on the fundamental stances, blocks, punches, and kicks. My dojang's white belt students practiced two stances, four simple blocks, three punches at different heights, and five basic kicks over and over until the movements were ingrained into their bodies. The techniques seem simple, and it can be tempting to bypass them, but they are absolutely essential to building a solid foundation. Without learning to add and subtract, you can't do calculus. Without learning an effective back stance, you'll lose your balance trying to perform swift and strong defense against an attacker. Without learning an effective low block, you can't quickly deflect a kick during free sparring (which I will refer to in the rest of this book as just "sparring") or perform one of the forms with compelling grace and strength.

White belt training can feel like a slow and plodding process if the student (child or adult) is used to rapid progress and instant payoff. It's doubly trying if the student is the lone adult in a class full of spazzy, inattentive little kids and awkward teenagers who would rather mess around than work. These first few weeks of training are a vulnerable time. Many students lose interest and give up before they really get a taste for taekwondo, what their particular talents and interests are, and what the rewards are for all that hard work.

After Grandmaster was satisfied with our front and back stances, which look respectively somewhat like a yoga Warrior I pose and the typical bent-kneed, angled fighting stance used by boxers and mixed martial arts competitors, he began meticulously demonstrating what we would do with our arms and legs.

Blocks are deceptively difficult, even for advanced students. Sloppy placement or lack of power and follow-through can result in an ineffective defense and a nasty blow to the head or chest. Piece by piece, Grandmaster taught us the four fundamental blocks, illustrating how positioning the shoulders just right and twisting the wrist just so could be the difference between a dud and a powerful, snapping defensive block. We clenched our fists tightly and tried as best we could to move our forearms with power and speed, as much as white belts could anyway. We learned to protect our heads with the angled high block, our chests and abdomens with the twisting inside and outside middle blocks, and our lower torsos and legs with the straight-armed low block.

Kicks were a welcome reprieve from the frustratingly intricate blocks we learned during that first class. I still remembered the basic kicks from my childhood taekwondo training and had taken a smattering of kickboxing aerobics classes at the gym, so I felt more at ease than I had with blocks. We began with straight-legged stretch kicks. A stretch kick requires the student to sling the leg straight into the air and bring it down with force but land with a final softness. While stretch kicks aren't actually used in self-defense, they are great for warming up the body and also for developing powerful axe kicks that can be wielded during sparring. We then practiced front snap kick, which is performed by sharply lifting the knee and then snapping the foot out and up toward an attacker, and finally roundhouse kick. Ah, this felt familiar!

Roundhouse kick proved to be more difficult than I'd thought. This kick requires a sharp pivot of the supporting leg in order to hoist the hips up into the air and pop the target with the top of the kicking foot (or in other circumstances, with the ball of the kicking foot). The thing they don't tell you about this particular kick is that performing it with no shoes or socks will produce a nasty blister on the big toe and ball of the foot of the standing leg until a callus forms over it. I was surprised at the pain of scraping my foot across the mats and prayed quickly for a rough layer of skin to cover my aching feet.

The way we closed my first white belt class was utterly charming. After bowing to the flags, seated meditation, and a final bow to Grandmaster, we applauded and milled around the room, shaking hands and greeting every person in the class with the Korean term for thank you, *gamsahamneda*. Any tension or frustration we may have felt during class was brushed aside. It was our own little *namaste* lovefest after spending an hour kicking and screaming.

"What, you're sweating already? You sure you want to come back?" Grandmaster asked with a smirk as we filed back into the lobby.

"Oh yes, sir, definitely!" I chattered, nodding nervously and bouncing around on my toes.

"Good. Come back tomorrow. Here, you need this." He shoved into my hands a piece of paper that listed the requirements for testing for first degree black belt. The two-sided document was full of swirling black text: lines of Korean terminology, over two dozen kicking combinations, and an impossible number of forms and self-defense techniques.

My eyes skimmed the document as my brain tried in vain to comprehend the fact that if I stuck with my training, I would someday be testing for a black belt. I couldn't worry about that right now. I just knew I *had* to come back. And besides, I had several other belt levels to get through first: orange belt (this was a level added in more recent years), yellow belt, yellow belt with a green tip (denoted by a strip of colored tape), green belt, green with a blue tip, blue belt, blue with a red tip, red belt, red with a black tip, and finally red with two black tips, which is referred to as *bo dan*, roughly translating to "black belt candidate." Wow, that could really be me someday. Let's give this a shot. I folded the paper neatly in half and tucked it into my bag.

After that first night, I knew without a doubt I wanted to be in the dojang, no matter what I was doing or what my belt rank was.

My bones, muscles, and nerves remembered enough from my childhood training that I could quickly incorporate smaller details into my technique. My hands formed tight fists when I punched, I curled my toes back when I popped my leg into a front snap kick, and I was careful to rechamber my kicks just as I remembered from my young training days in Snyder. As when I was a child, I was militant and precise, punctuating the air with my loud *ki-yahps* (yells) and barking a brisk, "Yes, sir!" when given instructions or feedback. It was as if the dormant taekwondo gene in my body was slowly beginning to awaken.

As I attended more classes, I noticed I became more relaxed in my daily life, perhaps due to the endorphin rush of slamming a kick into a practice pad, or simply because I'd found something to pique my interest and motivate me. I woke up feeling excited, especially on one of the three days of the week I had class. I sweated more than I ever had in my life, and I became more conscious of eating well and getting enough sleep. During work, I found myself secretly grinning when I remembered that in a few hours I would get to scrub off my makeup, slip into a clean dobok, and learn with a passion and a hopefulness I hadn't felt in years.

All right, let's get real. In case anyone thinks the white belt months were a 1980s movie montage of me doing push-ups and high kicks and high-fiving other students set to cheesy inspirational music, think again. Good feelings and rising self-esteem aside, those classes were slow, picky, and at times painfully repetitive and boring. Who knew a half inch made such a difference as to where I placed my middle punch? When I first practiced my roundhouse kick, I moved jerkily as I pieced together the kick rather than doing it in one swift movement. I held my breath when I was supposed to exhale, I wobbled in my stances, and for the life of me, I couldn't nail down that subtle wrist twist with the inside-to-outside middle block.

I felt like I was balancing a teetering stack of messy dishes as my body tried to keep track of all the fussy details. I thought I would find comfort in side kick, which was introduced a few weeks after my first class and had been my favorite kick as a child, but I was wrong. Instead of kicking straight out with the blade or side of the foot, which can result in a nice high kick to the face, we were supposed to twist our foot in a cramped flexed position to our knee, poke out our hips, and lock the leg forward with the heel pushing outward and toes pointing down. Although I've come to rely on it as a favorite tool in sparring now, at the time, I was frustrated with all the difficult details. I always dreaded being put in what I called "side kick jail," when Grandmaster would position me at the barre and make me do side kicks over and over again until it was to his liking.

To top it all off, I developed a searing irritation at the tops of my hamstrings whenever I did a kick. Taekwondo was literally a pain in the ass! Thankfully the pain in my hamstrings subsided (for a while anyway), but it was just the first of many injuries. Armed with the application of ice packs, Epsom salts, ibuprofen, and stubborn determination, I continued attending class.

Taekwondo was well-suited to a high-functioning crazy like me. Once again I was mired in the discipline and singular focus I had been lacking for so many years. I never quite got over being a perfectionist, but the extreme pressure I put on myself began to lessen as I continued my training. Performing the trusty old blocks, punches, and kicks was less like riding a bike and more like cracking the spine of an old high school yearbook. I hadn't thought about taekwondo in decades, but when I was reunited with it, I was flooded with joy and fuzzy familiarity.

Being a white belt gave me a chance to start over. I was ready to be fresh and innocent again. I was ready to be humble and forgive myself. For years I had focused on the absence of certain achievements in my life (romance, the perfect body) and could not see the positive side of anything. The anxiety and sadness would still linger as I mastered low block, middle punch, and roundhouse kick, but as it quieted, I knew I had found something special. My true self, which had been buried for decades under darkness, began furiously kicking her way to the surface.

PART TWO:

YELLOW BELT (Sort of)

CHAPTER 6

New Ventures

" I want you to test for green belt next month," Grandmaster murmured as he clasped my fingers and adjusted my knife-hand block a millimeter to the left. It was a month into my training, and my love for taekwondo was heating up along with the May temperatures outside. I had been working very hard, chipping away at my techniques and ignoring the searing blister that developed as I pivoted during roundhouse kicks.

I was still a white belt, but Grandmaster had casually begun introducing more advanced techniques from higher belt levels (knife-hand strikes, side and spin kicks, and two forms) before he dropped this little bombshell on me. Normally students test for one level at a time every few months, but his reasoning was that since I still had a good grasp of the basics from my childhood taekwondo training, I could advance more quickly through the lower ranks. This would include testing for orange belt, a new level that had been added since my childhood training days; yellow belt; yellow belt / green tip; and green belt. I would be performing testing requirements for all four levels rather than just one at the June color belt test.

Suddenly I felt the same rush of panic I'd felt when my father first told me he had signed me up for taekwondo lessons as a child. Wait a minute, this is happening too fast! I can't test for green belt! How am I going to remember all those extra strikes and self-defense techniques and do a *spin kick*? I'm not good enough to test for green belt! I'm not good enough for anything!

Then I calmed down and tried a different tactic I've used when I want to weasel out of something: I crawled all over his logic and asked incessant questions.

"Are you sure that's the right thing?" I asked sweetly as I batted my eyelashes. "I have a lot going on with work. Do you think I'll be able to memorize everything? Can't I just go at a normal pace so I can really get the feel of everything? Have you *seen* my spin kick?" Spin kick, also known as spinning hook kick, is exactly what it sounds like. In an ideal world the taekwondo student whips around, torqueing the upper body downward while slashing through the air with either a straight leg or a more sophisticated snappy hook aimed for the opponent's jaw. In reality most beginner students tentatively turn around in a tight circle with a stiff leg trailing behind halfheartedly through the air rather than doing the more advanced, whip-like spinning hook kick. Guess which version I did?

"You're testing for green belt next month. It will be fine. I'll help you," Grandmaster said, smiling cheerily, but his eyes were firm, shutting down any attempt to argue or beg for mercy. I mumbled a defeated, "Yes, sir," and started mentally ticking off a list of everything I'd have to do at the test:

White belt requirements testing for orange belt: stretch kicks, front snap kick, roundhouse kick, Korean terminology, punches, and blocks . . . okay, I felt comfortable with these.

Orange belt requirements testing for yellow belt: front snap kick, roundhouse kick, side kick, knife-hand blocks and various hand strikes, more terminology . . . Um . . . well, my side kick still wasn't up to snuff, but I could handle these.

Yellow belt requirements testing for green tip: sliding versions of snap kick and roundhouse kick, turning back side kick, the yellow belt form, five one-step sparring techniques (simple self-defense combinations) against a right-hand punch, and a little more terminology . . . Seriously? This was making me nervous, but hey, I'd gotten two master's degrees and had tons of experience memorizing things. How hard could this be?

Green tip requirements testing for green belt: combinations of kicks and punches *plus* the dreaded spin kick (Noooooo!), another form, five one-step defenses against a left-hand punch, and yes, more terminology . . . Nope. Nope nope nope nope nope. This was just too much pressure, but I had already learned that it was very difficult to say, "No, sir," to Grandmaster Kim. I accepted my fate and began to attend extra classes to learn and practice the higher-level requirements.

I would be free from sparring during the test—which I still regarded with the same, though not quite as pronounced, dread I'd had as a child—and also from board breaking, which was only performed at green belt and above at our dojang's tests. I was especially thankful for my fighting reprieve because I was worried I would react in a sparring match the same way I had as a child: frozen and desperate for it to be over.

I was happy to get to learn two forms, which I had excelled at as a child and had looked forward to practicing again as an adult. Forms, or poomsae, are an integral part of the taekwondo student's repertoire. Using the body and breath's energy as momentum, the student moves through a series of predetermined strikes, kicks, punches, and blocks that make up the pattern of the form. The student learns how to balance the softness of preparation with the bold power of striking, how to fall into the unique rhythm of each form, and how to intellectualize what appears to an outsider as a random cluster of techniques.

There is a form for every color belt and every black belt level, and each form is a story in motion. If performed with the correct speed, interpretation, and precision, one can imagine the invisible opponents the student is deftly fighting. Forms put the "art" in martial art.

In addition to offering an opportunity to hone self-defense techniques, each form provides a unique philosophy on mental conduct. Using imagery from Buddhism, Korean tradition, and the powers of nature—thunder, fire, mountains, and the universe, to name a few—forms offer a means for the student to grow emotionally and spiritually along with developing physical prowess. I had found my sweet spot with forms.

I spent the next several weeks staying late after class, coming to the dojang at off hours for extra practice, and practicing at home, taking care not to whack my foot on my coffee table or recliner. My fear of testing began to subside as the reality of this wonderful opportunity to advance to green belt sizzled in my mind.

In my martial arts reverie, I'd nearly forgotten I'd rejoined a popular dating website. Romance had once appeared essential to my happiness, but now that I was entrenched in taekwondo, it seemed like an inconvenient afterthought. Before shutting down my online profile, I agreed to a date with Ricardo, a divorced forty-year-old software analyst who had most recently lived on the East Coast and had found his way to Texas a few years earlier. In mid-May on a Friday evening, we met at a crowded pub in downtown Fort Worth.

"Melanie?" a soft voice rang out behind me as I sat hunched on a barstool, playing with my phone and waiting for him to appear. Ricardo opened his mouth in delight when he first saw me, and the skin around his brown eyes crinkled as he drew me in for a warm hug. He was tall and lithe, with a hint of a beard surrounding his grin. He settled onto a barstool next to me and ordered a beer.

I was shy at first, wondering if I'd been too hasty about jumping back on the dating scene, but I was already one beer in, so I decided to stay. I leaned in to listen to him over the din of chattering voices and clinking glasses.

"I'm the king of first dates," Ricardo moaned. "Nothing's worked out for me yet. I was starting to give up when I saw your profile. I was intrigued. I hope there'll be a second date?" He lightly touched my hand. I was a little taken aback by his being so forward, asking for a second date less than ten minutes into the first one, but I was so flattered that I just nodded.

The beer has since scrambled my memories, but I know we ended up having a very deep intellectual discussion, complete with mutual therapy and medication confessions. Ricardo told me the story of the Buddha inviting the demon Mara to tea, and I mused that I was long overdue for a tea party with my demons. While I had healed quite a bit emotionally with taekwondo training, I still wasn't out of the Anxiety and Mood Swings Woods yet. I was still not as confident in the dating world as I was becoming in the dojang. In hindsight I realize I was also still carrying a fading torch for Salad Guy and halfheartedly still hoped for a reconciliation. Nervously I tried to convince Ricardo that I was bad news as he increased his intensity in campaigning for a relationship.

"I'm crazy!" I said in a stage whisper, half-joking and half-miserable. In a flush of sympathy, he leaned forward off his barstool, clasped my shoulders, and pressed his face toward mine for a kiss, but I pushed him away. I wasn't ready. We both leaned backward, chuckling awkwardly and looking at the floor. He settled for gently cupping my fingers, and I felt ... nothing, at least not anything I was used to feeling. No rush of hot air to my throat, no butterflies, no desire to possess and obsess. Had I lost my mojo, or was this just normal dating? Was it possible *not* to feel the all-consuming flame of obsession on the first date and still have potential for a relationship? The discomfort of feeling nothing was more unsettling than the typical heat flush and butterflies that usually accompanied the first moments of attraction.

"Would you rather know or not know?" Ricardo asked, sipping his beer and wiping foam from the curved upper lip I had just refused to kiss.

"Know what?" I replied, taking the bait.

"Anything. When you're going to die, whether someone is being unfaithful to you, whether we're going to see each other again, if we're going to be together for a long time?"

"I'm not sure. I wouldn't mind knowing my death date. That would give me some motivation to clean out my closet."

"What about that last question: Am I going to see you again?" Ricardo raised a thick eyebrow and lifted his glass.

"Okay! Can I invite my demons, or is this a non-tea date?" I tilted my head comically.

"How about just you this time? I can meet your demons later."

"You sure you want to? I have a lot of them. Even more than I have skeletons in my closet." I raised my eyebrow back at him and squinted in mock seriousness. I was testing him. I'd never been that open about my mental health struggles with a man before, and I wanted to see if he really wanted to spend time with me, demons and all.

"Definitely," he said, nodding and widening his eyes. "I want to know everything about you. So . . . when am I going to see you again?"

Again with pushing for a second date! Not knowing how to respond, I stiffly agreed to brunch the following Sunday, and we got back to discussing the finer points of martial arts and mental health.

While I couldn't bring myself to kiss Ricardo that night, I began to secretly look forward to his gentle touch. Whenever he returned from the bathroom, he would place the flat of his palm against the middle of my back when he rejoined me. I was wearing my favorite dress, a white-and-teal cotton sheath. The back of my dress was a low-cut V, so every time he touched my back, I felt the dry warmth of his palm against my skin and the subtle pressure on my muscles and vertebrae. His hand never slid downward or lingered too long. Every time he touched me, the gentle firmness of his gesture made me consider him just a little bit more. It was so unusually intimate that in spite of myself and my collection of fears about dating, I found him interesting.

After our date ended, I drove home and burst into tears, afraid of the future and frustrated that I didn't know what I wanted. Ever since high school, I had either been consumed by a relationship or pining painfully for someone just out of reach. I'd had long bouts of being single in college, but it wasn't like I was out making friends or doing anything fulfilling or exciting during that time. Instead I was binge eating, binge drinking, and contemplating suicide. I had never truly accepted being alone, although the older I got, the more I shied away from commitment. By thirty-three I hated to admit to myself that I *wanted* to be alone and self-sufficient, free to run rampant in my mental prison of self-centered madness.

So here came Ricardo, who claimed to think I was perfect for him after only one date and ached for me to reciprocate his affection. There was something intriguing about him, though, a vulnerability under the surface that piqued my curiosity. On the other hand, I didn't want to force myself back into a relationship just because I was lonely. I didn't trust myself to be any good at dating because I'd felt like such a failure with men in the past.

As I washed off my makeup and brushed my teeth, it occurred to me that perhaps I could finally rest with Ricardo. I'd never admitted my mental health problems to previous boyfriends. I was too afraid that they would judge me and toss me aside for being the "crazy" girl. I'd hid my medication when they visited and smiled at them with tight lips and dead eyes rather than admit I was anxious or upset. Maybe it was time to stop punishing myself for past mistakes and see what could happen with Ricardo. Not only had he been casually introduced to my demons; he was willing to get to know them on a first-name basis. Besides, I kind of wanted a date for my upcoming green belt test.

CHAPTER 7

Brunch and a Boyfriend

S everal days after our first date, I had an impromptu dinner date with Ricardo. We'd been flirtatiously texting every day and had spoken on the phone a few times, but this was the first time we would see each other in person again. Regardless of the little high I got from each text message, I was still heavily doubting whether I was ready to pursue a real relationship. Something felt forced and false, but I couldn't quite place it.

We met at a colorful Mexican restaurant on West Seventh Street, a trendy Fort Worth hot spot of cafés, bars, and shops conveniently located a mile from my condo. I was sweating through my purple cotton dress and clicking my cartoonish yellow pumps as I scurried into the bar after driving through rush hour from work. Ricardo curled me into a hug and patted the stool next to him.

This time I came to the date prepared. I had written on a sticky note a list of red flags about myself. I couldn't decide whether I really liked Ricardo and wanted to keep seeing him or whether I wanted to run away to lick my anxious wounds in private. The note read:

1. No friends
2. Depression, anxiety [I wasn't ready to admit the bipolar part just yet]
3. Addiction to love and attention
4. Juxtaposing intimacy with selfishness
5. Boundary issues
6. Not sure I'm over the last one

"I don't want to see it," Ricardo said with a flick of his wrist. "I want to get to know you on my own time. But perhaps you're not ready to date, and maybe you should take some time to figure things out before venturing out into the dating world. I don't want to be your rebound. I want to be your boyfriend." Oh no, he was calling my bluff!

"Uh, no, that's not what I meant!" I said hurriedly. "I like you! I'm just not very good at dating."

"Why don't you give yourself the benefit of the doubt? Try me," Ricardo purred and patted my shoulder. "Let's order some chips."

I nodded weakly, but internally I was panicking, feeling as if I were rushing into a situation that could end in more heartache but also tired of holing up at home to mope. I'd made a nervous fool of myself, probably raised a hundred red flags, and he *still* wanted to date me! *Now* who was the crazy one? He never did read that note.

After dinner Ricardo suggested a walk. As we were about to step off the curb in front of the restaurant, he pivoted to face me and rested his slim tan wrists on my shoulders.

"Do I make you nervous?" he asked, his bright teeth flashing as he leaned in for a kiss.

Yes! I wanted to scream. *Everything makes me nervous right now! I suck at relationships! Run while you still can!* Instead I kissed him back and felt the kitten heels of my shoes lift off the gritty curb as I leaned into him. The kisses were soft and sweet, tasting like rain and papaya. It still didn't feel right, but I didn't trust myself to go with any other options.

As on our first date, I didn't feel that instant explosion of attachment that I usually did when I met someone I liked. My brain wasn't screaming, *Yes! Now you are* mine*! You must spend every waking moment worshipping* me*!* I did, however, feel something inside me lurch, but it didn't make me want to devote all my energy into possessing him. Is this how normal people date? Maybe it was the price to pay for achieving some tiny bit of inner peace, sanity, and a sense of self that had been growing since I began taekwondo training. Just as I had to trust myself to be able to test from white to green belt, I had to trust myself to be able to handle this budding relationship differently.

In a panic I blurted out, "I like you! I just have to take this slow!"

Ricardo intertwined his fingers with mine and replied, "I understand. You can lead this dance."

A dark anxious mood permeated my Saturday afternoon as I ran errands. It was Memorial Day weekend, and I was traversing the highways and strip malls in search of a baby shower gift for a coworker. Miles away from home, I had that awful feeling of both having to pee and feeling really thirsty. Every measured sip from my water bottle aggravated my full bladder.

Just as I was arriving home, Ricardo texted me an invitation to watch a televised baseball game at a bar. By this time we'd had our two dates, the first at the downtown pub and the second at the Mexican restaurant, where we'd had our first kiss, and we'd been communicating by text several times each day. We were still set for our brunch date on Sunday, but he was eager to see me sooner. Although I had agreed to start dating him, I still worried that I wouldn't be able to handle a relationship without becoming too clingy or having a meltdown.

Ricardo came to the house around eight, and his white linen shirt and khaki pants hugged his wiry frame, making him look even taller. He led me into the second bedroom I used as a library, leaned against the black bookshelf, took his hands in mine, and looked me dead in the eyes. Uh-oh.

"Melanie, I really like you," he began, "but I'm not sure what's going on. You've been pulling back and giving me mixed messages. You say you want to date me, but then you say you need more time and need to go really slow. You even said the other day that you weren't sure you should be dating at all. Look, I think there's a good thing between us, but if you don't, you need to let me know so we can both move on."

I panicked. This was my way out. I didn't *have* to date this guy just because he was interested. He was offering an escape, and I could wallow in peace and tormented quiet. The next few seconds dripped with anticipation. Should I say yes or no? What the hell, let's try something new. It's not like I had any other options (other than staying single and focusing on taekwondo, which didn't seem like a viable option at the time). I looked into his eyes, gave him a long hug and a kiss, and clasped his hands.

"Let's go watch that game," I murmured.

In the crowded, cacophonous bar with its sticky tables and spectators shrieking every time the Texas Rangers scored a home run, I caught myself sneaking admiring glances at Ricardo's profile. He grew more and more handsome as the night wore on. Every time I looked, I noticed something new: a slight wave in his thick graying hair, the softness of his closed-mouth smile, the blue-black whiskers of his day-old beard. He was good-looking, very smart, sensitive, and loved martial arts as much as I did. Why not step off the ledge and into a relationship with this guy?

The next day, the date of our scheduled brunch, Ricardo showed up looking like a rainbow. He wore reflective aviator sunglasses, a blue-and-white-checked button-down shirt, faded rose-colored pants, and genuine blue suede shoes. His lightly tanned skin complemented the pastels and bright colors perfectly. Before I could even think, I leapt up into his arms, swiftly wrapping my legs and bare feet around his waist and giving his neck a friendly hug. Good morning, indeed.

We went to a charming French bistro on the main street of a quaint oasis nestled in the concrete mass of highways known as the Mid-Cities area between Fort Worth and Dallas. We lingered over eggs and chocolate croissants, and our conversation never stopped. The dormant butterflies in my stomach began to stretch and tentatively flap their wings. Something was happening, and it was happening much faster than I had anticipated. I was starting to fall for him, and at this point I didn't care how far I fell.

We strolled hand in hand down the cobblestone street, marveling at the beautiful spring day and the pleasant morning we'd had so far. We popped into a resale shop, and he talked me into buying a twenty-five-dollar pair of teal-and-purple satin peep-toe pumps I later referred to as my "peacock shoes." Ricardo suggested we go back to his house, which was closer to the café than mine, to listen to music and watch movies.

As we coasted along the spiderweb of highways to a house he shared with some coworkers, he told me stories about his teenage years living in the Washington, DC, area and the adventures he'd had traveling the country. Somewhere on an overpass he glanced at me out of the corner of his eye and blurted out, "I could see us being together for a long time." Apparently, I wasn't the only one falling fast.

I blushed and smiled down at my hands.

"Well, great," I said sarcastically but still grinning. "You're older than me, so you'll probably die before I do, and where does that leave me? Square one!" Secretly I was thrilled that a man was actually suggesting a future with me. I couldn't get the last guy to look away from his work e-mail.

I enjoyed the last stretch of our drive after we'd gotten out of the maze of concrete and whizzing cars. The empty rolling fields and train tracks surrounding the small community where he lived reminded me of Snyder, where the open road was a sea of possibilities and a gentle means of escape from city life. I could see the full horizon and big Texas skies again, something I didn't realize I missed deeply until I got away from my everyday urban dwellings.

We stopped at a gas station to buy some cold drinks, prolonging our time alone just a little longer. His car didn't have air conditioning, and by that time of year, it was already roasting outside. I put the icy water bottle between my thighs to let the condensation cool me off as I gazed out the window, eager for the drive to end and our relationship to begin. After a few minutes spent chatting with his housemates, Ricardo and I sequestered ourselves in his tiny bachelor bedroom to listen to music. We spent the entire afternoon glued to each other's sides and talked until our mouths turned to cotton and our voices croaked.

"I'm starting to fall for you, babe," Ricardo murmured as he kissed the top of my head. My heart did a hundred joyous spin kicks. In retrospect, jumping into another relationship was the last thing I should have done, since I was finally on a healthy path to healing, but like pills and alcohol, an old addiction had suddenly become irresistible.

"I was starved for affection in my last relationship," he said as he looked out the window.

At once I wanted to scoop him into my arms and assure him that things would be different with me. I was just as hungry for someone who genuinely wanted to spend time with me. We were two broken dolls who had found solace entangled in each other's hearts.

"We appear to be a perfect match," he murmured, his lips brushing my forehead as we cuddled. "Thank you for making yourself emotionally available."

I burrowed my head into his shoulder.

That night we went out for a light dinner and then to a massive grocery store to pick up items for a Memorial Day cookout. We were doing one of those "couples" things I love to do. Anyone can go to a bar or to a restaurant, but *couples* go to the grocery store. They go to the gas station together. They go to the dry cleaner. Going grocery shopping with a woman means you want to spend actual time with her, you want to break bread with her, and you'd rather be at home with her eating overcooked chicken and limp vegetables than be anywhere else in the world. I had been so desperate for something beyond superficial dating that it meant more to me that Ricardo would go grocery shopping with me than if he'd taken me to any of the posh restaurants and bars I'd visited with my previous dates.

Ricardo had been hinting at "the exclusivity talk," and somewhere between the tomato sauce and canned corn I suggested now was as good a time as any.

"Well, I certainly don't want to date anyone else," I said, raising an eyebrow and tilting my head.

He hugged me from behind and sighed. "You're my girlfriend now?"

"Yes. And does that make you my boyfriend?"

He nodded emphatically and grinned with those chalk-white teeth.

"Brunch and a boyfriend. It's the perfect Sunday."

So now it appeared I was in a relationship. As much as I'd fought it in the beginning, now it seemed so easy. Ricardo said the things I'd been aching to hear from other men. He told me over and over how beautiful I was, how he could see us being together for a long time, and how he was falling in love with me. It almost seemed insecure, as if he were seeking reassurance, which wasn't unlike something I would do.

The things you want the most often happen when you least expect them. One night in early June, shortly after our brunch and exclusivity conversation, Ricardo and I had returned to his house from another trip to the grocery store. I gingerly asked him if he'd like to go to my upcoming green belt test.

"It'll be long and boring," I warned.

"Of course I'll come," he said with a shrug as he turned to trudge across the lawn. "I'm your boyfriend. That's my job."

I gazed at the back of the yellow polo shirt stretched across his back. I wanted to place the flat of my palm against his back the way he had with me on our first date and shout, "I love you!" Still a little gun-shy based on my past experience with men who didn't feel the same emotional connection with me as I thought I had with them, I stayed silent.

Ricardo did not.

"Do you love me?" Ricardo asked, shyly ducking his head and grinning as we huddled together inside his room.

"Yes! Yes, I do. I wanted to say it outside!" I gushed.

"I want to hear you say it."

"I love you!"

"And I love you! Aren't you happy that I said it back immediately, that it's reciprocated?" That was an odd way to word it, but . . . yes! He kissed the back of my hand and we fell into a pile of pillows and giggles. I was in love, and this time it was with someone who loved me back, not someone who dodged my phone calls—hooray! We had officially become one of those couples I hated.

CHAPTER 8

Green Belt Test

When I wasn't moonlighting as a ninja, I spent my days as an organizational development consultant for a large healthcare company in the DFW Metroplex. I began my career with the company in 2004 as a librarian in one of the company's hospitals, meaning I did research for clinical staff and patients on surgeries and drugs and cool stuff like that. For a number of reasons, I knew I needed to change careers around the end of 2010, so I went back to school for an MBA and took a job in my company's training and development department. By the time I started taekwondo, I had been at my OD job for three years.

My duties in the training and development department included facilitating workshops on various leadership and professional development topics. On June 7, 2013, the day of my green belt test, I was leading a process improvement workshop at one of our largest hospitals. During a break, I noticed I had a voicemail from Ricardo. His voice sounded gentle and calm, as usual, but the message was ominous.

"Hey, baby. Big changes are happening," the recording said. "Don't worry, we'll be okay. I'll see you this afternoon. Love you."

I could not get ahold of him all day, and as the hours dragged by, the little dark voice in my mind started to get restless. What was the "big change"? Was he suddenly "too busy with work," which was an excuse I'd heard from men in my past? Had something terrible happened? And in a moment of selfishness that made me cringe, I thought, *Is he still coming to my test?*

By late afternoon I had still not heard from Ricardo, so I grimly went home, changed clothes, and did a few stretches to prepare for my green belt test. At the dojang I smiled and chatted with the instructors, but internally I was a quivering wreck over my test and the wild speculations about Ricardo's voicemail. At six o'clock sharp, the students were ordered to line up and bow to Grandmaster; then we filed against the wall and sat quietly.

Color belt tests include the lowest-ranking white belts all the way up to a red belt / black tip for students testing for bo dan, the rank just below black belt. Black belt tests are conducted separately from color belt tests. We sat in order of rank, so I was at the end of the line with the white belts and the farthest away from where Grandmaster and two masters sat stonily at the judging table beneath the two large hanging flags. Instinctively I glanced at the area near the door where a small audience of parents and friends had gathered. There was Ricardo smiling broadly, and I felt a flood of relief. We wiggled our eyebrows at each other, and I quickly turned my head back to face the front before anyone yelled at me. It was time to begin.

"Miss Gibson!"

"Yes, sir!"

I scrambled to stand up and take my place in line with the other trembling white belts. I performed my white belt–level kicks, punches, and blocks, and then I sat down only to be called back up to repeat the process with the orange belts, yellow belts, and yellow belt / green tip students. Although by this time I felt confident in my ability to execute everything as well as a hardworking white belt could, I was sucker punched by anxiety and a little bit of stage fright. The only part of my childhood belt tests I could remember was snapping a board with a side kick, and that wasn't going to do me any good right now. I wondered how I'd made it through those tests without falling apart.

I did everything correctly, even though my brain was on overdrive. I was trembling so badly my movements were stiff, and my voice was a shaky whisper when I was asked to recite my Korean terminology. Nothing mattered at this point other than taekwondo. My job, my education, my condo, my relationship—these were all secondary to the one thing that had saved me from mental destruction. If I thought about how much this test truly meant to me, the gravity would weigh me down.

As an advanced taekwondo practitioner, I now have over two dozen forms and even more self-defense sequences swirling around in my mind, and I could be asked to perform or teach them at any time. These days it doesn't seem too difficult, although at the time of my green belt test, having to perform *two* memorized forms and *two* sets of one-steps seemed to be an insurmountable feat.

The irony wasn't lost on me that just a few hours earlier, I had presented a four-hour workshop to a room full of strangers. While facilitating was never something I particularly enjoyed, it was part of my job, and I happened to be good at it. Why couldn't I tap into some of that stage presence for my test? Here's the difference: You can't bullshit your way through a belt test. Taekwondo is very black and white. You either do the kick or you don't. You know the form or you don't. You can't turn to your partners and say, "So what's been your experience with practicing one-step sparring? Let's all pair up for discussions, record some notes on a flip chart, and then rejoin the large group to report out our findings." This was going to be a long night.

After I had completed my required kicks, blocks, strikes, forms, and self-defense, I could finally relax and watch the higher-ranking students continue testing with their own requirements, plus sparring and breaking. Even though I was greatly relieved to not have to spar, I found it fascinating to watch. There are rules to sparring, including bans on punches to the face, blows to the back of the head, and of course, hits below the belt, but it is much less formal than one-step sparring. You do not hear commands from one partner to another. Instead you simply hear the smash of feet against chest protectors and the hoarse yells of the opponents as they land blows. The excitement was infectious.

During my later tests as a more advanced student, I actually began to look forward to the sparring portion. Sparring, despite my complicated relationship with it, was the only part of a test when I wasn't overcome with nerves, as it forced me to focus completely on what I was doing. There is no room for extraneous thought when you're trying not to get hit in the face. Sparring is like meditating and beating the crap out of someone at the same time, so it's the best of both worlds.

Board breaking is the grand finale of any taekwondo belt test, whether it's a color belt or black belt test. There is some debate in the martial arts community over the usefulness of breaking boards or bricks. Some argue it is a great way to demonstrate focus and precision, while others claim it is downright fraud. Bruce Lee is often credited with the droll dismissal of breaking: "Boards don't hit back." While I don't see myself ever skipping onto a construction site and side-kicking plywood for grins, in my experience breaking has been an essential vehicle for honing concentration, precision, timing, speed, and follow-through. Besides, it feels . . . well . . . it feels fucking amazing. It's just so *cathartic.* That same experience can't be met through ghost kicks to the air or even blows to a bag (or other people). At the time of my green belt test, though, all I needed to do was watch.

During the breaking portion, the advanced students were called up to the front of the room in order of rank. We nodded and clapped weakly in support of the little kids who threw clunky hammer fists and side kicks at thin boards, but the real show-stoppers came from the higher-ranking students. A big teenage boy testing for bo dan was the final performer. He broke multiple thick boards with three different techniques, finishing his set with a beautiful spin kick that crashed through the boards with a satisfying snap. I shook my head in amazement. There was no way I could ever break with a spin kick.

After the breaking portion of the test, the students lined up in order of rank and stood quietly while Grandmaster cracked a few jokes and praised the hard work and discipline exhibited by the students. When my name was called, Grandmaster clapped a hand on my shoulder, turned me toward the audience, and announced, "She's testing from white to green belt today. That's why she got up to test so many times. She started taekwondo twenty years ago, and now she's back!" I blushed and grinned as I clutched my stiff new green belt. I shook hands with the masters before I flashed Ricardo a huge smile and trotted to the back of the room.

"Okay, what's this big thing you've been keeping from me all day?" I said casually, placing my hands on my waist and jutting my hip to the side. I gave Ricardo a big kiss and pulled him to his feet. "Are you sick? Did your car break down? You lose your job or something?"

He smiled grimly and slowly nodded.

"Oh, I'm sorry!" I gasped. "I was just joking! Shit, what happened? Oh, I'm such a selfish jerk for making you come to my test!"

"I wanted to come to your test. I'm your boyfriend, remember?" Ricardo replied.

We went to a pub next door and rehashed the day over fries and patty melts. That morning he had been called into his boss's office and was informed that, due to recent layoffs, he had been terminated. He was still in shock and hadn't quite formulated a game plan.

"I was wondering if you still wanted to be with me after I told you about losing my job," Ricardo said tentatively, looking away while he sipped his Diet Coke.

"What kind of bitch would I be if I broke up with you for losing your job? That would be a pretty low blow if I dumped you over that. We just started dating," I said through a mouthful of fries. Although we were very early into our relationship, we had both fallen hard and fast for each other. There was no way I'd give up on him this quickly; I'd just "got" him.

Before resigning ourselves to frugal home-cooked dinners in order to help Ricardo save money, we had one last hurrah at a quaint French bistro the next night. As we sipped wine and munched on garlicky escargots, we chose to celebrate not only my green belt but also our budding relationship. In spite of this setback, the summer was off to a great start. We were in love, so what could stop us?

Part Three:

GREEN BELT AND

GREEN BELT / BLUE TIP

CHAPTER 9

Splats and Sparring

"Oof!" *Splat*!
During my very first attempt at a flying side kick, I landed squarely on my bottom in a collapsed pile of thick rectangular kicking pads. The Monday after my green belt test, I graduated to the later evening class, which was informally referred to as "cardio night" since the focus tended to be on kicks, jumps, and aerobic conditioning. The commands were louder, and the pace was much faster than I'd been used to in my low-key white belt classes, which were so small I often had time for one-on-one practice with Grandmaster.

For this particular gravity-defying drill, one of the masters set up a stack of pads about three feet high and told us to do flying side kicks over them, as if that were something normal people did on a daily basis. Flying side kick requires a running start and a strong liftoff from the standing leg, and then the student must quickly turn their hip in the air and jut their kicking leg out into a strong side kick before landing. Easy, right? I barely made it past the liftoff before I fell.

I reddened as I clumsily climbed to my feet and wondered if this was the end of the line for me. This wasn't fair! Didn't the master remember I was only a white belt three days ago? I hadn't had the advantage of training through the orange and yellow belt months before being promoted to green belt. He had just thrown me immediately to the wolves!

Maybe I was deluding myself. I was a thirty-three-year-old office worker with a bad hip. Who did I think I was, swaggering around with my new green belt and nothing to show for it? It had been a mistake to promote me so many levels so quickly. If I can't do this kick now, will I ever be able to do it? Come on, did I *really* think I could ever be a black belt? Oh, God help me, I had to *spar* on Wednesday, and I knew I'd be even worse! I'm such a failure!

Then I began to worry about how the master and the other students would react to this pratfall by a brand-new green belt. My classmates were a gaggle of goofy teenage red belt boys who seemed to move together as a chattering hydra of hormones. While I eventually came to enjoy their company, being around them was at first jarring. Did they *ever* shut up? How did I *ever* think boys were attractive and charming when I was their age? I was dreading their jeers and giggles after my fall, but they averted their eyes politely and continued sneaking in jabs at each other when the master wasn't looking.

"I think that's enough for today," the master said, letting me save face as he had us line up and practice a few hand strikes before closing the class. My mixture of embarrassment and hot sense of injustice at having been asked to do a very advanced kick after only two months of training subsided as we slowly breathed and bowed to each other.

"Well, Green Belt, how was your class?" Grandmaster asked, popping out of his office and smiling impishly.

"Oh, uh, it was fine. Lots of fun! See you Wednesday!" I ducked my head and rushed out the door before he could say anything else. I hoped my first sparring class two days later wouldn't be as embarrassing as my first color belt class.

That Wednesday I went back into the dojang feeling both excited and nervous about facing what I'd hated so much as a young taekwondo student: sparring.

"Green Belt, you're back! Time for sparring!" Grandmaster said, winking at me as I lined up with the other students. My classmates and I scurried into line and warmed up with a few kicks and punches before we scattered to pull on our sparring gear. I had not yet bought my own gear, other than flimsy foam wrist and shin guards, so I tied on a faded, borrowed chest protector and squeamishly smashed a cracked and yellowed plastic foam helmet onto my head. My heart was already pounding, and I wondered if I would be stricken with the same frozen mind and frantic body I'd had in my old childhood sparring classes. The worst part about sparring as a child (or now, frankly) wasn't the fear of being hit; it was the fear of not knowing what to do. It was the same reason I'd hated improvisational acting in high school theater classes: my mind didn't work that way. I didn't know how to effortlessly react to a situation and, more importantly, trust my instincts to carry me through it.

Grandmaster barked at us to get a partner and form a line. We all stood facing each other in a line that snaked to the back of the training room. For the first ten minutes, we worked on simple reaction drills: One person did a roundhouse kick, and the other blocked and did a turning back side kick, which is turning backward and shooting out the kicking leg, heel first, into the opponent's torso. It's one of the most effective kicks in sparring and is often used to counter another student who is off-balance or has simply left themselves open for a hit. Other times one side of the class could only use kicks while the other side could only use punches during a short sparring drill. I enjoyed the drills because the more time we spent doing them, the less time we would spend actually sparring in real matches.

We maintained our lines and then sparred our partners for a minute or two before moving to the next person. This time it wasn't a drill. There were no teenage girls or women my size, so I was paired with little kids, grown men, or teenage boys. Greg, a bo dan who attended class with his two young sons, was gentle for his hulking size but also wily and swift. He liked to trick me with a fake roundhouse to the side before quickly popping it up to my head or jabbing the ball of his foot into the middle of my chest and swatting me backward with a forceful push kick.

Greg's young sons, also bo dans, were much more timid, and I soon learned that even though they were higher ranking than I, they spooked easily and could be quickly overpowered, even by a newbie like me. Since I was one of the few adults in the class and had the added responsibility of setting a good example and looking out for the kids, I chose to back off with the boys rather than become a bully.

As if on a conveyor belt, we moved down the line to switch partners every few minutes. By the time I got to Ricky, the big teenage boy who had tested for bo dan during my green belt test, we were giving each other pleading, tired stares and slowly hopping around marking time until Grandmaster shouted for us to stop.

I had never felt so exhausted in my life. Sparring is kind of like tennis, sprinting, and boxing all at the same time: it requires high cardiovascular endurance and the ability to make short, quick movements every few seconds. My heart pounded unrelentingly in my chest and seemed to be banging away in my stomach and head as well. I was so drenched with sweat that my hair was a heavy, dripping mop. I didn't remember feeling this tired as a youngster in sparring class, but to my relief, the gripping anxiety that had accompanied my childhood sparring days seemed to have lessened considerably. I wasn't afraid of being hit or not knowing what to do. It was quite the opposite—I loved the adrenaline rush of landing (and receiving) blows.

After that first night, I developed a love-hate relationship with sparring that still remains with me as an advanced student.

It's the same feeling I've had toward facilitating a workshop or team-building event—I'm grumpy up until the event, feel euphoric during the actual event, and am flooded with relief when it's over. Sparring was (and still is) the most physically and emotionally difficult aspect of taekwondo for me, and it's also where I've seen the most improvement over the years. Unlike when I was a child and frozen in fear, I tended to *think* too much as an adult student, especially during those first months as a green belt. My brain was in overdrive as it tried to come up with kicks and punches that could land effectively.

By the time I became a black belt, I'd finally found my groove with a few favorite tactics, an improved ability to read my partners' patterns and weaknesses, and a marked viciousness if they played the old kick-and-run-away game. My chief instructor (you'll meet him later), in an attempt to make me comfortable with up-close fighting, regularly goaded me into shoving matches (which sometimes unintentionally resulted in a fit of giggles from both of us), and we spent much of our sparring time furiously punching each other in the stomach. With the rush of endorphins, I usually drove home from sparring class feeling more blissed out than if I'd done two hours of yoga.

But back to that first night sparring as a green belt: I still had a long way to go from slinging halfhearted roundhouses to the land of head shots and chasing down opponents. I was clumsy, clunky, and frustrated, but I also realized sparring class was the true test of applying what I was learning. That night it was all I could do to will myself to stay upright until I could stumble like a drunk out of the dojang and into the summer twilight.

I spent the next few weeks both dreading and looking forward to sparring class. I was eager to try out what I was learning, but I was frustrated with how slowly my progress seemed to be going. My brain knew what I was supposed to do, but my body didn't always respond appropriately. Toward the end of June, I felt like I was plateauing, even sliding backward. Meanwhile, in my relationship, I seemed to have hit a similar snag.

Ricardo had come over to visit on one of my off evenings. He was leaning against my kitchen counter as I told him about my most recent experiences in taekwondo class.

"I haven't been around this many kids in a long time," I said as I sipped from my water glass. "They're pretty funny, but I'm glad to come back to a quiet house."

"So . . . do you want kids?" Ricardo asked.

Crap. He asked the question I'd always tried to avoid in relationships. "No . . . um . . . not really."

And on that note, let's just get this out of the way now: I don't want children.

For those of you who have not thrown this book across the room in self-righteous, huffy indignation, thanks for sticking it out, even though you were warned at the beginning that I'm sometimes the villain of this story.

I've never wanted kids for a myriad of reasons. I didn't like being around children, even when I was a child. I dreamed about being an artist rather than a wife and mommy, and at this point I was dreaming about being a black belt. I didn't want the exhaustion or the daily life challenges of being a parent. Those stressors are very real, yet like mental illness, they're often hushed up and glossed over in polite conversation.

I was in a secure place with my finances, home, and career and finally feeling like my emotional and mental health were on track for the first time in my life. Pregnancy and caring for a newborn would send my physical and mental health into a destructive tailspin.

I don't think I need to justify my choice any further. I simply don't want children. My choice has no impact on anyone's well-being and future but my own. Parenthood, despite popular social norms and pressure, is *not* for everyone. It is not for me.

Let's continue. . . .

As adamant as I was in my desire *not* to have children, I'd also never treated the desire for kids as a deal breaker in relationships and instead shied away whenever the topic was brought up. Come to think of it . . . I'd never set any deal breakers or boundaries. I usually held on to relationships as tightly as I could, whether the relationship was healthy or not. Like sparring, I hadn't quite gotten the hang of making wise choices when faced with a challenge from another person.

"Well, I guess we'll have to go our separate ways." Ricardo crossed his arms and gave me a prissy smirk. I panicked. It looked like he had set the deal breaker for me.

"Wait, what? You already have three kids. I thought you didn't want any more. And you know I have mental health problems. I don't want to deal with that being pregnant or postpartum. I'd probably end up killing myself!"

"You read my online profile. I said I'd like to have more kids in the future, and I was hoping it would be with you. Now it sounds like we're incompatible." He tilted his head to the side and pursed his lips smugly. Shit. Shit shit shit, I did *not* want another relationship to fail, especially one that seemed to be going well. I didn't want to be alone again. I *had* to make this work.

This is probably when I should have stood my ground and walked away from what I dreaded (and knew) would be an ongoing fight, but of course I didn't. Even though my confidence and self-reliance were growing thanks to taekwondo, I still valued and needed a man's love and validation above all else. So I told a little white lie that would haunt us for the next two years.

"Okay, I guess I'll think about it. Maybe," I said as I fidgeted with my drinking glass.

"Good. Think about it. How about we try in the next five years?" Ricardo kissed my forehead and trotted into the living room. I smiled wanly and excused myself to the bathroom.

Five years . . . a deadline . . . a mandate. I shot my reflection a grimace. Who was he to dictate what I did with my body? What would happen if I refused? Could I handle being single again? And since my story is an accidental romantic comedy, let me use a cliché: "Sword of Damocles over my head," I muttered. I could actually see the blade swinging back and forth above me like a clock hand, ticking away my years of freedom, counting down to an ultimatum I'd given myself no choice but to meet. I was going to lose this sparring match.

CHAPTER 10

Didn't You Know the First

Six Months Don't Count?

After the summer setbacks of Ricardo's job loss and my shaky consideration to have a baby I didn't want, I caught a nasty bout of strep throat that I swear to this day was brought on by running around barefoot with a bunch of children in taekwondo class. Autumn seemed more promising when, in September, I began training with a new instructor who had returned from a job stint in Arkansas. At just twenty-three, Alex was a fourth degree black belt and had returned to his post in Fort Worth as our dojang's chief instructor.

Alex's youthful face, shock of light brown hair, and big blue eyes belied a serious demeanor and commanding voice. Frankly, I was terrified of him when I first saw him. While I was still recovering from strep throat, I had visited the dojang to watch a sparring class and was surprised to see a new teacher shouting and growling commands at the students. Who *was* this guy? I wasn't sure what I would be getting myself into when I was well enough to rejoin my classes with this new instructor.

After politely interacting with each other as teacher and student for a while, Alex and I eventually became good friends, sharing the same sarcastic sense of humor, political leanings, and taste in movies. During class, though, we were all business. He shouted orders and demanded perfection, and I was quick to follow his guidance and answer him with a crisp, "Yes, sir!" His teaching style was detailed, mindful, challenging, and just what I needed to help me grow. He watched me closely and helped me fine-tune my technique with changes that were subtle to the untrained eye but made a huge difference in my precision, fluidity, and power. Although my progress in sparring went at a much slower pace, through his guidance I was able to develop a more aggressive and strategic style of fighting.

I envied Alex's no-nonsense attitude and emotional maturity. If I had been like him at age twenty-three, I would probably have saved myself years of crushing despair, irrational anger, and throwing myself at the wrong men. Throughout my teens and early twenties, I was a drama queen with poorly placed priorities: I looked good on paper with my degrees and my budding career, but internally I was a wreck. I had no confidence or self-respect, hated everything about myself, and stacked all my self-worth on the approval of others—namely the men I dated or wanted to date. Perhaps if I'd had something like taekwondo to boost my confidence, challenge me in a healthy way, and just get me out of the damned house, I might have turned out differently.

On the home front, things were also looking up . . . or so I thought. Ricardo and I had bonded over his recovery from a surgery he'd had that summer and my recovery from strep throat, deepening what he called our "nesting" tendencies.

"We're pair-bonding!" Ricardo cooed as he stirred a pot of milky steel-cut oats on my stove one Sunday morning in late

September. Although we still lived roughly twenty miles apart, we spent as many nights during the week together as we could, and we would either camp out at his place or mine for the entire weekend. I beamed and buried my face into his back as I hugged him from behind.

"It's an official relationship day!" he declared as he slung his arm around my shoulders and kissed my forehead with a loud smack. We cuddled on the couch to watch the morning news as we cupped warm bowls of oatmeal and mugs of tea in our hands. It was mundane, low-key, and perfect. This is what I'd always wanted in a relationship: security, comfort, and the feeling that I was very much loved.

Later that afternoon we went to a nearby hardware store, since Ricardo insisted some of my outlets needed to be rewired, and he needed electrical supplies. I secretly cheered that a man actually wanted to do repairs around my house. I was lucky if my previous suitors could even remember my street address. Before going back to my place, we settled on a fast-food Chinese restaurant near the hardware store for a quick lunch.

"Oatmeal, hardware stores . . . we're starting to act like a boring married couple," I joked as I speared a glob of greasy noodles with my plastic fork.

"No, we're not. You've never been married; you don't know what marriage is like. I . . . I don't think I ever want to get married again or live with a woman," Ricardo blurted out through mouthfuls of brown rice. Although at this point in our relationship we hadn't discussed living together and hadn't seriously addressed the issue of marriage, we'd brought it up casually in conversation. Ricardo had, in fact, been the first to bring it up several weeks prior, jokingly calling it "the merge word." Now everything had come to a screeching halt. I almost choked on my noodles, and tears clouded my eyes. I was shocked, furious, and devastated. Here we go again with another man afraid of commitment.

Ricardo was usually very loving and romantic, but there had been red flags about the darker side of his personality before this incident. Without any warning, he would sometimes turn gruff, pouting and snapping at me with criticisms and corrections. In July, after spending several days together, he'd coldly told me he wanted to be "on his own" and then changed his tune and begged for forgiveness the very next day. Still unemployed, he would moon over daydreams of moving to Seattle, New York City, or back to DC without any consideration of how we would continue our relationship. I was always a little bit on edge around him and terrified of being abandoned by him. I should have seen this coming.

"But . . . but what about all the things you said after we first started dating?" I gasped after I swallowed my food. "You said you wanted to get married! You were so romantic, and you still tell me every day that you love me! You even said that you broke up with your last girlfriend because you wanted to live together, and she didn't want to commit! *Remember?* You told me you wanted something more substantial, and that's why you started dating me! What was all that crap about 'pair-bonding' and having a 'relationship day' this morning? Were you lying?"

He blinked and shrugged.

"I've been thinking about this," Ricardo said, maintaining his poker face. "Marriage didn't work for me. I don't like someone telling me what to do. I like doing my own thing."

"Why do you assume it's going to be like that with me?" I asked, feeling insulted and by this time quite panicked. "And if you don't ever want to live together, then what is there for us? Just keep driving back and forth to each other's houses forever?"

"Well, maybe we should go our separate ways if you think differently." Ricardo sniffed as he shrugged, pursed his lips, and raised his eyebrows, indicating this was the most obvious choice.

"Maybe we should go our separate ways" was a phrase Ricardo liked to toss around when we were having an argument, whether it was major or minor. He first used it when I balked at the idea of eventually having a baby and occasionally threw it at me when he daydreamed about taking a job out of state. So far it had been a bluff and a means to control me and the situation, but he'd never taken it this far before.

"I'm right here in front of you giving you a committed relationship, and you're pushing me away! Your ex-wife made you hate marriage, and you're turning into a flake just like your ex-girlfriend! Those bitches ruined you!" I snarled.

By this time in our relationship, I had developed a deep and irrational jealousy of Ricardo's ex-wife, the mother of his three children. Even though he had no warm feelings toward her, and I didn't view her as romantic competition, I still felt her influence hovering nearby, and I seethed with envy. *She* got to be married to him. *She* got to take his last name, and she didn't even appreciate it. *She* was responsible for his ill feelings toward marriage and left me with the scraps of his commitment fears. Meanwhile, on the other end of the spectrum of my misdirected hatred, his ex-girlfriend was very loose with the boundaries of fidelity, and she and Ricardo had maintained a long-distance off-and-on relationship for many years. I wondered if he wanted to go back to that "arrangement."

I despised his ex-wife and ex-girlfriend, those faceless creatures I'd never met, for "making" him shy away from committed relationships and therefore stealing my future. I couldn't bear to place the responsibility on him, where it squarely belonged. These women were easier scapegoats.

"You and I were in the honeymoon phase. Talking about marriage didn't mean anything," Ricardo said with another sanctimonious shrug and purse of his lips. "Nothing you say in the first six months of a relationship counts. Everybody knows that."

"What the hell is that supposed to mean?" I stammered. "How can you say that? Do you mean that the first six months of our relationship mean nothing? You told me you loved me. I guess that didn't mean anything either?"

Ricardo just shrugged again. "Baby, I'm afraid of commitment. And what would I tell my kids if I were living with you out of wedlock?" He crumpled his napkin in his hands.

"Oh, now all of a sudden you're Mr. Holier-Than-Thou. I was raised Catholic too; don't pull that hypocritical moralistic crap on me," I spat. "First of all, I didn't ask you to live with me, but it would be nice if we were headed in that direction. Second of all, *you* said all that bullshit about wanting to get married, and now you change your mind. You make up the rules when it's convenient for you." I pinched my lips together and turned away, my nostrils flaring as I tried to fight back more tears.

"Sorry, baby, that's the way it is." Ricardo sipped his soda and looked out the window.

Too stunned to say anything else, I drove us back to my condo as I wept and refused to look at him, although I secretly entertained the thought of strangling him by wrapping his seat belt around his skinny neck. We arrived home, and I melted onto the couch. Ricardo quietly joined me and put an arm around my shoulder. I continued to sob heavily, soaking the shoulder of his soft T-shirt with tears.

"You lied to me!" I sniffled hoarsely. "And now you're being so cold and condescending. This hurts so much. I don't know what to do now!"

"I . . . I feel bad for you," Ricardo said quietly and stiffly.

I looked up at him and glared wildly through loose strands of hair and hot tears. "Oh, you're actually feeling *empathy*?" I choked bitterly. "Welcome to the human fucking race! I thought you weren't capable of feeling empathy. Or did you change your mind about that too?"

During one of our deep conversations near the beginning of our relationship, Ricardo remarked that he was incapable of feeling empathy. I had brushed it off as a self-deprecating comment from a self-conscious man, and I was so desperate for a relationship that I didn't want to accept it as truth. Now I realized I should have taken it as a severe warning of heartache to come.

"I'm not good at being married," he pleaded.

"You only married that harpy because she was pregnant!" I spat viciously. "You two never loved each other! It was just a meaningless hookup that lasted five years. How can you compare that to the love we have? You just run and run and run, leaving a trail of pain behind. With that mindset you'll be alone forever."

"But you *have* me now. What else do you need?" Ricardo protested.

"I want to be with you more than anything in the world," I said as I sank farther into the couch. "But now it seems like it can only be on your terms. It's your way or the highway. I'm just along for the ride." I glared at him with glassy eyes.

"I need to finish rewiring that outlet," Ricardo said with a frown. He abruptly stood up, padded to the hallway by the front door, and crouched by the electrical outlet to continue the work he had started earlier. I shut myself in my bedroom and sipped angrily on a glass of wine until, out of exhaustion, I passed out in the clothes I'd been wearing that day.

Around 4:00 a.m., after a fitful, sweaty sleep, I bolted awake to find Ricardo lying still next to me.

"I love you, baby," he murmured in his sleep.

"Bullshit!" I snorted and shoved myself away from him. I pouted for another two hours and then quietly showered and dressed for work.

"You look beautiful. Have a good day," Ricardo mumbled when I poked him in the shoulder and told him I was leaving.

"Whatever. I'll never be able to do that again," I grumbled and stomped out of the house, hoping a busy day at work would keep me distracted from my anger and sadness.

CHAPTER 11

Blue Tip Test

Following the meltdown with Ricardo over his sudden change in intentions, I went to taekwondo that Monday night as usual, which took my mind off my relationship troubles. Trying not to fall over or get kicked in the teeth were always good motivators to keep my mind keenly focused. As we neared the end of class, though, I started to feel sad again. I didn't want to leave what had become my second home to go back to my dark, lonely condo with only my thoughts for company. I wondered if Ricardo would be waiting for me, ready to pick up the argument where it left off. Conversely, I wondered if I was going to come home to a "Dear Jane" letter and find he had simply vanished from my life.

Stinging tears poured down my face as I drove home, and by the time I took my exit from the highway, I was numb and couldn't cry anymore. I opened the front door with a creak and flipped on the foyer light. Ricardo had left his black tool bag by the gutted outlet in the foyer of my condo. I sighed with a muted sense of relief. That meant that he wasn't clearing out of my life for good. At some point he would have to come back for the bag and, more importantly, for me. I was still angry with him, though. I narrowed my eyes as I considered the bag for a moment, leaned over, and spat a fat, foamy droplet of saliva into its open maw.

Moving mechanically, I showered and plunked down in front of a jigsaw puzzle I'd started the day before. I welcomed the distraction and had just finished fitting together all the edges when my phone dinged. It was a text message from Ricardo:

Just got home, honey. How was your day?

Ugh, *really*? I glanced at the spat-upon tool bag and smiled. I flipped my middle finger at my phone and continued to work on the puzzle. He called a few minutes later.

"Baby, I've been thinking about you all day," Ricardo said with a resigned tone. "I'm really sorry."

"Hmph," I grunted. I felt all talked out at this point, and I wasn't going to let him off that easily.

"You're my everything right now," he continued, ignoring my response. "You get the good and the bad."

Ah, I see. I get the good with the bad. Jekyll and Hyde. I didn't realize I'd signed up for the Flaky Boyfriend Deluxe Package.

"When can I see you again?" he asked. I sighed and waited a beat.

"I really need some time to myself right now," I said stoically. "I'll call you later this week."

"Okay," he replied quietly and hung up. I smirked, rolled my eyes, and returned to my puzzle. Now I had the upper hand. Let's let him sweat for a while.

I was cheered up by a private makeup test that Grandmaster had scheduled that Thursday. Finally, after illness, injury, and months of waiting, my chance to advance to the next level was here. There was a small class of green and blue belts, so Grandmaster sent the rest of the group to the front of the room to practice self-defense techniques with Chief Instructor Alex. Meanwhile he corralled me to the back of the room to run through my testing requirements.

"Sliding front foot snap kick, back foot roundhouse, double punch," Grandmaster commanded, unsmiling as he watched me expectantly.

I inhaled sharply and slid forward, popping my left leg up into a front snap kick and feeling relieved that my sweating feet didn't catch on the mat. Sliding kicks are especially effective during sparring to catch an opponent who is backing away or is caught off-balance. Plus, the feet make a satisfying noise when they scrape against the rubbery-textured mats. By the time I repeated the series with sliding roundhouse kicks and sliding side kicks, my heart was pounding from nerves. As emo as this sounds, it was nice to feel sweat stinging my eyes rather than tears . . . ugh. I told you this was a romantic comedy from hell, didn't I?

I stalked through my form, hoping I wouldn't tumble into the stack of mats at the back of the room as I blocked and punched. A young blue belt student joined us so I could do my one-step sparring sequences with a partner. Green belt self-defense introduces elbows, arm breaks, and takedowns into the student repertoire. Slinging my pointed joints through the air felt like a cleansing after that horrible, bottomless Sunday with Ricardo a few days earlier.

After completing my self-defense requirements, Grandmaster shooed the other student away and trotted off to the storage room to select a board for my first break. While he was gone, my brain frantically flipped through mental index cards of the kicks I'd learned so far. Maybe I should use one of my sliding kicks as a thoughtful nod back to my testing requirements, or maybe I could use a side kick, which is usually an easy win for breaking. Side kicks may look simple, but if done correctly, they deliver devastating power and force. I could just bend my leg up toward my standing knee and slam it heel-first into the board, problem solved. . . . No, no, I was sick of side kicks. I always used them when I was a kid. What about a spin kick? Absolutely not! I could barely do a spin kick at all. There was no way I could break a board with one.

I finally settled on using a kick I had planned on using as a twelve-year-old blue belt / red stripe for the next belt test that never came, since my family had stopped going to taekwondo around that time: axe kick. While I was seeking the comfort and safety of a fairly easy kick, my decision was also based on nostalgia. What better way to reenter breaking technique than to pick up exactly where I had left off when I quit taekwondo as a child?

When performing an axe kick, the student slings their leg up into the air and slams the heel down like a guillotine. It can be quite vicious and effective as a head shot in sparring. However, it's often regarded as a little kid's kick for breaking (other than the jumping version), since it's a fairly simple movement that relies more on brute force than focus and precision. Let the taekwondo snobs shake their heads in dismay; I was doing an axe kick. Grandmaster agreed to my simple choice, crouched on one knee, hoisted the flat board into the air, and waited for me to yell to signal that I was ready.

I took a deep breath, barked a loud *ki-yahp*!, threw my leg high into the air . . . and my foot slapped the unyielding board and flopped to the ground limply.

"Concentration!" Grandmaster shouted at me with a glare and not-so-playful swipe of the board at my head. I blushed and quickly repositioned myself.

Crack! The board popped cleanly in two, and I sighed with relief. I returned to a quiet home with a new piece of blue tape on my green belt, a fire in my belly, and an angry determination to not let anything deter me from getting my black belt. Not even my broken and bitter heart.

CHAPTER 12

The Click

After spending a week trying to convince myself that I was just fine on my own without Ricardo and his wishy-washy ways, I had finally started to believe it. I was finding peace I didn't know was missing beneath the thundercloud of my relationship. I awoke the following Sunday, a week after The Chinese Restaurant Incident, to the following text message:

I miss you. Weekends are just not the same without you.

Well, well, well.

Not trusting his sentiments, I ignored Ricardo's message and busied myself all day with household chores and errands. What if he was going to change his mind yet again? I didn't want to take that risk. He finally called late that evening after I'd returned from the gym and the grocery store. Our conversation was hesitant and formal.

"I want to apologize," he began. "I'm in a very dark place. I'm not happy here. I don't fit in. I always clashed with people at work, and I know that will happen again if I get a job here in Texas. I can't even take you out because I don't have any money. But I miss you. I really love you."

I calmly eyed the sizzling pork chops I had just slapped onto an olive oil–drenched frying pan. I wanted to scream at him, grab him by the throat, and tell him to get a goddam job and stop complaining and criticizing everything every waking moment of the day. But I also loved him and needed him so much that I wasn't ready to strike a fatal blow. After a few beats of silence, I attempted to lighten the mood.

"I'm making pork chops," I said with a tiny upswing of hope in my voice.

"I'm coming over," he replied before I could take a breath. Thirty minutes later he was at my door.

"Look at me," he pleaded when he arrived, taking my face in his dry, rough hands and walking me backward into my living room. "I'm really in love with you, more than ever. Do you still love me?"

"Yes," I whispered, tears streaming down my face.

"How much?" he said, pressing his lips to my forehead.

"With all I have."

"I want you to be mine."

"For how long?"

"Pretty much always."

The next few weeks of September and October were a delicate dance of fragile feelings, ruffled feathers that needed soothing, and soulful-eyed declarations of love. Ricardo became increasingly concerned about his "hang-ups" around relationships while also showing more affection and attachment. I didn't trust him, but I also wasn't sure I could function on my own without a relationship. Perhaps I could accept the good with the bad.

"Do you know that I love you?" he would whisper often as he pulled me into a tight embrace.

We began to spend as much time together as we could, and he said everything I thought I wanted to hear. Silently I wondered when the foundation was going to crack again, but I was also surprised at my resilience, relatively speaking. In past relationships where there was even less commitment and certainly no love or deep feelings, I'd fallen apart much earlier in the game when a man got flaky. This time, when much more was at stake, I was stronger than I ever had been . . . relatively speaking.

~

"Long time no see," Grandmaster said sarcastically as he tapped his foot in mock impatience. It was about a week after Ricardo and I had reconciled over pork chops, and I was at the dojang warming up before class. I had taken some time off from classes to live inside my swirling head for a while and ruminate on my relationship woes. I was kind of dreading returning to taekwondo, as I always did after a long break, but at the same time I knew I desperately needed the mental focus and emotional high that I was only able to find in the dojang. I didn't care what we did—flying kicks over a stack of thick pads, cardio drills, a thousand and one spin kicks, an hour of nonstop sparring—it didn't matter. I needed that familiar sting of sweat on my brow to remind me of my purpose and my source of hope.

I had arrived thirty minutes early thanks to especially light traffic, so I had some time to kill. Grandmaster was preoccupied with planning an upcoming tournament, so he pulled me away from my stretches and asked me to work with Josh, a chubby-cheeked preteen who had once been in my white belt class and was now an orange belt. Since I had been skipped ahead to green belt, I was now senior in rank to him and therefore responsible for encouraging him to practice and learn. Any student, regardless of rank, is expected to help lower-ranking students.

"Just work on kicks with him," Grandmaster said quickly, shoving a teardrop-shaped focus pad into my hand before he raced into his office and plopped down behind his computer with a sigh.

I'd never coached or taught technique to any fellow students, but I figured if I could handle workshops with brash, weary adults in my day job, I could handle an eleven-year-old kid. Without thinking, I went into facilitator mode and broke down spin kick and turning back side kick into their mechanical pieces. I cheered every time Josh slapped the pad with a spin kick. I was coaching! I felt powerful and confident, something I was sorely lacking at home.

Grandmaster and Chief Instructor Alex dragged me away so we could begin sparring class. I was so emotionally high from working with Josh that I danced dreamily through the sparring matches, not worrying once about how I looked or how crappy and clumsy my fighting was. It was the most fulfilling moment of my week and planted the seed of desire to give back to other students as much as I had received from my instructors. Ever the nurturer, I found my opportunity to be a caregiver in some form.

The elation of my reconciliation with Ricardo and new opportunities in the dojang hit a wall in October. He continued to struggle with joblessness, and the elephant in the room over whether he would stay in Texas with me or seek employment elsewhere grew larger and more ominous. Meanwhile, I had severely injured my back while lifting weights at the gym and had to take two weeks off from taekwondo to recover.

When I finally returned to taekwondo after my back injury, not only had I seemed to have hit another plateau in sparring, but I felt like I was sliding backward. I didn't fight smartly or move efficiently. My moves were too clunky and slow. I winced and closed my eyes instinctively when the harsh blows came at me.

I reassured myself that one day I would feel "the click" when my body and brain connected, just as I had with swimming, ballet, classical guitar, and other physically demanding endeavors. As I'd learned with my past activities, I knew it took time to build up not only muscle memory but also keen intuition. "The click" was that moment when my body suddenly snapped into perfect symmetry and performed with ease. After "the click," my body would forever hold a memory of what perfect performance could be. For example, I could never go back to a clumsy, slow freestyle stroke, even if I spent years out of the pool, nor could I unlearn the technical tools of the musical trade when I watched a classical guitar performance. I hoped I would soon feel "the click" in taekwondo, because it sure as hell wasn't happening at the present moment.

Since I had barely recovered from my back injury and was dissatisfied with my sparring performance in taekwondo class, I decided to postpone testing for my blue belt. I found myself just wanting to get it over with, which was missing the point entirely. I wasn't one of the little kids forced there by a parent who wanted a quick return on investment. I was serious about learning taekwondo and retaining it so I could help others learn. I needed to take my time so my body and mind could truly absorb everything.

Several weeks later, I started to get what I wanted, or at least what I'd told myself I wanted at the time, both at home and in the dojang.

"Should we live together?" Ricardo asked one night when the autumn air had finally turned crisp and cool. We were holed up in my condo, eating beans and rice and snuggling on the couch while we watched movies.

Instead of hearing a choir of angels singing, I was stunned into silence.

"Um . . . this is quite a change," I replied tentatively as I played with a gold tassel on a throw pillow. Even though we had made up since his declaration in September that he never wanted to marry again or even live with a woman, I still didn't fully trust him. I wondered if this was just a spur-of-the-moment thought that he would conveniently forget when the moment suited him, or if he was actually serious.

"I know. I'm just looking for ways for us to be a team. I *do* want to get remarried," he said, kissing my forehead. "You're so good to me. Sometimes I don't know why. You're restoring my faith in people. You're mine, and I'm yours. I don't think you know how much I love you."

"Let's figure out this job thing of yours first," I replied quietly and shifted closer to him. It felt like a weight had been lifted, not entirely removed but picked up and softly placed outside the door where it wouldn't bother me as much.

As if to add an exclamation point to Ricardo's declaration of commitment (for now anyway), the following Monday's tae-kwondo class was fantastic. I felt light and strong and began to feel that I was rising out of my plateau. One of the masters pulled me aside and broke down the mechanics of flying side kick. He was the same one who had seen me land gracelessly on my ass into a pile of pads during my first color belt cardio class, so now was my chance to redeem myself. I didn't quite feel "the click," but I was starting to inch closer to it.

We ended the class by hitting the bags with hand strikes, and afterward as I sat at home icing my shaking paw with a bag of frozen corn, I mused about where I might be in six months. Hopefully I'd be a high-ranking red belt (or very close to it) and in a loving, promising, healthy, and more stable relationship with Ricardo. No more plateaus or steps backward. I wanted everything to move onward and upward.

CHAPTER 13

Goodbye . . . Just Kidding!

Texas winters seem to alternate between a balmy seventy degrees on Christmas Day or an ice storm that comes without warning and shuts down the entire state. At the end of 2013, Texas got the short end of the weather stick. For nearly a week in mid-December, Ricardo and I were trapped in my condo by several inches of thick ice. We had planned it that way so we could ride out the storm together, or at least I'd hoped it would bring us together. Once again, Mr. Hyde paid a visit.

During the first hint of a thaw, I went to a hotel in Grapevine for a week of training and certification in the Myers-Briggs Type Indicator (MBTI), a decades-old personality assessment that had given society the popular "introvert" and "extravert" terminology, among other things. I would use the tool for coaching and team development at work. I hadn't felt this excited about a work-related topic in quite some time, and I was also relishing all the alone time Ricardo and I had had together the previous week (other than him making an offhand comment that I was eating too much. I figured I could starve off a few pounds. I'd show him!). I felt like things were on the up and up.

The night before my final day of MBTI training, I was studying for the certification exam when Ricardo called around nine thirty.

"I'm moving back to DC. I just wanted to let you know that," he said nonchalantly.

"Whoa . . . what?"

"You knew this was coming, baby. My unemployment money has run out, and I still haven't found work in Texas. I'm moving back East."

"You call me late at night when you know I have an exam for my certification tomorrow, and you drop this bombshell on me?" I was too stunned to be angry . . . almost.

"Sorry, baby. That's the way it is. I have contacts on the East Coast that I don't have here. Things are just easier for me up there," he replied. I felt helpless, in checkmate. I knew he wasn't having luck finding a substantial job, but did he have to pack up and run back to DC as if it were some magical promised land? Did he have to flake out on me again the way he had in September when he'd said he never wanted to get married, after months of professing his undying love and commitment to me?

"I don't know what to say," I said weakly. "I have to study. Good night." I hung up the phone and sat on the hotel bed feeling mentally exhausted. He had threatened for months to move out of state and shamed me whenever I protested and got upset, but it never seemed like he would actually do anything. Now, seemingly on the spur of the moment, he was making it a reality. I trudged through the rest of my evening like a zombie and slept fitfully that night.

I was thankful for the distraction of my final day of MBTI training and for the fact that my parents were waiting for me at my home in Fort Worth when I returned from the hotel in Grapevine. I was the designated pit stop during their trips from their new home in Tulsa, Oklahoma, where they'd moved in 2011, down to the to the Texas Hill Country to visit their friends or to Austin to visit my brother and his wife. When I arrived home, my parents greeted me at my door with pizza and wine, and I burst into frustrated tears.

"I don't know what to do!" I moaned. "Ricardo called me last night and said he's moving back to DC! He's been threatening to move for months and keeps going back and forth on his word. I don't know how much effort he put into really looking for work here. He said he wanted to stay here and make it work, and now this! This is so frustrating!"

"Sorry, pumpkin," Dad said as he poured me a glass of wine.

"Maybe this is for the best. This back and forth stuff has been going on for a long time," Mom chimed in over the clicks of her knitting needles. Suddenly my phone dinged. It was a text from Ricardo.

Do you want to work out tomorrow? the message said. Really? He's moving across the damned country, and he's acting like things are normal?

I think I need some time on my own to process what you told me. I'm still a little in shock, I texted back.

What is there to process? It is what it is, he responded sharply, or as sharp as one can be via text message.

It's just a lot to take in, I typed quickly. *We can still do something tomorrow after my parents leave.*

Oh no, I wouldn't want to take away from your precious time to 'process,' Ricardo's return message read. I began to panic. I left my parents to their pizza and wine and holed up in my bedroom so I could call him. Perhaps this could be worked out better over the phone than via text message.

"Hi," I said tentatively after he answered his phone.

"Oh, shouldn't you be 'processing' right now? I thought you needed time to do that," Ricardo growled.

"Come on!" I was stung by his rare foray into sarcasm. "Things aren't black and white with me like they are with you. This is really hard to deal with. Can't you understand that? You're moving across the damned country!"

"I don't like Texas. I never liked it here. I don't fit in," he spouted, a sneer barely contained in his voice. "Baby, we're drifting . . . and you're . . . well, you're too needy."

Wait a minute, he was calling me "needy"? The word "needy" scrapes just as grittily down my back as the word "bitch" does, possibly even more. "Needy" implies impossible to deal with, a burden, an unwanted annoyance, and a person who is weak. At least a bitch has some implied power. And besides, *he* was the one who always seemed to be seeking reassurance with his cutesy little questions: "Do you love me today?" "Do you know that I love you?" "Do you think we'll be together for a long time?" Unfortunately, I was still too stunned by his coldness to spit out a response. I was also too afraid to say anything that would push him further away from me.

"We'll have a long-distance relationship. I think I'm more comfortable with that anyway," he said, sounding colder with every word. I started to squeak in protest.

"I don't care if I only see you every few months," he added.

"In fact," he continued, "I don't care if I ever see you again."

I collapsed onto the bed in tears. I couldn't believe someone who claimed to love me so much could be so incredibly cruel. I would like to say that I screamed at him to fuck off and take his lazy ass back home with his tail between his legs, but I remained silent. My brain was shocked into denial. What did I do to deserve this hatefulness?

"You could always move to DC and continue to date me," he said calmly, throwing me a scrappy bone of hope.

"What?" I sniffled. "Where would I live?"

"We'd live in separate residences, of course. I don't want to live with anyone ever again."

I pictured myself in a tiny overpriced apartment with yellow cracked walls and unhung paintings gathering dust on the floor. I started calculating the hours it would take for us to get to each other's "separate residences" if we happened to live on opposite sides of the capital. It didn't make any sense, and it was the first time I truly despised him.

"No. That's ridiculous." I started to shake and cry again. "If I'm going to throw away my life here and move across the country for someone, I want to live with you. I'm worth it, even if *you* don't think so."

"I do think you're worth it," he replied quietly.

"Did you mean what you said when you told me that I was helping you 'believe in love again'?" I asked through muted tears.

"No. I lied. Mel, it's time to say goodbye," he whispered.

After I hung up the phone, I kicked open my bedroom door and crumpled into my parents' waiting arms. For the next few hours I sat limply on the couch with my head hanging forward and hot tears splashing from my eyes as they sat on either side of me gently patting my shoulders.

That night as my parents slept in my bedroom, I twisted and turned on the fold-out couch. I tried to console myself and my insomnia with nighttime TV. About two in the morning, a text popped up from Ricardo:

I'm sorry I am being so difficult. My thoughts have been all over the place trying to plan out what to do. I am crashing against you because you are one of the few people who care about me. I suspect this is my way of rebelling. Please don't give up on us. I rolled my eyes, drifted into an exhausted sleep, and didn't move for two days.

A few days later, Ricardo contacted me via e-mail. While I did stand up for myself a little bit in my response (calling him out on his cruel comments and his unwillingness to look for work), I couldn't resist opening my heart to him again. What would I do without a relationship? I still felt like I needed to be loved (or at least liked) by someone to find happiness and security. After a flurry of e-mails and negotiations, we had a whirlwind reconciliation. Ricardo decided to stay in town and accepted a part-time job, and we shakily took things day by day. My words had been strong, but he had a stronger psychological hold over me. Who was the wishy-washy one now?

Three days before Christmas, when I showed up at the dojang holiday party with Ricardo on my arm, Grandmaster looked surprised (I had told him about our mini-breakup) but said nothing. I won the student of the year award and proudly tacked the small certificate on the wall in my home office next to my university diplomas. Maybe 2014 would usher in happier times.

CHAPTER 14

Blue Belt Test

Ricardo and I spent every day we could together during the Christmas break and into the beginning of 2014. The mini-breakup, instead of freeing us to follow our increasingly different paths, had instead given us a sense of urgency and hunger for each other's company. I returned to taekwondo in January after the holiday break and promptly injured my left shoulder so badly doing a simple block that it took nearly a year to heal (probably thanks to being too stubborn to see a doctor). I hadn't had a good injury in a few months, so I suppose I was due. I felt relieved that some things in life were going on as usual.

While I was recuperating, Ricardo invited me to his house to hang out on a gray Saturday afternoon in mid-January. I was also still recuperating from the Great Four-Day Breakup of December 2013. I didn't know where our relationship was going; it seemed like he was holding all the cards. Ricardo was padding around barefoot in his workout clothes and gave me a peck on the cheek when I entered the house. I perched on the couch to watch a movie while he did abdominal exercises on a workout ball.

"The new part-time job at the bicycle shop is okay for now, but I'll need to find more substantial work," Ricardo said as he leaned back on the ball and stretched his chest. His voice was distorted as he stretched farther back and extended his throat. "I'm glad I stayed, but I still need money, baby. I might need to find another place to live."

He knelt beside me and said with a smirk, "Maybe I could move into The Garden," referring to a tumble-down apartment complex on the opposite side of the street from my posh neighborhood. "Or . . . maybe I could rent a room from you."

This is the part where the needle jams on the record: *Screeeech!*

I was delighted, surprised, a little scared, but mostly in shock.

"You mean . . . move in with me?" I asked tentatively, and we clutched each other's fingers. He rested his chin on the soft arm of the couch and tilted his face up toward me.

"I've been looking deep inside myself and realize that I've been directing some anger that I have about my ex-wife toward you instead. I want to stop the cycle of giving up and moving back to DC every few years. I love you, and I want to be with you. I want to change," he said.

"I don't want to get my heart broken again. That last one was pretty bad," I muttered darkly, tugging my hand away.

"You have to feel secure in our love," Ricardo pleaded, widening his eyes as he continued to look up at me. "Our love supersedes arguments or cross words or whether or not we say 'I love you' every day. Let my actions prove that I love you." He climbed up over the arm of the couch and wrapped me into a hug.

We talked quietly about repairs we wanted to make in my condo and things we wanted to buy together. Later that day we went to the grocery store, my barometer for coupledom, and bought cashews and Diet Coke, which would become staples in our little shared household. I really didn't think I'd be in that place—a real, messy, but growing relationship. Okay, sure, there was all that tension over the summer, and let's not forget the little breakup in the winter, but I had big bright blinding stars in my eyes: I had a man who was *in love with me*. I'd never really had that before. When things were good, they were wonderful, so maybe I just had to settle for the disappointments to ensure I kept getting that hit of love, like a drug that's ultimately dangerous but feels so damned good in the moment.

I remembered that in previous relationships (if you could even call them that), I would *live* for receiving a text message once a week from my *amour du jour*. I used to beg for scraps, and now a man I loved was telling me he wanted to wake up next to me every morning. This was so different. Flawed, for sure, but different.

When I returned home, I immediately began cleaning out the closet in my second bedroom, shoulder injury be damned.

Meanwhile, a thought began to germinate. I wanted to write about taekwondo and all the life lessons I was gleaning from it. At the moment my thoughts were just fragments of ideas. Did I want to write a book? Should I start a blog? I had so much narrative floating around in my head—not in a manic way where I couldn't switch off the fire hose of monologue in my brain, but it was bubbling up so quickly that it was harder and harder to capture. I wished I had a little stenographer on my shoulder. Would I be jumping on the year-in-the-life bandwagon that seemed to be the model for so many recent memoirs? Could I be funny and poignant at the same time? I was excited, but it would be another two months before I launched the blog I named Little Black Belt as a tongue-in-cheek homage to the ubiquitous little black dress.

In the midst of my cohabitation planning and blog scheming at the beginning of February 2014, I'd put my upcoming blue belt test on the back burner. Grandmaster encouraged me to go through with it, and I was more than eager, since I'd been a green belt / blue tip since late September 2013. The night before the test, I sat cross-legged on my bed and visualized the entire test. I smiled as I imagined how I would creep out of work early to scrub off my makeup and stretch out my nervous limbs at the dojang. I closed my eyes and saw myself marching confidently to the front of the room to face the judges' table. . . .

The test begins with kicking requirements. I crouch into fighting stance with a loud ki-yahp! and spring into the air to execute a jump front snap kick. I repeat it on the left side even though there's a familiar twinge of pain deep in my hamstring. I execute the three other required kicks—jump roundhouse kick, jump back kick, jump side kick—with precision and power. Then it's time for my form.

I am alone in ready stance in the center of the room. My heart races and my breath quickens, but I remember I have done this form beautifully and flawlessly countless times before. I dart my head to the left and whip my balled fists into a high block and inside middle block, making a crescent moon with my arms. Each breath is intentional. Every position of my body is deliberate. I catch a spectator's eye as I face the back of the room and smile slightly as I jab a spear-hand thrust directly toward them. I am bold and ominous, like thunder rolling across the night sky.

One-step sparring is crisp and swift. My partner steps forward with a punch. I knock their offending fist away with a block, swipe a knife-hand strike toward their neck, and jab them in the gut with an elbow strike. Four more one-steps, three more, two more to go. And then I free spar for the first time at a test. I suit up, simultaneously dreading it and curious about how I will perform. I make it through my fight, panting through my mouth guard.

And then the finale—breaking. I have chosen to break a board with an elbow as a nod back to one of the self-defense techniques in my one-step sparring series. I inhale sharply, and with a shriek I slam my right forearm through the board with a clean snap. The audience applauds, and I smirk shyly with satisfaction. I bow to the masters, exhale deeply, and trot back to my spot on the floor. After it's over, my name is called. I race to the front and bow as I'm handed my blue belt. I shake hands with Grandmaster and the other masters and quietly revel in my accomplishment.

... Twenty-four hours and a Whataburger patty melt later, I was sitting on my bed, gently unfolding my new blue belt in my trembling hands.

It felt like I had been a green belt forever (eight months, to be exact). The green belt represents a plant growing from the earth, just as the taekwondo student is growing from a solid and fertile foundation. My relationship with Ricardo had grown too. We had been through major moments and milestones, good and bad, in a matter of months rather than the years that some other couples take to have those same experiences. I was becoming more and more confident and skilled in my taekwondo practice. Now I was reaching for the bright blue sky.

Part Four:

BLUE BELT AND

BLUE BELT / RED TIP

CHAPTER 15

The Amazing Walking Uterus

The four months I spent from February to May 2014 as a blue belt and blue belt / red tip was the shortest period I'd spend in a particular color belt level (not counting the two months I'd spent as a white belt). While fleeting, the blue belt months felt more relaxed than any other training period.

If the white belt months felt like freshman year in high school, the blue belt months felt like junior year: you don't have the responsibilities and the pressures that the seniors or higher-ranking belts do, but you get to have a lot more fun than the underclassmen, like driving and going to the prom. I was edging toward the halfway mark between white belt and black belt and would be considered "high ranking" when I reached red belt, but I could still get away with the clumsiness and slowness attributed to lower ranks.

During this period, my confidence in my taekwondo performance began to solidify and take flight. I began to trust myself more, and that aura of confidence even bled over into other areas of my life. My boss told me that I was "intense and intentional" in my performance at work, and it was evidenced by what he saw as an insatiable desire to learn. It was also around this time I began to really appreciate the mental and emotional stability my taekwondo practice brought me. I now had a clarity, focus, patience, and emotional maturity I'd never experienced before. I learned to laugh off (and learn from) mistakes and not put so much pressure on myself to be perfect. I began to pay more attention to the important things in my life and less to the other stimuli and clutter. Physically I was in better shape, although it wasn't a huge transformation. I had actually gained a little weight since I first started taekwondo, mostly because I was no longer starving myself and drinking myself to sleep, but I looked much healthier, more muscular, and shone with a bright glow.

Another thing I'd grown to appreciate over my time in the dojang was the mentality of men and boys. I had grown up with a brother, worked on a team of all men who were much older than me but respected me as an equal, was closer to my male friends in graduate school than I was to female friends, and trained with several male taekwondo students and instructors, so I'd had more than one glimpse into the male mind. While I was never really "one of the boys," I'd missed the girlfriends' boat. I wasn't even sure what I was missing out on—maybe boozy brunches and torturously drawn-out shopping trips? I've never made the effort to endear myself to other women. I've always figured if I ever get married, my bachelorette party would be spent hanging out at home by myself eating cupcakes, drinking whiskey, and watching mafia movies.

Maybe I've been more drawn toward male friends because I haven't figured out how to handle the rich complexities of female friendships. Men have always been easier to talk to, at least on a superficial level. Perhaps I subconsciously enjoyed being the only alpha female in the room. Besides, if I hung around a bunch of guys, then that meant there was always someone else who could reach for the kicking pads on the highest shelf.

Being the only adult female in the dojang, however, heaped some responsibility on my shoulders. I discovered through hastened conversations with parents of other students that their daughters looked up to me. I was a little embarrassed but secretly delighted that the young girls had someone they could relate to and aspire to emulate. I was educated and financially independent and had a pretty sweet roundhouse kick. If I were a seven-year-old, I'd look up to me too. I wanted to encourage them to believe in their own magic before they're crushed by the realities of the world. This added another layer to the expectations of me as a future black belt, and I've been honored to carry that torch. I would be even more honored if more girls and women donned doboks and joined me. (Hint: put this book down now, and go sign up for taekwondo lessons. I'll wait.)

I had a harder time figuring out the twists and turns of the male mind in my personal life.

Late one night when Ricardo and I were going to sleep, his voice floated up in the darkness: "Hey, listen, if I get my affairs in order, I want to have a kid."

I sighed and rolled my eyes at the ceiling. The topic of a baby had come up sporadically since our first discussion shortly after we started dating. I had hoped that his interest had waned. After all, he was over forty, already had kids, and had seemed to be very comfortable with his bachelor lifestyle in Texas. He was also still mostly unemployed since his termination the previous June. Besides, ever since our little meltdown in September, he'd stopped talking about marriage. Was I good enough to impregnate but not good enough to marry?

"Really?" I replied. "Or will you change your mind tomorrow like you have about marriage or wanting to live in DC?" A cruel little bubble surged up into my throat, and I smiled at my comeback. To be fair, I had acted like a fence-sitter with children the same way he'd debated whether to stay in Texas or move back to the East Coast. I was still paying for my lie to "consider" having a baby within the next five years, and I clung even harder to all the reasons why that would be a terrible idea.

Accurate or not, at thirty-four I thought my eggs were already cooked, and having what I feared would be a dangerous pregnancy and delivery was not a risk I was willing to take. I was also not willing to go off my psychiatric medications and risk suffering debilitating postpartum depression. As for Ricardo, I didn't understand why he would want the cost and the care of a new baby. He already had (and was still paying for) three kids. He also didn't seem to have a realistic view of how much time caring for a newborn would consume. Had he made his ex-wife do all the hard work while he did the fun dad stuff? Is that why he had such an idealized vision of parenthood? An image of Ricardo trotting off to the gym while I rocked a screaming, vomiting infant flashed in my mind. I hated him.

There was also the question of Ricardo's ability to truly commit. He often changed his mind about marriage and where he wanted to live: Some days he'd declare his everlasting love for me and swear that he wanted to put down roots in Texas. Other days he would pout about how much he disliked Texas and wanted to move back to the East Coast. Why should I make the biggest commitment of all in what I hated to admit was an unstable relationship?

As I waited for Ricardo to respond to my little jab, I mused more about my decision to remain childfree. The more Ricardo pushed me, the more I wanted to dig in my heels and defend my right to the life I wanted.

I've had my moments of wistfully daydreaming about what it might be like to have a child . . . but those are just daydreams. I can make a meaningful contribution to the world in many other ways besides popping out one more mouth to feed on an overpopulated planet. I loved working with the students in taekwondo class and the people I served in my day job. I had so many things I wanted to learn in addition to taekwondo. Turning into an exhausted, resentful, mentally unstable, sad, and likely alcoholic and pill-addicted mother would not allow me to live as fully as I did now. Why should society or one man in particular demand that I give up my happiness?

Sometimes I still want that daughter, though—the one with flowing hair who screeches with a wild laughter I never had as a sullen and quiet child, who picks out her own clothes and wants to play with my makeup, who has a no-nonsense attitude and kicks the crap out of other kids in sparring class.

In other words, I'd love to have a daughter as long as she isn't anything like me.

Back to our regularly scheduled program. . . .

After a few moments of awkward silence, Ricardo cleared his throat.

"Well, maybe I won't get my shit together, and you won't have to worry about it," he muttered as he turned over, barely containing the hurt in his voice.

"So that's all you care about?" I asked. "If all you want is a baby, then am I just a walking uterus to you?"

"Well, you're not getting any younger."

Ricardo was never adept at picking up on my sarcasm. I stared at the ceiling and fumed.

"Do you still want to move in with me?" I asked after a few minutes.

"Yes," he replied and turned back to face me as he snaked his arm under my neck and shoulders. What I couldn't bear to tell him then or ever was that I didn't trust him to provide the stability I knew I needed if we were to have a child. I didn't want to willingly take on his life of struggle and self-imposed impoverishment. I did trust him to love me and our hypothetical child, but I didn't trust him not to change his mind on a whim about sticking around. I didn't trust him to get his finances in order and be able to save for the future. I didn't want to take the risk, but would I have to compromise my physical, mental, and financial well-being to ensure he wouldn't leave me? In hindsight it seems ridiculous to give in to a demand I didn't want. At the time, I felt I had no choice. I didn't see an alternative to being in this relationship. Being single again seemed too distant and unknown.

As I lay quietly in the darkness, I tried to burn the reality of moving in together into my mind. If Ricardo really did move in, I would be the primary breadwinner, the owner of the house, bringing home triple his income, and keeping us afloat. I wondered if he would feel weird about it. He'd be under my roof, squeezing in among my stuff, and adjusting his schedule to mine. I hoped both our egos could take it. I hoped it would be an exercise in humility and love for both of us. I just didn't see how using a baby as a relationship bandage would make our budding life together any better. I groped in the darkness for his hand, tucked it under my chin, and finally drifted off to sleep.

CHAPTER 16

Home Life

Ricardo officially moved into my condo the weekend of Valentine's Day 2014, and for the next few weeks, it seemed surreal. We'd poke each other giddily and giggle: "We live together!" This was such a paradigm shift for both of us that we almost couldn't believe it had happened. Both of us were vulnerable and gun-shy when it came to relationships, and Ricardo's moving in symbolized a new step for us both. After questions of commitment, the Four-Day Breakup of Christmas 2013, and the renewed pressure on me to have a baby, we were both seeking some semblance of stability.

Everything was a milestone: the first time Ricardo received mail at the condo, adding his name to the dry-cleaning ticket, hearing the click of his key in the lock, yelling "Roomie!" at each other when one of us came through the door. I would huddle on the couch wrapped in a blanket waiting for him to come home from his late-evening workouts. He would turn over expectantly under the covers each morning as I leaned down to give him a kiss before I went to work. When he bought a membership at my gym, he blurted out in front of the sales rep, "Our lives are becoming more intertwined!"

Sometime in early March, the newness began to wear off. As I brushed my teeth early one morning, I started to resent Ricardo in a way I hadn't before. I resented him for settling for part-time work while I held down a professional full-time job. I had goals. I wanted to pay off my mortgage. I wanted to get my black belt. I resented him for cutting me out of his search process for more substantial work. I resented him for pressuring me to agree to a baby when he seemed to regard the actual process of child-rearing with only dreamy idealism. I scowled at my reflection in the mirror.

Just then Ricardo woke up and shuffled to the bathroom to brush his teeth. My heart softened. He hugged me from behind and cooed, "My roomie!" I sighed and leaned into his embrace. We'd work it out. Perhaps I could express my concerns from a place of love, not hostility. Maybe that would soften the nagging feeling of dread.

And then I started to lose my mind . . . well, sort of. It got worse in the summer, so hang on for that.

I began to have body-image problems again. Along with bicycles, books, and designer shirts, Ricardo had also brought with him a digital scale that was more accurate than my cheap plastic drug store scale and let me know that I was five pounds heavier than I'd thought I was. According to the readout, I was 119 pounds, which to me was unacceptable. I thought I was at least down to 115. It sent me into a tailspin. I became depressed and short-tempered, and my foul mood seemed to draw out even more self-defeating behavior: I reached for comfort food when I was bored or distressed, and I reached for the covers when the early alarm buzzed for me to get up and head to the gym.

In retrospect, I imagine my stress and inward dissatisfaction stemmed from the sad fact that my relationship with Ricardo was more flawed and much less stable than I wanted to believe it was. I also hadn't forgotten his fondness for very thin women and panicked when I saw the numbers rise on the scale. I thought I was getting everything I wanted—a domestic partnership and a protective, attentive boyfriend who claimed to love me. I felt like it was my responsibility to keep everything running smoothly.

There was also the matter of Ricardo's employment, or rather underemployment. He had a part-time job at a bike shop, but he still seemed to be having no luck finding more substantial work. The one-year anniversary of his job loss was looming. Ever since he'd pushed me away during his early job search, I was afraid to ask him whether he'd had any leads or if he was looking at all. I could have taken the chance to express my unease about his lack of finding full-time work after nine months of unemployment, but I stayed silent. Ricardo admitted to glossing over situations when he was in a tight spot, which could make conditions worse. At times he would beg me for feedback and communication, but I clammed up. I just couldn't do it. I was so afraid to express my fears, concerns, desires, and even anger because I didn't want to scare him away or, worse, make him turn on me with an attack. When he was in a bad mood, he was quick to criticize and be condescending about anything: my choice of words, my choice of clothing, my opinions, my weight, my supposed inability to make decisions (or at least that's what he had me believe), the supposed physical tremors that he attributed to either my anxiety medication or my anxiety itself. I was terrified of his impossibly high and ever-changing standards, something I'd brushed aside in the name of making this relationship work at all costs. I was terrified of *him*. All that did was heighten the wall of mistrust and miscommunication between us. And yet, I remained because he told me he loved me, and I'd become dependent on that fragile reassurance.

In early April I had another pressing item on my plate besides my nagging relationship worries: my next color belt test. I would be testing for blue belt / red tip, which is the final rank I had reached as a child. As usual, Ricardo was my loyal spectator and official belt test photographer. I still wasn't quite able to quell my nerves the night of my test, but I performed my jump kicks, difficult form, and self-defense with precision and held my own in a sparring match with a teenage girl who had a good three inches and twenty pounds on me. I did two clean board breaks with a left-hand knife-hand strike and a right-foot sliding side kick and trembled with relief when Grandmaster ceremoniously placed a piece of shiny red tape on my blue belt.

"We're living a love story that's still being written!" Ricardo exclaimed as we arrived home from the belt test, our bellies full of chicken fingers and fries from a nearby chain restaurant. I threw my taekwondo uniform in the washing machine and turned to him.

"Do you feel like this is your home now?" I asked.

"Yes, baby," he replied, wrapping his arms around me and kissing my cheek. "I like doing repairs and buying new things for the house. It makes it feel like it's our place." I'd never been with a man before who dragged me around to buy bath mats and kitchen utensils. Although we were tiptoeing around each other's flaws and hair-trigger tempers, we claimed that we'd found a more solid love than we'd ever had in the past. As the water in the washing machine began gushing over my taekwondo uniform that was still damp with sweat, Ricardo turned me toward him, covered my forehead with kisses, and told me over and over again how beautiful I was.

Maybe the complications of this relationship were a test that I could work through, just as performing the complicated pieces of my blue belt form helped me graduate to the next level in taekwondo. I could do this. I could navigate through the contradictions and surprises.

CHAPTER 17

Getting Fat Shamed as a Size Four

"What would you do if I held on too tightly for you to escape?" Chief Instructor Alex asked, grabbing me from behind in a bear hug. It was early May and my first class after returning from a two-week vacation Ricardo and I had taken to visit his family. Now I was back to work in the dojang with a new red stripe on my blue belt and more difficult skills to practice.

Uh . . . what to do . . . the index cards in my mind were flashing blanks. I shrugged my trapped shoulders and bent down low, doing little other than lifting Alex an inch off the ground and eliciting giggles from my classmates.

"Remember?" He gave me a little shove. "Kick the knee!" It was so obvious and yet so elusive! He turned his eyes to the rest of the class.

"In a real-life situation, you need to be prepared with one or two really simple things you can do well and do fast so you can get out of there. It's not about fancy kicks or complex combinations. You won't have time to think about it." Alex raised his dark eyebrows to emphasize his point. "Get back in line. Shoo!" He flicked his hands at us and cracked a tiny smile.

It looked like my taekwondo instincts hadn't quite kicked in yet, red tip or not. Taekwondo has always been a humbling experience. For example, no matter how badass, toned, or agile I thought I was, my left foot spin kick was slow and sloppy, and my flying side kick was more of an apologetic hop. I could deal with having crappy kicks, though. What bugged me was when I couldn't respond intelligently to a spur-of-the-moment attack. I still didn't feel confident in a sparring match.

I was trying too hard, trying to play by the book and do what was "right." I didn't trust myself or my instincts. Ironically, when I needed to think clearly, I was thinking too much.

As I drove home, I thought about my botched attempt to escape Alex's hold. How would I respond if I felt trapped in a seemingly impossible situation and couldn't come up with a way to defend myself? Fate brought me that opportunity later that week. Despite my chief instructor's urgings to trust my training and my instincts, I froze in the face of adversity right in my own home.

"I liked you better skinnier." Ricardo sighed as he stretched his body across the sun-dappled bed and rested his head in my lap. It was a Friday morning, the last day of May, and a year after the memorable Memorial Day weekend that had spurred our romance.

"Wha—what?" I was stunned and deeply hurt. He turned to face me with wide puppy eyes and a pouty frown.

"You've changed so much since we first started dating. You were so thin when we met. I mean, baby, you match me bite for bite now when we eat. I've told you before that I might look elsewhere if you continue to put on weight. Did you . . . sell me a bill of goods?"

Little volcanoes of hatred erupted violently in my head. Coupled with them was the crushing self-consciousness that always swept through me when a man expressed disapproval. Just as when Alex had grabbed me in taekwondo class, I was too unnerved to think clearly and fight back. I was terrified of Ricardo's criticism and his threats to leave, although the threats had been hollow so far.

"First of all, I *don't* 'match you bite for bite,' so don't lie! Second, I was *sick* when you met me!" I snapped. "I was getting drunk every night and starving myself because I was *miserable!* I wanted to die! And I have *not* put on that much weight—maybe a few pounds, which I *needed to gain.* I'm a size four fucking petite! And *you* always push fries and pizza on me, so don't complain about how much I eat. I can't believe you'd say something like that!"

He shrugged and pursed his lips sanctimoniously before adding, "While we're at it, that brings up the elephant in the room—I want a child and you don't."

"Oh, this again," I growled. "What the hell does that have to do with my weight? By the way, have you realized I'd gain weight if I were pregnant? What would you think of that?"

"Supermodels lose baby weight in five or six weeks. You could do that too."

"Why are you doing this to me when I have to leave for work in fifteen minutes?"

Ricardo never did have a good sense of timing. He brought up topics late at night or right before we had to go somewhere, just like when he'd called me late in the evening during my December Myers-Briggs training to announce he wanted to move back to DC.

"You didn't answer my question. Do you want to have my baby?" Ricardo asked with a frown and doing his best to make his eyes look large and sad.

"I *had* to agree to a baby," I said through tears. "You threatened to leave me if I didn't! And why are you so fixated on a baby? You're romanticizing something that would be *very* hard on our finances *and* our relationship. You're a *parent.* Have you forgotten you have three kids already? How have you not thought about these things? I think you just want the fun daddy times. Babies are hard work, which you should know unless your ex-wife was the one who did all the daily grunt work. You don't even care about marrying me.

I'm just an incubator to you." I started slamming around the room, slapping on my watch and grabbing my purse.

"Mel, please, it's not a deal breaker! I'm sorry I'm harsh sometimes. I don't know any other way to be!" Ricardo called. God, I hated him.

"Who is going to pay for this magical baby that you want so goddamn badly?" I asked. "Where are we going to put it? My place is a good size, but it's not that big."

"It can sleep in a drawer!"

"Are you stupid? You know you can't do that."

"You're being very First World about this."

"Then go live in the Third World if you don't like it!"

I stormed down the stairs of my condo, jumped into my car, and pouted and cried as I drove to work. It was a quiet day that thankfully went by quickly. My closest work friend, Madeline, asked me what was wrong as I moped around the office, but I brushed it off as nothing. She had always been my closest ally and cheerleader, an extravert who adopted me from the day we met. By this point, though, I had been withholding my problems lest she tell me something I knew was true but didn't want to hear.

As I brooded at my desk, I thought about everything that had led up to this latest insult.

Ricardo had dropped hints about his displeasure with my weight before. He often criticized my choice of swimming over other forms of exercise because (in his mind) it was supposedly less effective. He mused nostalgically about his Belgian ex-girlfriend subsisting on one meal a day. Early into our relationship he'd admitted that he preferred the waif body type—the flat chests, slim hips, and thin, spaghetti-like arms of his typical European girlfriends. He would often remind me that he was dating against type because (1) I was American and (2) I was a little rounder than his former paramours. I wasn't sure if that mindset came from his pseudo-European snobbery or his own disordered body image honed by years of cutting weight for high school and college sports.

Between his threats to move out of state and harsh judgment of my body, I felt like I was living on borrowed time with Ricardo.

I was tired of feeling paranoid about a man who said one thing but demonstrated another. How could he turn up his nose at my slight weight gain when all the while he was chasing me around the house for kisses and cuddles, clucking like a grandmother if I didn't help him finish all the rice in the pot, and complimenting me on how muscular I was looking? He was so sweet and loving at other times. Maybe if I dropped a few pounds he'd drop the subject.

Let the record show I weighed 116 pounds at the time of this incident.

Ricardo was at work by the time I returned home, so I changed clothes and went to the dojang. Taekwondo was usually a welcome distraction in times of stress, but I couldn't concentrate that evening. I felt fat and rejected. Ever since Ricardo's digital scale had found its home in my guest bathroom, I'd become obsessed with weighing in every morning. No matter what I did, I still had that little spare tire around my lower abdomen. Whenever I got fixated on my stomach, I forgot to notice my sculpted shoulders, my powerful legs, and the new lines marking muscles in a deep V just above my hip bones and just below that hated little pooch.

In class that night, Grandmaster focused less on me and instead directed his stern attention to another student. It was just as well; I couldn't have borne another man picking me apart that day. As we slid through the form I'd learned for the blue belt / red tip rank, I wondered darkly if there was a phenomenon of disordered eating among female martial artists as there was in other sports. Maybe I'd be the first. I'd show Ricardo! I'd get so skinny my bones would break during sparring. Then he'd feel sorry!

No, I needed to concentrate! Mastering this form marked a major turning point in my taekwondo career: I would soon be testing for red belt, which is a hugely important milestone among the color belt ranks. As a red belt I would truly be considered high ranking and would be on the fast track to black belt. I also wondered if this was a major turning point in my relationship with Ricardo. What should I do? As I blocked and kicked, a list ticked away in my mind:

I could just leave and let him come home to an empty condo . . . even though I'm the homeowner . . . never mind, scratch that one.

I could kick him out.

I could develop anorexia and blame him.

I could tell him I'm not changing my body to please him.

I could do nothing.

I felt trapped. I didn't know what to do. I knew I needed to confront Ricardo, but I couldn't let go of my overwhelming need for him. I could lose him if I stood up for myself. The confidence I was building in taekwondo didn't seem to be transferring very well into my personal life. The challenge was that I still had to overcome a lifetime of sensitivity and self-subjugation. Whenever I felt confronted or criticized, I would go into full primal lizard-brain panic, blame myself for the other person's assholery (or for simply having a different outlook than mine), and do anything I could to avoid being abandoned.

I wasn't very good at handling conflict. Sometimes I'd go on the offense and strike before the first blow had even been dealt. Sometimes I'd take feedback as a fight to be picked, and I was especially sensitive to Ricardo's more abrasive style. It wasn't the first time I felt hatred for Ricardo, but I still loved him so much that I was trapped by my own confusion and codependency.

Ricardo arrived home about an hour after I had finished taekwondo class, and he found me in my bedroom sulking and listening to rap music. Once a die-hard classic-rock snob, I'd lately begun to find odd comfort in hip-hop music, especially artists from the late 1990s and early 2000s. Tupac Shakur, Jay-Z, Dr. Dre, and The Notorious B.I.G. often accompanied me on my workouts at the gym or provided background music when I was home alone.

Rap music gave me the bravado I needed to fight with people half my age in sparring class and leap over obstacles with flying kicks. When I listened to the clever lyrics and drum-heavy beats, I felt like I could go toe-to-toe with the men in my office and be just as strong and powerful in the dojang. It offered me comfort when I felt like I was faltering in other areas of my life, especially in my relationship. When I listened to rap, I felt like the most badass woman in the world. I switched off "Get Money" by The Notorious B.I.G. and turned my narrow, reddened eyes to Ricardo.

"Mel," he said softly and sat behind me on the bed. He patted my shoulder and pulled me into a hug. I leaned into him stiffly and stared at the floor. "I'm not happy here. I think that's why I'm tough on you. I'm tough on everybody," he said solemnly.

My heart leapt into my throat. Not the threat of moving again! "I'm sorry you're stressed out, but I will not be your punching bag," I replied hollowly as I trembled. "You keep saying mean things to me when it's not my fault."

"I feel like I'm drowning," Ricardo pleaded. "I don't trust anyone. I purposefully impoverished myself because everyone kept asking for a handout—my ex-wife, my family, my friends—"

"I don't ask you for anything," I protested. "You live in *my* house!"

"I know, baby. That's how I know your love for me is real. You've been with me through everything. You're an angel. You're so good to me."

"Then why do you talk down to me and criticize me?" I sniffled.

He shrugged. "I have high standards, Mel. I'm hard on the people I love. You have low self-esteem, and you're always trembling. I get impatient with you sometimes. You seem paralyzed by fear. You struggle with making decisions. I'm trying to build you up."

I gaped at him. Had he really just justified his cruel comment by blaming my anxiety? "One of these days I'm going to treat you the way you treat me," I mumbled.

He kissed me on the forehead before leading me into the kitchen to eat dinner. A shaky truce had been reached. Once again, we'd righted ourselves after another wobble on the tightrope, but we were still in a precarious position. I didn't stand up to him. He never apologized.

For the rest of the night, we sat on the couch and watched movies. I felt spent and subdued. I was trapped and out of options. The opportunity presented by that turning point of standing up to him had vanished.

"I love you, Mel," Ricardo murmured in his sleep that night. "I want to have your baby."

Ugh.

The following Friday, the first Friday of June, I had my chance to prove myself. I was physically ready for my red belt test but was still processing the psychological weight of it. I had stopped tae-kwondo as a child right before I would have tested for red belt. I'd never reached this level before. As I drove to the dojang, I thought about the men in my life who were questioning my confidence: black belts whispering to Grandmaster within earshot, "She just needs more confidence"; a male coworker telling me I should give myself more credit as if I were a meek little girl; Ricardo telling me with pity that the reason he was constantly telling me I was "beautiful" was because of my purported low self-esteem. The hell with them! I'd show them!

"You're going to be a good black belt," Grandmaster said, giving me a friendly jab in the arm when I stopped by his office to say hello before I changed into my uniform. Wrapped in the compliment was an expectation of serious responsibility but also a huge amount of faith and trust. Finally, here was a man who believed in me. I marched to the front of the training room and readied my mind and body for the test.

No confidence? Watch me throw people to the ground during one-step sparring: *Blam*! (Sorry, Alex. He was my partner that day.) Low self-esteem? Watch the steely glare of my eyes as I wind through one of the more lyrical and dramatic forms in the student repertoire: *Kazaam*! Don't give myself enough credit? Watch me spar a girl half my age and beat her to a pulp: *Pow*! Paralyzed by fear? Watch me punch through three boards: *Crack*!

Ricardo took a photograph of me at the end of my test when I was awarded my red belt. It's one of my favorite photos of myself, not only because it marked a very important day in my life and a turning point in my taekwondo career but also because I saw my true self shining through: confident, beautiful, and strong.

PART FIVE:

RED BELT AND
RED BELT / BLACK TIP

CHAPTER 18

Welcome to Red Belt Class

In taekwondo a red belt means things just got real. Gone are the cool-toned, mid-level green and blue belts. Red is the color of war and blood. Red is bright and bold; you're in the spotlight whether you want to be or not. A red belt means it's time to hunker down and work hard because that black belt test will be here sooner than you know it. As a red belt, it's time to show your instructors what you're made of and set an example for the lower-ranking students.

A red belt is considered high ranking in most taekwondo schools, so I faced additional pressure—or let's put a more positive spin on it and call it "responsibility"—to attend as many classes as possible, work hard, and hone my skills. If blue belt was like the more lax, carefree junior year of high school, the red belt period was like senior year: taking advanced courses, developing a more mature rapport with instructors, and feeling a combination of excitement and anxiety about the not-so-distant future.

In order to test for black belt, there would be two more ranks I needed to achieve after the initial red belt test: black tip and, several months later, a second black tip signifying the bo dan rank, or black belt candidate. The total time I spent at various levels of red belt was about a year and a half, and every day was a reminder that I was ultimately training to trade in my bold, bright red belt for the steely, somber black belt.

After I completed my red belt test in early June 2014, I took stock of where I was as a newly minted red belt. My roundhouse kicks were high, and my forms were graceful. My self-defense technique was precise, and my board breaks were clean. My sparring, which I felt was my weakest area, was showing improvement. Even when I stumbled or looked awkward, I was having fun and was always ready to work hard and try again. Yeah, I could do this red belt thing.

After the high of earning my red belt wore off, I was faced with the reality of *being* a red belt. I would now be allowed to attend the advanced red and black belt class on Wednesday nights after sparring class. This class included students who had reached red belt, red with a black tip, bo dan, and various degrees of black belt. As a lower-ranking student, I'd wondered what went on during that class but also kind of dreaded the day when I would have the pressure of performing at a more advanced skill level.

Even though by the time I became a red belt, and was quite comfortable with the instructors and advanced students, I was actually nervous the first night I was to attend the advanced red and black belt class. What were we going to do for that magical hour? What did they expect of me? Would I look like a clumsy fool trying to master more complicated forms or self-defense techniques? Would I pass out after the high intensity of sparring class? Would I fall onto a stack of pads again just as I had as a brand-new green belt?

"Welcome to red belt class!" chirped a first degree black belt named Mr. Derrick as he bowed and shook my hand on the first Wednesday following my red belt test. Mr. Derrick was sixty-seven years old and had earned his black belt a few months earlier. He was soft-spoken and kind but had a grip like a vise and a brutal takedown that even my instructors feared. One of the instructors, a third degree black belt, padded over to the wall to stretch with me after Mr. Derrick and I finished talking. He was now a rare occurrence, since his job as a construction supervisor was taking up most of his time, so we chatted for a few minutes to catch up before class.

"Well, you're a red belt now. What's your plan?" he asked, tilting his head and looking at me as he hooked his left foot on the barre and leaned over his outstretched leg. I thought he meant my training plan for the year and a half I would be spending preparing to test for black belt. I was about to list some of the cross-training exercises I'd do, or maybe make a vague promise to cut back on wine, but I noticed a funny look on his face as he narrowed his eyes.

"You mean am I going to get my black belt and then quit?" I asked incredulously. "No way!"

"Good answer."

I didn't tell anyone that taekwondo had given me my life, my health, and my sanity back. I didn't tell him that quitting would veer me away from the new wonderful life of confidence and self-respect I had uncovered. The plan was . . . there was no plan. I just wanted to be there. I wanted taekwondo to be a part of my life for as long as I could still drag my body out of bed. Getting my black belt was now becoming a more tangible reality, but it wasn't the end goal. I had no end goal other than to be happy and, more importantly, to love and accept myself for who I was without desperately seeking approval or affection elsewhere . . . and kicking ass while doing it.

Even though I'd had some time to relax and stretch after sparring class, our most intense and physically demanding class of the week, I was still a swampy, panting mess as we began red and black belt class. Once the endorphin high wore off, I began to feel sleepy and drained, both physically and mentally. Thankfully we worked on forms in the advanced class, so I could move at a slower pace. I yawned every time Chief Instructor Alex, who was leading the second class, turned his back. I was racing against the Sand-man, so once the class ended, I drove home quickly and showered before collapsing into bed with wet, tangled hair. Ricardo arrived home from the gym about an hour later and slipped into the dark bedroom to check on me.

"Baby, how was your first red belt class?" he whispered.

I opened one eye and croaked, "Awesome," before dissolving back into blackness.

Eventually my stamina improved, and I was able to make it through two back-to-back Wednesday night classes without feel-ing like I was going to collapse from exhaustion. Since most of us, including Alex, usually spent the first hour of Wednesday night classes hopping around and fighting, we all looked forward to a quieter class that involved more cerebral activities. Occasionally we'd pull out a thick mat and practice rolling or falling on the ground, leaping over obstacles to improve our flying kicks, or doing judo-like throws and takedowns. Most of the time, though, we worked on forms or paired up with partners for self-defense practice.

Sometimes we would add a few advanced twists to our regular practice. For example, for a fun challenge we would do the forms in super-slow motion to the point where it looked like tai chi (and had the same centering, relaxing effect). Or we did the forms with our eyes closed, which could lead to a lot of unintentionally funny moments, like when I went in completely the wrong direction and ran into the wall, much to the amusement of Alex, who had patiently watched and done nothing to stop the impending crash.

The advanced class opened up a brand-new world of tae-kwondo training. It was just the motivation I needed to keep striving for my black belt. We practiced more intricate, hapkido-based hand-to-hand self-defense, defense against weapons, and drills designed to improve reaction time. Just as important, the advanced class was also an opportunity for Alex to start grooming lower-ranking students to help him teach and coach. Sometimes he would split us into groups and have the other black belts and me, the lone high-ranking adult, teach small sections of forms or self-defense to other students. For those who think taekwondo is just a bunch of pretty but useless kicks, I invite you to join us in red and black belt class. Enjoy your bruised wrists and overloaded brain.

Taekwondo seemed to be the one place in my life where I hadn't set an "I'd be happy *when*" ultimatum. I'd be happy when I finally felt like I knew what I was doing at work, since I was still only a few years into the world of organizational development. I'd be happy when I had a flat stomach. I'd be happy when the ups and downs of my relationship with Ricardo finally settled into a steady wave of commitment. I'd be happy when . . . come to think of it, I wasn't sure if I'd ever been truly happy. Something in me, perhaps a protection mechanism or self-loathing or a combination of the two, never allowed me to be happy. Maybe now I finally had my chance.

Life was good as a new red belt. The tension I had at home with Ricardo receded to the background, and we began to enjoy the rhythm of domestic partnership. I felt more relaxed and confident at work. Taekwondo class was the highlight of my day and a constant source of positivity and motivation . . . until I had another mental breakdown.

CHAPTER 19

Obligatory Nervous Breakdown

While things were going well inside the dojang, I was mentally deteriorating at home. At the time, I thought I was stressed out because of increasing demands at work and planning an elaborate family reunion. Through most of June, I was on edge and entering into a state of what may have been considered mania or its lesser cousin, hypomania.

In retrospect I suspect my seemingly blissful domestic partnership was the true cause of my anxiety. Ricardo was very affectionate, but he was also very demanding. He always had to be *right*. When he was in a bad mood and feeling especially insecure, he would take it out on me with snide criticisms. Let's not forget the "I liked you better skinnier" incident or the pressure to get pregnant.

Ricardo constantly tried to convince me that my anxiety was a major problem, as if it would be the undoing of our relationship. From seemingly out of nowhere, he'd look at me with big concerned eyes and exclaim, "Baby, you're shaking! It must be because of your medication. You seem so anxious all the time." Other times he would threaten to leave if I didn't bring my energy level down a notch during times that I felt the need to buzz around the house with projects and errands. If I dared remind him of his parents or ex-wife or whomever else he decided to vilify, I was to blame if he disappeared. He would glare at me and lecture me as if I were a child. As much as I still loved him, I was growing to secretly dread him too. I felt stuck, but I also felt I could not let this relationship fail.

My sleep problems came back, but instead of having insomnia, I would become painfully drowsy early in the evening, often passing out shortly after dinner. During the day, I would become teeth-grittingly sleepy in the afternoon, so much so that I almost fell asleep driving home after meeting Ricardo for lunch on a day I was off from work. Whenever sleepiness would start to come on, I would be racked with tremors and began involuntarily clenching my jaw as a means to stay awake. In the morning, shortly after waking, my vision was blurry to the point where I couldn't see even while wearing my glasses. What was wrong with me? Narcolepsy? Diabetes? What the hell was going on?

It didn't help that the more I conked out early in the evening, the more Ricardo shamed and scolded me for it because it took away from our "quality time" together. Never mind that he usually slept until ten and never got up to have breakfast or visit with me before I went to work. After dinner or in the middle of watching a movie, I would pass out cold with my mouth open and eyes rolled back, only to wake up to Ricardo's frowning face. I was so terrified of losing him (and terrified of his admonishments) that my actual anxiety soared as I tried to find an answer for my strange drowsiness. The naps weren't enjoyable little snoozes. They were bullies shoving my head into a bowl of painful exhaustion, sucker punching me into disorientation when they knew full well I had stuff to do.

Only years later did I realize my bouts of profound sleepiness had coincided with my most controlling relationships, notably an unstable, possessive boyfriend I had in college and a horribly abusive man I'd dated while I worked on my MBA. At random times,

I would pass out and sleep deeply for hours and hours, as if my stressed brain had given up and forced me into unconsciousness to escape my situation. Even if I'd had this realization in 2014, I'm not sure I would have heeded the warning. I was too stubborn and shortsighted.

When I wasn't collapsing exhausted onto the couch or the bed, my mind was on fire with rapidly shifting thoughts. My normally organized, can-do mind had gone a little further into what I call the "Ray Liotta at the end of *Goodfellas* mode," the part where he's racing around town between packaging cocaine and cooking marinara sauce while he's being followed (he swears) by helicopters. The music switches from one track to the next, and the voiceover is chattering and choppy. I always think about that scene when I find myself racing from one task to the next and feeling overwhelmed by the rapid-fire monologue in my head. Maybe my life was becoming more like a Scorsese movie than a romantic comedy after all.

Some people in manic phases will go on buying binges and max out their credit cards on ridiculous purchases. My reaction was usually the opposite. For some reason when I'm manic, I tend to focus on cleaning, not the kind where I'm elbow-deep in a bucket of bleach for twelve hours but more of the decluttering kind. Perhaps in my state of clouded thinking, I believed that if I could control my environment, then I could control everything else. During that June, I felt like my skin was crawling at all the perceived clutter in my house.

I've always kept my home neat and tidy, but I had a lot of stuff, and I felt like it was suffocating me. I gave away bags and bags of items, most of which were meaningless things that needed to go, but I also impulsively donated several childhood mementos. At my most manic point of decluttering, a feverish thought took hold that if I didn't have anything to pass on to a child (clothing, decorations, old toys), then I couldn't very well have a child. I was so desperate to free myself of Ricardo's plan to coerce me into a pregnancy that in a sense I erased my own childhood. I also wanted to disconnect from the sad, lonely, angry child I had been. It made perfect sense at the time.

Once I came down from my high, I was racked with guilt and grief for years over the irreplaceable items I had so casually thrown out or given away. My pragmatism reminds me that those boxes would still be untouched, unloved, unused, and forgotten in my closet today, but I've had a hard time consoling myself with that simple truth.

On top of the sleep problems and the manic surges, the ever-present body-image storm cloud rumbled into sight, hitting me hardest as I hallucinated half-asleep most nights. I thought I had conquered this. I thought I had emotionally matured beyond the problems I had in my teens and early twenties. I thought—*I really thought*—that I truly viewed exercise as a pleasurable hobby that I did to be loving to myself and keep myself healthy, not a never-ending punishing pursuit of the "perfect" body that would guarantee me love and acceptance. I was also still aching from Ricardo's smug chiding that I had "sold him a bill of goods" for gaining a few pounds.

I was still seeing my therapist, Ramona, once a month, and I'm sure we had wonderful conversations, but I have no memory of them from this time. I know I didn't share the details of what was happening in my relationship any more than I had with my one trusted work friend, Madeline. Both Ramona and Madeline had seen me free fall over the years and nearly destroy my sanity over relationships, and neither of them was afraid to tell me to get out of dangerous situations. I knew they would tell me to leave Ricardo, and that seemed like an impossibility. This was my last chance at love. No one else would want me, and I couldn't bear to be unloved. I *had* to make this work. I had to keep my secret buried.

I did try to white-knuckle through it with some advice Ramona had once given me. She suggested I "sit with the discomfort" when my thoughts and emotions were running high rather than struggling against it. Observe, accept, let go. Perhaps that's how I could view the plateaus (or sometimes the two steps backward) that I experienced in my life—taekwondo, fitness, career, and my relationship. Just sit with it for a moment. A rest in music can be as profound as the most complex chord.

I had witnessed the power of letting go of expectations and outcomes too many times to not give it another shot. If only I could get my anxiety under control.

"I'm not that much different from the other psychos you dated," Ricardo said nonchalantly as he puffed on the raspberry-flavored tobacco in the hookah pipe. The thick headiness of the sweet tobacco mixed with the beer that was already sloshing around in my brain. It was early July, the night of my thirty-fifth birthday, and we were at a charmingly rundown nightclub about two blocks from my condo. For decades, what was now an eighties-themed dance club had been a family-owned Italian restaurant with dim lighting, a live jazz band, and excellent garlic bread. After the restaurant went out of business, the dining area was gutted and turned into a dance floor. The darkened back room, which had once been a private space for birthdays and rehearsal dinners, was now filled with faded, broken couches and hookah pipes-for-rent.

The topic of relationships had come up, although I almost never mentioned my exes. Ricardo must have latched on to whatever minor details I had let slip over the past year.

"We have patterns in our relationships and tend to attract the same types over and over," Ricardo continued between pulls on the pipe. "Maybe there's a reason why you've been drawn to me and those other guys over time. And that's why we're drawn to each other. You and I are each other's alter ego. I see you struggling, baby. Your self-esteem is so low, and I'm doing my best to help you and show you all the time how much I love you and want to be with you. Perhaps you should meditate on it." He hoisted himself up off the low tattered couch and sauntered away to the bathroom while I frowned and took advantage of having the hookah to myself to take some extra-long drags of smoke.

Meditate? *He's* telling me to meditate? *He's* telling me where my self-esteem is? That pompous, judgmental . . . or was he right? I appreciated that he was a fellow seeker like me, but at times I found his advice patronizing and dismissive. In my mind Ricardo didn't acknowledge or respect all the work I had done to improve myself. I felt like if I wasn't a walking cloud of bliss and enlightenment at all times, Ricardo was ready to cut me down with know-it-all Buddhist trivia and proclamations gleaned from his own emotional health journey. I sensed in him a strange delight when he pointed out the hypocrisy in my actions compared to what I preached on my taekwondo blog, which I'd launched a few months prior.

"Baby, you write about letting go of what worries you, and yet I don't see you doing that. I mean, have you *really* read *The Power of Now*?" he'd say, his voice brimming with icy sincerity. Ricardo had no idea the depths I'd trawled in exploration of my psyche. He never saw how, just as the Italian restaurant had been transformed into an eighties dance club, I'd gutted my own interior through self-reflection and the volumes of exploratory journals I'd written. He never heard the conversations I'd had over the years with Ramona and Dr. Kapoor. How dare he say that to me as if I were totally unaware and unawake?

"Unavailability," I whispered to myself while Ricardo was still in the bathroom. That was my pattern. For years I had attracted men who had some kind of barrier—a fear of commitment, a desire to play the field, an all-consuming job or no job at all, lack of money or more money than they knew what to do with. Even though Ricardo and I were (supposedly) in love and living together, he still fell into the unavailable category. He constantly changed his mind about whether he wanted to get married, whether he wanted to stay in Texas or hightail it back to the East Coast, whether he was going to continue pressuring me to have "his" baby or turn his focus back to the children he already had. His finances were a wreck, and the prospect of a full-time job seemed more and more remote.

To my horror, I found myself once again hating Ricardo and wondering if I had walked right into another emotionally abusive relationship. I took everything he said as a threat. I couldn't tell whether his cruelty was real or a fabrication of my own imbalanced brain that was desperate for approval and terrified of abandonment. Was my anxiety really as bad as he claimed?

I was tormented by my contradictory feelings for Ricardo. Sometimes I loved everything about him. Other days, which were beginning to be more frequent than the loving days, I silently resented him for micro attacks and threats: I'd better not be like his demanding mother or *else*. I'd better stay thin or *else*. I'd better not be like our high-energy fathers *or else*. I'd better agree to have a baby *or else*. I'd better stop falling asleep too early *or else*.

Some days I wanted to scream and put my fist through a wall if I thought too long about some of the things he said. I *never* asked him to change. I *never* gave him ultimatums. I *never* threatened that he'd better change his ways . . . or did I? All the times I whimpered and cried and played the victim—could those have been my own forms of psychological manipulation?

Of course I feared if I told him any of this, he'd snobbishly say what had become a pat line for him: "Perhaps we should go our separate ways." That was his answer to everything: We went to sleep at different hours; let's go our separate ways. I wanted to get married, and on that particular week, he was anti-marriage; let's go our separate ways. He wanted more kids, and I didn't want any; let's go our separate ways. He decided once again that he didn't like living in Texas after all; let's go our separate ways. I dared to show emotion; let's go our separate ways. I wasn't sure what was real and what was just noise in my head.

I took a greedy drag on the hookah and desperately wished the pipe could fill me with something more mood-altering than the pleasant but subdued buzz of tobacco. I spied Ricardo padding out of the bathroom and grinning at me.

"Now, where were we?" He sighed and put his arm around my shoulders. "It's your birthday, honey! Aren't you having a good time? We're making a home together. This is a perfect union." I smirked with resignation and snatched the pipe for another puff. As emotionally trying as our relationship could be, I thought I had finally gotten the love I had been craving. Maybe Ricardo and I were meant for each other: vulnerable, longing for validation, hungry for companionship, and craving love from one another when the pain inside became too intense. We were two miserable peas in a pod.

Like a fever, my manic state eventually subsided toward the end of the summer. I felt like I had been an entity separate from myself, and when I've since tried to reflect on what it felt like to be in that altered state of mind, it seemed distant and inaccessible, like when you immediately begin to forget a very vivid dream the moment you wake up. I was able to piece together warning signs so I'd be ready next time: racing thoughts; obsessions, such as my panicked desire to declutter; explosive and angry fantasies about arguments with Ricardo or even with random strangers; and of course, the physical problems, such as blurred vision, muscle tremors, the clenching jaw, and the constant drowsiness that sometimes alternated with insomnia. At one point during that summer, I wished I could just get sick and be totally incapacitated for a few days so my mind and body could slow down. I wanted to stop having to feel so damned responsible for every moving piece of my life.

It's amazing that this weird little breakdown didn't adversely affect what was happening in taekwondo. In fact, taekwondo was my saving grace from it all. Taekwondo was the richest part of my day and the moments where I felt most free and authentic. Certainly no one there made comments about my weight or my questionable state of mind in the dojang. I wished the sense of calm I had in class could be more constant throughout my day.

CHAPTER 20

Will This Be on the Test?

As September 2014 drew to a close, the test for my black tip was drawing nearer. I'd been training hard for the last four months and was eager to move to the next level. When asked by my instructors what I wanted to work on in taekwondo class, I immediately jumped to testing requirements. Was it my responsibility to practice outside of class? Absolutely. Did it happen every day? No, but I did my best. I mentally ran through my self-defense techniques often and practiced all the forms I'd learned on the weekends. It was a little harder, though, to work on my jumping and flying kicks with a creaky floor and downstairs neighbors. I would look silly if I practiced them outside on the parking lot of my condominium complex.

Preparing for a belt test could sometimes give me tunnel vision. I was so focused on practicing the particular kicks, forms, and self-defense techniques I'd have to perform that I let the rest of my technique slide. Ironically, my schoolmates and I used to admonish our tenth-grade English teacher for "teaching to" the state standardized test. Here I was, twenty years later, doing exactly the same thing with my taekwondo practice. That's not learning; that's regurgitation. Taekwondo practice draws from a comprehensive body of knowledge. It's not a single kick or form existing in a vacuum, but that's how I was treating it.

As if God and the Universe were listening, I got a little bit of a reprieve when Grandmaster changed the date of the test from the first Friday of the month to the end of the month so we could all concentrate on the upcoming tournament, and I could temporarily set aside my obsession with testing for black tip.

～

Our annual taekwondo tournament was held in mid-October in the Fort Worth Convention Center, a huge colorful building located on the corner of downtown near a gothic Catholic cathedral I attended occasionally (okay, very rarely) and the hotel where President Kennedy stayed the night before he fatefully made his way thirty miles east to Dallas on November 22, 1963. Ricardo, who at that point had attended most of my belt tests and taekwondo social functions, was by my side at the 6:00 a.m. call as we stood in matching blue volunteer T-shirts and wiped the sleep from our eyes. We filed into a side room near the convention center arena to sip coffee and munch donuts with other volunteers who were there to coach, referee, run the scoring software on computers at each of the fighting rings, and be on hand to run errands or fix problems as needed.

Ricardo and I had volunteered to staff the computer stations at the fighting rings. Modern tournaments typically rely on a computer system to help tally points from judges. During sparring matches, two to three judges sit at the edges of the ring, and employing a controller not unlike one used for video games, they award the competitors points for shots to the body or to the head. Volunteers use the computer software to start and stop the timer for the match based on the referee's commands, as well as deduct points when a competitor does something against the rules or add points when it is warranted.

You'd think sitting at a computer and clicking a mouse would be a breeze, but it required solid concentration and quick response time. The next eighteen hours were a cacophonous blur of Korean commands, the thump of feet smashing against chest protectors, and yells from the competitors and spectators. Once in a while I sneaked outside to squint into the sun and thaw out after turning purple and gray due to the extreme cold inside the building (Texans like their air conditioning blasting at frigid temperatures from March through November).

Ricardo and I were first paired up together at a table with a computer running the software that tracked points and timed the matches. Inwardly I said prayers of relief that (1) I didn't have to add up the points myself, as would have happened in the old days, and (2) unlike some volunteers who were parents or friends of our school's students, I had a background in sparring that allowed me to quickly keep up with the pace and rapid-fire commands.

Eventually Ricardo and I split up to take over different fighting rings and met up hours later when we filed back into the side room with the rest of the volunteers to devour a late-night communal meal of homemade Korean food, courtesy of Grandmaster Kim's wife.

I thought about my reluctance to compete for fear of being annihilated during a sparring match. Perhaps I would compete the next year. Getting beaten up in a three-minute sparring match would probably be much less exhausting than the physically and mentally draining job of a volunteer glued to a computer for hours on end. Too tired to speak, Ricardo and I drove home quietly and passed out together in a tangle of clammy arms and legs.

"Baby, I think we want different things," Ricardo said morosely Sunday morning as he stared at the ceiling and clasped my leg, which was draped across his waist. We had just woken up and still felt groggy and spent after our long day (and night) volunteering at the taekwondo tournament. My stomach dropped. What had changed? The day before we were a team. We were the go-to martial arts power couple. The referees loved us for our work ethic and quick thinking.

"Mel, I'm not happy here. I don't like Texas. I want to go back to DC, and I want you to go with me."

"Nooo, I don't want to have this conversation again," I moaned, burying my face in the sheets. This topic had hiccuped to the surface so many times over the past year. Ricardo would toss around the threats of moving but balked whenever he saw the tears spring to my eyes. Returning to the East Coast seemed to be his answer to solving all his financial problems and a way to soothe his restless spirit. At this point it seemed like Washington, DC, was the third party in our relationship, and I was feeling like the third wheel. "You keep running, and you'll never be satisfied anywhere. You move from place to place and keep hoping you'll feel better. You keep chasing happiness hoping to find it on the outside, and you and I both know that's not how life works," I muttered.

"And I really want you to have my baby. Doesn't that show you how much I love you if I want you to be the mother of my child? If we have a baby, we can be together forever," Ricardo whined.

"Forever? Yeah, how'd that work out with your ex-wife?" I snapped.

"Well, you're not getting any younger." He slinked off to the bathroom to sulk in private.

Why did my boyfriends always seem to get all primal and broody during times of relationship instability, as if a baby were the magical solution to all our commitment and money problems? It wasn't romantic or sexy when Ricardo enfolded me in his arms and told me he wanted me to have "his" baby. It was demeaning and creepy. I felt like he saw me as nothing more than a human incubator, a means to an end, and something that might help him get over the sting of being separated from his existing children.

I was annoyed we were having this conversation once again. Did he not understand how much stress and work came with a baby? Where was he when his children were small? I thought darkly about how funny it would be if he left me and moved back to DC only to end up without a job or anyone willing to procreate with him . . . or even funnier if he knocked up some anorexic, thin-hipped broad (I assumed he would return to the stick-figure set if we ever broke up), separated from her, and ended up paying even more child support.

As Ricardo began running a shower in the guest bathroom, I burrowed under the sheets and wondered if I were making a wise decision to choose my life over Ricardo's vague promises of life in the capital. I had now lived in Fort Worth for ten years and loved it. I felt at ease with the city's slower pace compared to its larger metropolitan counterparts and its sweet-as-pecan-pie western charm that tugged at my small-town roots. I also adored Fort Worth's world-class art, old money, and vibrant culture amidst the boots and barbecue. I had bought a home with my own hard-earned cash and was enjoying the beautiful neighborhood near the arts district that I loved so much. I was starting to feel more comfortable and confident in my job and worked with a great team and supportive boss. I was really growing in taekwondo and becoming a part of our little tight-knit, ass-kicking family. In the not-so-distant future, I would be testing for black belt. I was in a much better place mentally than I was a few years ago.

I was living my dream in Fort Worth, Texas, but I wasn't so sure it was Ricardo's dream. I wasn't the one who was a thousand miles away from family and friends. I knew he was much more extraverted than I was and needed that social interaction to thrive. Maybe I was keeping him isolated so I would be happy. Maybe I secretly hoped he wouldn't find a full-time job so he would be ready and waiting for me whenever I arrived home. He was my own little prisoner locked in a tower.

Was this what I really wanted? Was I choosing Texas and taekwondo over love? It didn't seem like the end of this love story would be anything close to "happily ever after."

When I am under serious stress, it often manifests in physical pain or discomfort. As I lay among the rumpled sheets contemplating my fate and waiting for Ricardo to get out of the shower, I felt the right side of my neck burn with an ominous tickle. My head felt flushed and light with the pressure of a ghostly headache, and my jaw clenched and unclenched jerkily. Then I felt what I only feel in dire straits: a tiny squeeze in my chest, the telltale sign of my telltale heart breaking.

At the end of October 2014, we held our delayed color belt test. At the dojang I warmed up and chatted with another red belt. Suddenly our conversation was interrupted by a blast of screeches and giggles. The gaggle of little yellow belt boys who rushed in behind me must have been freebasing their Halloween candy right before the test. Soon the training room was filled with cackling, tumbling little monsters as Chief Instructor Alex scurried around angrily and tried to keep them from bashing themselves into the mirrors.

Now that I was high ranking, I calculated that I'd have to wait for five white belts, four orange belts, about five thousand yellow belts, and two blue belts to test before my turn came around to test for black tip. I decided to set a good example and show how an advanced student should sit quietly at attention. I perched prissily in half lotus with a smug smile of contentment on my face. Thirty minutes later, after watching kids with glassy stares plod through heavy front stances and weak blocks, I was bugging my eyes out at Ricardo in desperation and pointing an imaginary gun at my head. So much for setting a good example.

Two hours (*two freaking hours*) later, it was finally my time to test! Thankfully, my hips hadn't tightened up too much, and I was able to scramble to the middle of the room without tripping over myself. I was proud of how I performed my form, which was called Palgwe Chil Jang, the seventh form in a repertoire of eight color belt forms. Relationship problems be damned, I was determined to make this form as powerful and strong as it deserved to be. I was nervous during one-step sparring but got through it without forgetting anything, and when it was my partner's turn, I did a decent job of landing properly during a face-forward takedown . . . which means . . . well, I got thrown on my face.

Breaking was a fun, cathartic way to end the test. I did a palm-heel strike, jump side kick, and turning back side kick. All those years of smacking my steering wheel in a fit of anger while driving in rush hour traffic had prepared me well for my hand strike. I stumbled out of the longest belt test ever with a new black stripe, signifying the next step I had taken toward black belt. Ricardo and I celebrated with Whataburger patty melts, and for the first time in months, I collapsed into a dreamless and worry-free sleep.

CHAPTER 21

Frustration and Resignation

I began learning my new form, Palgwe Pal Jang, in early November. This was the final form in the set of eight Palgwe forms our school taught. Taekwondo students typically learn a different and more popular style called Taeguk, whereas my grandmaster's preference was to maintain the older Palgwe forms. I loved the style of Palgwe, which has strong stances and powerful strikes. The new form I was learning was heavily steeped in self-defense movements and was much more complex than the lower-ranking forms. One night I nearly teared up with frustration as I tried in vain to master its many complicated movements. The form wasn't really the problem as much as the threat to my little snow globe of a life being shaken up again by Ricardo's seemingly inevitable departure. He was still throwing around halfhearted threats to leave Texas, and I was desperate for him to stay with me in my quiet, contained life.

I was tempted to deal with my constant fear that Ricardo would leave through starvation, alcohol, and Klonopin, but taekwondo gave me a reason to take care of my body and fuel it properly. I didn't want to purposely weaken myself as my training was becoming more and more important. In a few months I would test for bo dan, the last color belt rank in preparation for black belt.

Was I in or out? Did I want to continue kicking and punching and ki-yahping as if my home life weren't crumbling? I wanted to either explode or shut down and hide from the world. I had a lot of time to think during my torturously long black tip test at the end of October, and it sent me into a bit of an existential crisis. I didn't think it was the mental illness demons whispering in my ear, and I didn't think it was burnout with taekwondo or work. The stress of my relationship had sent me over the edge, and I was at a loss over what to do.

Was I choosing my taekwondo classmates and instructors in Fort Worth as my adopted family over Ricardo and his family on the East Coast? Could I give up a life of certainty that I had built for myself in Texas for a stability that Ricardo had yet to prove he could provide in DC? Did I want to stay in a troubled relationship, or did I want to end the pain before it got worse? Was I in or out? The darker part of my mind began to frequently ask, "What's the point of any of this . . . of your life? It's all meaningless, isn't it?"

Lately I'd had a nagging sense of foreboding. The stress of Ricardo's inability to find a full-time job was reaching a breaking point, although I still continued to hide my head in the sand of the bliss of cohabitation. Thursdays were our nights off from working out, and on one particularly chilly November Thursday, Ricardo sank down into the recliner and gestured for me to sit on the couch. I knew something was wrong when he didn't claim his usual spot right next to me with his arm around my shoulders.

"Mel," he began, clasping his hands around his knees, "I've been invited to interview for a job."

"Oh, good!" I exclaimed. "Finally!"

"Mel . . . it's in DC."

I swallowed, blinked once, and grabbed the slippery black arm of the leather couch.

"When did you apply for this job, and why didn't you tell me?" I asked sharply, feeling too stunned and slow to react the way I really wanted to. My inner Medusa awoke. Her snakes began writhing and snapping, but she wasn't ready to unleash her stony fury.

"Mel, please, this is really hard for me," Ricardo pleaded. "I don't think you know how much I'm struggling here. I'm barely making enough to cover my child support payments. I know I've backed myself into a wall, but I've tried everything, and no one will hire me. I didn't want to tell you because I've seen how upset you've gotten when I've talked about leaving before. I really didn't think I'd get an interview."

"I bet you didn't even try to get a full-time job here," I said softly as I stared at my intertwined fingers.

"Mel, don't say that. You know I did. I miss my family. I have baby nieces now, and I want to be there for them. I want you to come with me. You'd like DC. There's so much culture and nightlife and so much history."

"And it's cold, crowded, and expensive," I said sulkily. "What about my home? I can't just walk away from it. I worked so hard to buy it, and I haven't even been here three full years. I want to enjoy it."

"Baby, the market's really good right now. You could sell it or even rent it out! Besides, it's good to have challenges." Ricardo joined me on the couch and hugged me. "If you never go anywhere, then you never grow. You strike me as a flower bud waiting to blossom, but you're afraid to . . . you're a cherry blossom!"

"Why do you East Coast people think that someone should live in New York or DC *at least once* to prove that they have street smarts or bravery or whatever other bullshit?" I grumbled. "I don't need to prove myself to anyone. Unlike you, I haven't hopped from city to city. I've lived in DFW for sixteen years. I've built a good life here. Why go through all that hardship? I'm not some couch-surf-ing twenty-year-old who can just move around on a whim."

I never could understand the appeal of Ricardo's nomadic lifestyle. Ever since his divorce, he'd run the gamut of crashing at his parents' place and renting rooms from strangers all over the country. It was so different from the predictable, solitary life I'd lived since graduate school. As soon as I could afford to live with-out roommates, I was happily on my own, and my steady job had blessed me with the ability to stay in one city for over a decade. Maybe losing the false sense of security he'd had as a married family man made him wary of putting down roots again. I saw no sense of adventure in his tendency to hop homesteads and cities every few years, though. I saw only inconvenience and uncertainty.

As for my aversion to moving to the East Coast—I realize some of my dear readers may feel slighted at my not wanting to move to DC. I never said DC or New York City or Philadelphia or any of the major East Coast cities were "bad." I just don't want to live there for my own reasons and preferences. I like what is familiar to me. I'm accustomed to the culture, climate, and cost of living in Texas. I love Fort Worth. This, like being childfree, is once again a very personal choice. If you want to live on the East Coast, knock yourselves out. If you think Texas is terrible, that's fine. I don't care. Back to the conversation. . . .

"Honey, I don't want to lose you. I love you very much. You know that, right? I know you want to stay here for a while to get your black belt. We have to work as a team to figure this out," Ricardo said gently, rolling his forehead against my shoulder.

This was my chance to stand up for myself the way I hadn't been able to so many times before. I had the opportunity to tell him off for not trying harder, fight back at his insinuations that I didn't care about him when I had opened my home to him for eight months, and berate him for constantly changing his mind about what he wanted to do and where he wanted to live and whether he even wanted to be with me. I had my chance to lay into him for being irresponsible, impulsive, and for seeking out-of-state jobs behind my back.

But instead . . . I stayed silent. As I had in the past, I deferred to the destructive habit I had of deflating into submission when whichever man I was worshipping at the moment expressed displeasure or, worse, threatened to leave me. I buried my face into his chest and began to cry.

My line of defense when I felt my relationship was being threatened was to turn the swirling destruction inward on myself with an odd mixture of manipulation and self-loathing: If I played the meek little woman who didn't question his decision, perhaps he wouldn't leave after all. If I played the victim *just right,* I would be absolved of any responsibility for whether Ricardo stayed or left. As much as I eagerly debated with the men on my work team or fought ferociously with the guys in taekwondo class, I couldn't shake the tendency for my self-worth and confidence to crumble when I was around the men in my love life. The fear of abandonment was a constant burning flame. If I lost that external source of love, it would leave me to face the cold void I had inside me.

"Mel, I have to go. I'm out of options. It'll be a year, two years at best," Ricardo said as he reached for my hand. "I'll stay with my parents to save money. I'll come back to you. Or maybe you could move up there. The interview is next week. Are you okay with that?"

"Fine," I mumbled. Who was I kidding? He would never come back. I couldn't believe I was swallowing my own lies, but I thought agreeing with him was the only option if I wanted us to stay together. My mind started to wander as I thought about the other compromises I might need to make in order to quell his threats of moving away or suggesting we "go our separate ways," as he'd said so many times before. Maybe I should accept his impending move to DC. Maybe I should give up everything I'd worked for and loved to follow him. Maybe I needed to force this relationship to work, no matter the cost to either of us.

I'd even begun to wonder if I should just give in and have a baby, which Ricardo had romanticized to the point that he implied our relationship couldn't continue without the promise of a child. I'd often heard about women so desperate for a child that their husbands gave in and resigned themselves to parenthood, but I never thought the baby ultimatum would be used on me. Why don't we ever hear about the women who are pressured into unwanted motherhood by their boyfriends or husbands? Did they subjugate their bodies to the wills of their men? Where were their stories? Did they suffer in silence? While Ricardo waited for me to answer him about the interview, I continued fretting about the ever-present baby pressure.

Even though Ricardo was a father three times over, he seemed to be unrealistic about the daily demands of caring for a child. When I'd point out that babies cost a lot of money, he'd shrug and brush it off, although he often complained about the expenses he incurred from his demanding teenagers. If I did have a baby, perhaps I could just be pleasantly drunk during the whole postpartum period when my depression was sure to surge toward the suicidal end of the spectrum. Perhaps I could talk his mother into babysitting as often as possible.

For now, though, I didn't have to worry about being coerced into pregnancy to save our dying relationship. At the moment we just needed to worry about Ricardo finding gainful employment. I had no choice; I had to give in and let him go to the interview if I wanted to stay in this relationship. My inner Medusa lowered her stony gaze and bared her neck for Perseus's sword.

CHAPTER 22

Conversations in the Jewelry Box

In mid-November 2014, Ricardo flew to Washington, DC, to interview with a small privately owned software company. The day he was to return, I woke up sweaty and crying. I was still a little drunk and high from the mixture of wine and Klonopin I'd consumed the night before out of loneliness and misery over my troubled relationship. Later I'd had a dream that Ricardo and I became separated at an amusement park. I paged him over the loudspeakers for hours, but he never showed up. When I woke up, I knew for sure he would leave me.

All day my neck was burning, and my body trembled with anxiety. I had planned on making a light dinner of teriyaki-doused chicken and vegetables before I went to the airport to pick up Ricardo, but I was too impatient and nervous, so I shoveled down my ultimate comfort meal: a peanut butter and jelly sandwich with Cheetos smashed in between the pieces of gooey bread. I munched noisily on the sandwich and dredged the sticky bitten end in the orange crumbs that dusted my plate. It was the first sense of solace I'd had all day. Ricardo had promised he would text me when he boarded the plane, but he never did, which sent my mind racing.

What if he decided to stay in DC, and I would be stuck at DFW International Airport driving around the terminals like small circles of Hell all night? I wiped my mouth with a napkin, grabbed my purse and keys, and decided to take my chances.

While I waited for Ricardo at the airport's Terminal C, I people-watched. I saw a red-faced businessman try to restrain his temper as he craned his neck in search of a cab that was apparently very late picking up his Japanese colleagues and himself. He started cursing and stomping around like a flustered cartoon character. I almost expected him to start shrieking like a tea kettle, with steam coming out of his ears. In light of everything that was happening with my relationship, it made me laugh. A handsome young man in army fatigues rested his fingers on the handle of his rolling suitcase. A gray-haired woman in a blue sweatshirt that said *The Spirit of St. Louis* lit a cigarette. Finally I spotted Ricardo walking quickly toward my car. He grinned and grabbed me in a bear hug.

"Baby, I missed you!" Ricardo shouted. I climbed into the passenger seat, and he gobbled down the pretzel sticks I'd brought him as a snack as he drove us home. When we got there, we shuffled into the bedroom to talk, and he turned on the bedside lamp. I'd always loved how my room looked under the glow of a lamp. The soft light against the deep teal walls made the space feel like a velvet-lined jewelry box. We were both lying on our backs and twisted our heads to face each other.

"Baby, what if I get offered the job in DC next week? I don't want to be without you," Ricardo said. He tilted his head against my shoulder and softly stroked my wrist.

"Then we'll deal with it when it happens," I answered. I was in deep denial and still didn't believe it could actually happen. We shifted to our sides so we faced each other and rested our hands flat on the pillows.

"You never want to talk about it. I feel like the bad guy pushing you to make a decision, and you refuse to tell me what you're thinking." Ricardo let out a frustrated breath.

"I don't like that I'm in this situation at all and *have* to make these decisions."

"Mel, I need a job. It's just not happening here in Texas. I don't fit in. Back East they value experience and new ideas. Down here it seems to be all about running people through the degree mill and getting that piece of paper. I don't have a degree. Experience doesn't matter down here. It's really holding me back."

I blinked and remained silent for a long time.

"You're struggling and suffering here. I feel so guilty that you're staying here because of me," I said. Perhaps if I acknowledged his struggle, he would realize the safest place to be was snug at home with me.

"Don't worry about that; I'm here with you by choice," he replied. "But I'm kind of going crazy by myself here all day."

"I feel like I'm responsible for that," I choked as the tears began welling in my eyes. "You've taken on my lifestyle of being a hermit. I don't care about going out and spending time with other people, but I know you do."

"Well, I feel guilty for you paying for everything and taking care of us. I feel terrible about that." Ricardo rubbed my shoulder. I covered his fingers with mine, wondering if each touch or kiss was going to be one of my last.

"There seem to be a lot of guilty feelings on both sides," I muttered with a sniffle.

"Maybe I should have left Texas right after I lost my job." Ricardo twisted to his back to stare up at the ceiling. "But I chose to stay here with you. Don't blame yourself. I love you. I wanted a serious relationship, and I found it with you. This is the most stable relationship I've ever had."

"Really? With my goofy ass?" I grinned mischievously and clasped his hand.

"I don't want to leave you," he groaned. "I'm afraid if I move back to DC, then we won't survive as a couple."

"We can try."

"I was thinking about this the other day," he began. "I know you really don't want a baby. And I don't want to have a baby with someone who feels that way. I'm not going to force you."

"Oh," I stammered. "Well, uh, I've been thinking about it too, and I kind of like the idea of having a kid." It was a lie, but I was desperately trying to convince myself that I could go through with it as a means to stay together. "I think it would be fun. I just don't want to, you know, *have* a baby. Like, the being pregnant part. That sounds awful."

"Just be true to yourself," he pleaded. "I've heard the things you say—you don't want to be impoverished because of a child. You don't even like them. It's okay. We're okay."

"But if you really want another kid, then I don't want to hold you back," I said. "Maybe you should go find someone who's willing to have a baby with you."

"Nah—I don't think I really want a new baby either. I feel like I missed out on a lot of my kids' childhoods when my ex picked up and moved so far away with them. I wanted another chance to raise a child. I liked being a dad."

"You're still a dad!" We both laughed and intertwined our fingers.

"So what do we do?" Ricardo asked quietly, pulling us back from our moment of levity. I gulped and took a deep breath.

"You're drowning," I said, trying for the moment to remain objective. "If you can't find a job here and decide to stay, it's only going to get worse. You're going to sink lower and lower. But I also think you're going to be unhappy anywhere, and that's why I'm afraid to leave Texas and follow you. I'm afraid you'll keep changing your mind."

"So . . . are we breaking up?"

"What? No!" I slowed my breathing. "I'm just telling you how I feel. You always want me to speak my mind and tell you what I'm thinking. Well, that's what I'm thinking."

"I don't want to lose you, baby," Ricardo said softly as his brown eyes flicked up to meet mine. "But I think our ideas of 'stability' are different. I don't know if I can give you that.

"I don't trust myself to make good choices," he continued. "Every choice I make seems to be the wrong one. I seriously feel like there's a dark fucking cloud following me." He furrowed his brows and threw up his hands in frustration.

"I seem to have good luck all the time," I murmured. "I've never been without a job since college. Good things fall into my lap. I kept hoping some of my luck would rub off on you. I wish I could give you some sunshine."

"You'll see," Ricardo said. "I'll get hold of something, and I'll soar. We might even be in the opposite situation, where I'm the one working and taking care of us." We pressed our shoulders against each other and lingered in our own private thoughts. I appreciated the sentiment but could never imagine myself out of work and depending on Ricardo for income.

"I'm scared," I whispered as I clutched his hand.

"Me too." We looked into each other's eyes for a long time without saying anything.

"Are you hungry?" I asked with a yawn. We hoisted ourselves off the bed and went to the kitchen to make a late-night dinner of chicken, rice, sweet potatoes, and carrots. Ricardo used chopsticks to feed me Cheetos as an appetizer. I felt lightheaded and dizzy, and my blood still coursed with residue from the tingly stress that had been pinpricking across my entire body all day. I felt relieved that we'd broken the ice and talked about the very real possibility of him leaving, but at the same time reality came crashing down. I started to cry again.

"I feel so guilty," I sobbed as I wiped my nose with a napkin covered in orange Cheetos dust. "You're selling all your things so you have money to stay here with me, and I know you're not happy." Maybe I *was* holding him back. We rarely went out, we didn't have friends we regularly visited, and Ricardo only had a low-paying, part-time job. What if the roles were reversed, if I were living with him in DC and either unemployed or working myself to death at a job I hated? Could I handle it?

"Come over here," Ricardo purred. By this time he was lying on the living room floor, which he often did after a long day because he claimed it made his perpetually aching back feel better. I gingerly knelt down on the carpet and rested my head on his chest.

"I'm either taking you with me or staying here," he said as he stroked my hair. "I'm very attached to you, baby. Are you attached to me?"

"Yes." I hugged him. I still felt incredibly uneasy. I wanted to mentally escape my current situation, so I clumsily stood up, popped a Klonopin I'd fetched from the bathroom, and threw back a shot of Southern Comfort.

"No, please don't start drinking! Sit with the pain. Sit with the discomfort," Ricardo pleaded. "Isn't that what your therapist says? It's not good to deny your feelings. Baby, I worry about you drinking so much."

"I'm fine," I muttered as I slurped the last drops from my shot glass. Too late. It was self-medication time. I welcomed the immediate numbing effect of the alcohol, something I would come to depend on more and more over the next few months. While I otherwise maintained a healthy lifestyle through diet and exercise, I turned a blind eye to the destructive effects of alcohol. I didn't care about the extra calories from wine or the headaches from whiskey. I didn't care that once I started drinking, I was too buzzed and lethargic to get anything done around the house. I didn't care how my growing need for alcohol might negatively impact my taekwondo performance. I fell asleep on the couch, dragged myself to the bed a few hours later, and was barely awake when Ricardo kissed my forehead before leaving.

CHAPTER 23

Down but Not Out for the Count

The Monday following Ricardo's return to Texas and our conversation about his inevitable departure, I drove to taekwondo class and listened to James Taylor's "Fire and Rain" playing on the radio. That song always gave me a sense of comfort, albeit bittersweet.

But at that point I wanted to give in. The tension with Ricardo was suffocating. I felt anxious and depressed, and there was an odd security in those emotions, especially for someone like me who had experienced them as the norm for so many years. I wanted those dark feelings to envelop me and let me rest. I didn't know if I was in a manic episode or a depression or somewhere in between in what some people would call "normal." I glumly strolled into the dojang, bowed at the entrance of the training room, and shuffled across the mats to the back so I could change into my uniform.

As I slipped on my dobok and tied my worn red belt snugly around my waist, I reminded myself that every year had gotten exponentially better, especially since I started going to therapy and even more so since I returned to taekwondo. Everything before making those changes seemed like a blur of tears and bad choices. I didn't know I'd be so skilled and strong in taekwondo, with a black belt becoming more of a reality. I didn't know I'd feel so free and comfortable with speaking my mind and being a true peer to my older male colleagues. I didn't know I'd have the courage and talent to write a blog (or write a whole book, whoa!). What would 2015 bring? I put my wandering thoughts aside as my classmates and I began stretching and warming up for training.

"You started doing taekwondo so you wouldn't be afraid, right? Don't be afraid of this," one of the black belts said after we had warmed up and moved on to kicking drills. He was holding up a two-foot-long, rectangular-shaped, soft blue kicking shield and coaxing me to hit harder with my turning back side kick. I was turning too much and letting my bent leg fly out too far instead of chambering it close to my torso, which threw me off-balance and diluted the power of the kick. I looked like a dog that was about to pee on a fire hydrant rather than a formidable martial artist.

"It's not a matter of being afraid." I laughed before chambering my leg again, this time being mindful to pull my bent knee straight in toward my body rather than out to the side. "It's a matter of reprogramming my muscle memory!"

I was actually a little offended by his assumption that I'd started taekwondo to fend off the bogeyman but later wondered if it had some truth to it. I didn't start taekwondo because I was a trembling little girl afraid of muggers or street gangs. I started taekwondo because I was afraid of losing myself to an eruption of anger, to despair, and to finally following through on my suicidal thoughts. I started taekwondo because I was slipping into addiction: before I donned a dobok, I was dulling myself into sleep with whiskey and pills every night and dancing closer to full-blown anorexia. I needed a drastic change and wanted to recover a piece of me that I had buried for over twenty years. I wanted to tap into that steely independence and confidence of my eleven-year-old self who just wanted to draw cartoons, listen to my parents' Beatles records, and go to taekwondo class without a care for what other people thought. Now I wasn't afraid to fight so much as I was afraid to stop fighting. I was afraid of losing my steam, my drive, and my life. I was afraid of erasing all the hard work I had done to uncover who I really was.

A taekwondo person doesn't give up. A taekwondo person deals with failure and disappointment with grace and determination. A taekwondo person doesn't erupt or walk away. A taekwondo person gets back up. I was in. Bring it on.

I faced the black belt holding the pad, pivoted on my feet, chambered my leg, and smashed into the center of the pad with a powerful back kick. He let out a surprised puff of air as my foot slammed the pad into his belly. We both looked at each other for a beat and then started laughing.

A week later, Ricardo accepted the job he had interviewed for and would move to his parents' home near DC before Christmas. I was barely hanging on to my newly found strength, but like a good taekwondo student, I was determined to fight my way back up again.

The day Ricardo left in early December, I was numb. I had cried, fretted, and raged for so many months that by this time I was exhausted. I was ready for resolution, even if it came in the form of the man I loved moving across the country. After the emotional roller coaster of mind games, threats, mini-breakups, and fragile declarations of undying love, I felt defeated. If this was how my relationship was going to be, so be it. I'd fight through the pain. Ricardo and I stood in the parking lot of my condo and looked at each other for a long time. We clasped each other in a tight embrace before he got in his car.

"No tears," Ricardo said, cupping my face in the same dry, warm hands that had lingered on my back during our first date. "Be good. I love you, baby. I hope you know how much. You're helping me believe in love again. You're helping me break the block of ice around my heart. Let me squeeze you one more time!" He wrapped me in a bear hug, kissed my forehead, and opened the door of his car. He started the engine, turned on the rap mix CD I had made for him, and drove out of the condo complex parking lot.

I watched detachedly until the car and trailer were out of sight. Then I went to work and stared mutely out the window for the rest of the day. When I got home from work, I mechanically trudged up the stairs to my condo and sat unmoving in the quiet living room until the sun disappeared, leaving me in darkness. Then I stood in the shower sobbing silently until my skin turned red.

He was gone. I was down but not out for the count.

I gave myself a few days off from taekwondo to get reacquainted with having the house to myself, although remnants of Ricardo's presence were everywhere: the dresser full of clothes he didn't take with him, his DVDs mixed in with mine, his tools in the storage closet. For weeks afterward I would tuck a second pillow by my side at night so I could feel the sensation of something next to me. It was very tempting to shut down emotionally and hide in my home forever, but I knew I had to get back to the dojang. To my delight, when I returned, I had one of the best classes I'd had in weeks.

I had felt a little bored lately, since most of the recent classes had consisted of me as the lone adult surrounded by little kids, maybe with a teenager or two if I was lucky. Being the only (or one of the only) adults in class for long stretches at a time could be discouraging. While I enjoyed helping the little ones and watching them flop around, I was hungry for a challenge and intellectual stimulation. My stressful relationship only added to my listlessness and discouragement.

In this particular class, the one that signified an upswing in my situation, were five black belts (three adults, two teenagers) and an adult bo dan in attendance, in addition to the two brave little green belt regulars who did a great job of keeping up with the big people. Our instructor for the evening was a seasoned sixth dan and master whose quiet, soft-spoken nature made his demands seem all the more sadistic. We kicked, slid, punched, and jumped for the entire hour. Even though we weren't doing very complicated moves, doing them several times in succession was quite tiring, especially the turning kicks. We were all stumbling into each other as we neared the end of each drill. The master just smiled calmly and told us to do it again.

When I had a moment to catch my labored breath and mop my tomato-red face, I smiled too. Somehow I'd made a lot of progress and had forgotten to notice! My spin kicks were finally respectable (at least on the right side), and my back kicks shot out with a satisfying pop. My balance was more solid, and my speed had improved. Even when I was running low on energy, I could still maintain decent technique and focus. Sometimes when I've gone on a short hiatus from a physical activity such as swimming—or in this case, taekwondo—I've come back stronger and more refreshed. The time I'd taken off to deal with Ricardo's departure had not been pleasant, but perhaps it had given me the physical and mental break I needed to return to the dojang rested, improved, and ready to work. That class was a good reminder of why I'd rejoined the martial arts ranks, how much I loved doing taekwondo, and how much I truly needed it to keep me going. It made me a better person inside and out, plus I was able to justify eating a leftover hot dog after class since I had burned all those calories.

Grandmaster cornered me after class as I was gathering my belongings.

"Miss Gibson, long time, no see. You haven't been here much," he said kindly. He must have noticed my sporadic appearance in class over the last month.

I nodded with a sheepish smile.

"That's okay," he continued. "It's normal to hit a plateau around red belt. Some students quit around this time because they don't see rapid progress. That happens to a lot of green belts too. They're in the middle."

My shoulders collapsed with relief. I hadn't told him I had been forced from a domestic partnership into a long-distance relationship, but he must have sensed that something was off with me.

"Be patient," he said, his voice softening. "It's not like this." He shot his arm straight up in the air. "It's more like this. Zigzag. Like stairs." He wiggled his hand to indicate little incremental stairsteps. One step at a time, one day at a time, one class at a time, it would all work out.

The Old Me would want to crumble under the sadness of my situation. Old Me would want to lie motionless on my couch for three days straight and watch movies. Old Me would want to become addicted to pills again and wash them down with whiskey every night. Old Me would want to alternate between dulling my brain with gooey sweets and gleefully hearing my starving stomach rumble day after day. Old Me would want to flirt with very dark thoughts that I hadn't entertained in a long time.

I was not Old Me anymore, although once in a while she tried to stage a comeback tour, especially during this unhappy phase of my relationship (and she succeeded a little while later). I was sure I'd have a few moments of hibernating with movies or going on some kind of detox to gain some sense of control after Ricardo's departure, whether it was another frenzied purge of supposed "clutter" all over the house or restricting my diet. The dark thoughts would likely flirt with me again, but I knew they would dissolve just as quickly as they appeared. I remembered the advice given so often by my therapist, Ramona, and even by Ricardo himself to "sit with the discomfort." This would be a true test to show whether I could actually do it or not. I would be lost, and I would find myself again. Guided by the indomitable taekwondo spirit, I would get back up again.

CHAPTER 24

New Year's Reservations

"Any New Year's resolutions?" Chief Instructor Alex asked, raising his eyebrows expectantly as we all stood at attention. It was early January and the first class after we returned from the Christmas holiday break. My classmates and I, still sweating from a hard workout, looked back at him with quizzical expressions.

"To not write 2014 on my school papers," remarked a teenage first degree black belt with a smirk.

Alex rolled his eyes and bounced his question back to the rest of the class.

"To get my black belt," said a classmate proudly. Noah, who had moved to the United States from Ethiopia and more recently from another taekwondo school, squared his shoulders and smiled.

Dammit! I thought. *He took my idea!* What would my New Year's resolution be? My mind wandered off to my usual internal hippie daydreams, like meditating more, being more mindful and present, starting to swim in the early mornings again like I used to, drinking homemade green juice when what I really wanted to do was pick up an order of large curly fries after class. I had forgotten what was so obvious and looming in the not-so-distant future:

Black belt.

This was it. This was the year.

Holy crap.

Contrary to popular belief, first degree black belt is still at the beginning of the taekwondo student's journey, not the end-all-be-all pinnacle of training. That's where so many people, including even some taekwondo students, get it wrong. The color belt years are basic training. You don't stop suddenly learning or advancing when you achieve a black belt, although sadly many students drop out of training at that point. In fact, first degree black belt is when the learning really kicks into gear, along with leadership expectations like teaching and coaching. There are several levels beyond first degree, and they take decades to attain. Even then the journey is never complete. Taekwondo would definitely keep me busy for a while, hopefully for a lifetime.

"Twenty fifteen is going to be a good year," Grandmaster chimed in as he padded quietly to the front of the room. "It's important to set goals," he added, glaring at each of us. This was a man who had run a successful business for over forty years, had survived the horrors of war in Korea, and had achieved state, national, and international recognition for his contribution to taekwondo and to the community. This was a man who was living proof of the power of focus and sticking to goals. We all shifted nervously and made silent promises to ourselves to step up our games.

I usually didn't make New Year's resolutions, but I thought about what I wanted to accomplish that year. Mentally I made my list of taekwondo resolutions for 2015:

1. To stop hopping on one leg during a 360 roundhouse. It does involve a jump but not a clumsy bunny hop.
2. To cleanly and precisely execute a turning back side kick. That meant keeping my chambered leg close to my body so my kick would go straight behind me and squarely into my opponent's chest.

3. To be able to run through all eight color belt forms by memory.
4. To be able to accurately teach and correct other students.
5. To improve my spin kick on my left and much weaker side.
6. To execute a flying side kick the way God and nature and all the taekwondo masters before me intended.
7. To really nail a flying turning back side kick instead of getting confused and just opting for a half-assed ballet *tour jete*.
8. To pull my partners in close to me during self-defense practice so I could effectively use my weight, even as little as I was, to toss them to the ground.
9. To improve my speed, stamina, and strategy during sparring.
10. To get my black belt. Duh.

Looked like I had my work cut out for me.

Two days later I was in the advanced red and black belt class practicing what we call "hand-to-hand," a hapkido-based technique that is, in theory, simpler and faster than one-step sparring but for some reason is much more difficult to master. I had to learn and perform five different ways—besides defending against a punch, which is the typical mode of attack in one-steps—of subduing an attacker who was grabbing my wrist. If done correctly, my opponent would be bent over in pain and begging for mercy while I twisted his or her wrist into an unnatural and very uncomfortable position. My instructors, classmates, and I all had gleeful moments of tapping each other out (the opponent signals surrender by tapping their partner, the floor, or their own leg) with wrist and elbow locks, but it took months of trial and error to perfect. On this particular night I was having some trouble with these intricate techniques.

"Calm. Down," whispered Chief Instructor Alex, who was my hand-to-hand partner for the evening. Even though I was physically exhausted and felt wrung out like a limp dishrag from the earlier sparring class, my mind was still buzzing with manic, jittery energy. I was breathing quickly, giggling nervously, and waving my hands frantically as I jerkily tried (unsuccessfully) to subdue my attacker. He glared at me and grabbed my wrist tightly, signaling me to try again.

"I'm not good with this technical mechanical stuff!" I shrieked in mock desperation. Maybe I was getting tangled up in my thoughts, which were moving faster than my body could respond. Perhaps I needed to be more patient as I waited for this particular technique to click.

Then it hit me—I was still a perfectionist. I naively thought I had squeezed out those tendencies from my life . . . and yet there I was, apologetic and fretful because I couldn't get the mechanics of a complicated self-defense technique exactly right. I was worried that I was frustrating my chief instructor, and more so I was frustrated with myself—the educated, fit, professional alpha female who *still* wasn't perfect. The desire for perfection wasn't even a conscious one; it was so deeply ingrained that I knew it would take many attempts to extract it and shake myself free of it.

It took a few minutes and a few thumping rap songs during the drive home to get my mood back up from the deep uneasiness I was feeling during class. I told myself silently that not every taekwondo class was going to be a breeze. Twisting the crap out of someone's wrist and throwing them on their face *was* what I signed up for, not just gliding through forms or hopping around in sparring class.

Sure, kicking someone's ass was a part of taekwondo, but even more so was the power of discipline over the body and mind. You can't have focus, precision, and . . . well, some semblance of perfection without keeping your mental shit in check.

"*This* is taekwondo, not pretty kicks. If I can't defend myself with my hands, then I'm just dancing," I muttered aloud as I took the exit ramp off I-30 toward my home. My disappointment about the challenges I was having with hand-to-hand weren't helped by my increasing challenges at home.

~~

Despite my positive moments in taekwondo, my depressed mood and sadness over my relationship followed me into February. The pressure to move to DC and join Ricardo began almost immediately after he moved in December, and it increased into the new year. (And wouldn't you know, the pressure to have a baby restarted as well, although there was still no talk of marriage.) Ricardo pushed me to discuss our troubles during every phone conversation and to hurry up and make a decision about whether I would stay or go. The fact that I had a very stable job and owned a home in a very affordable part of the country seemed to fall on deaf ears. I suspected the same impulsiveness that had made Ricardo so incredibly romantic early in our relationship had not only led to his decision to drop his job search in Texas and run back to his roots on the East Coast but also incited his anxiety about the fragile state of our relationship.

I knew how risky it would be for me to give up my life in Texas and move to be with him. I would have to quit my job and either sell or try to rent my home—and do what? Live in a tiny apartment that cost twice my mortgage and would likely come with a grueling commute to whatever job I would have to take out of desperation? Live with his parents? I would be inheriting his money troubles and job struggles while trying to acclimate to a very different way of life, and I'd never be able to get back the sweet, easy living I had in Fort Worth.

I wasn't about to give up my comfortable, predictable existence until I had solid proof he could offer me the same stability on his turf.

One morning in the early part of that unusually cold and dark Texas winter, I woke up with my favorite line from Franz Kafka's

Metamorphosis running through my head: "When Gregor Samsa woke up one morning from unsettling dreams, he found himself changed in his bed into a giant insect." I always silently recited that line after I'd had a bad night of crying, worrying, and nightmares or when I was in the midst of a bleak depression. Although I had not been transformed into a giant insect, I felt like I had gone through five brutal sparring matches in a row. Once again Ricardo and I had had a stressful conversation the night before. We fretted and argued in circles, never quite able to come to a solution for handling our new long-distance relationship. My face was puffy and nearly unrecognizable from poor sleep and two solid hours of heavy crying the night before. My head ached dully, and my mind felt like it was in a fog.

I regarded Washington, DC, in the same way I regarded San Francisco, New York City, and Chicago: fantastic to visit, but I knew I couldn't hack it living there, no matter how much money or comfort I had. If the circumstances were different—maybe if Ricardo had his own place and didn't change his mind about what he wanted so often, or maybe if I didn't have all the anchors that were holding me in Fort Worth—perhaps I could have made a home on the East Coast. But that wasn't my reality.

On the other hand, I knew Ricardo deserved to have his own life and not disappear neatly into the folds of mine as he had when he was with me in Texas. He had finally found a way to get back on his feet with a full-time job, and who was I to take that opportunity away from him? He was just as at home on the bustling, circular streets of the capital as I was on the sun-drenched, open highways of Texas. Every night after the endorphin rush of taekwondo class wore off, I asked myself these questions, and the twin devils of worry and fear that thrive in those dark, isolating hours of the late evening grabbed my heart and mind and wouldn't let go.

CHAPTER 25

Sparring with Demons

Exhausted from the constant pressure from Ricardo to follow him after he'd only been living in DC for two months, I figured there was no better way to lift my mood than to go to the dojang for taekwondo class.

I was wrong.

It turned out to be the last place I wanted to be. As soon as the first round of sparring began, my mood crashed. I felt clumsy, slow, and very irritable. Chief Instructor Alex was buzzing around me like an angry bee. His barking commands were coming at me too quickly for me to keep up. My partner's attacks felt like physical manifestations of all my shortcomings, an ugly mirror that showed just how unskilled I really was.

This, of course, was all in my head. Alex was just coaching as he normally did, and my partner was just a sweet-natured fifteen-year-old trying out some new moves. They just happened to be in my line of sight when my old friend Low Self-Esteem decided to play. All my flaws were exposed, and there was nothing I could do about it. I was failing in my relationship, and I was failing in taekwondo.

I. Was. Pissed.

"I'm tired!" I snapped as I glared at Alex, feverishly praying he would leave me alone and go bother another student. I had been looking forward to class all day in hopes that it would help ease my emotional pain. Even though my body wasn't really tired, my mind and heart were exhausted. I was tired of the instability and uncertainty of my relationship with Ricardo. I was tired of holding it together, being my own hero, and bearing my crosses alone. I was tired of being weak and ineffective when I sparred. I was tired of trying to live up to my own impossible expectations.

As my partner and I circled each other, I continued to throw nasty glares and mutter curses through the plastic of my mouth guard. For a split second I caught Alex's blue eyes glinting with a mixture of confusion and irritation. Even though I wanted so badly for him to go away, I secretly hoped he would say something jarring or suddenly stop the match. Maybe the shock would bring me back to reality. Instead he simply shouted commands at both of us until the sparring match was over.

I later felt thankful that Alex stayed with me and kept pushing me to improve despite my protests and pleading. He didn't know what was going on in my home life; all he was trying to do was help me. Even though I was reeling inside, he kept me focused on the present and shielded me from my own mental violence. I was a much more deadly opponent to myself than anyone else I've ever encountered. After the match was over, my sparring partner gave me a friendly (and slightly worried) pat on the shoulder and lingered for a moment before he walked away to join our classmates. I was so ashamed I couldn't meet his eyes.

"I'm sorry I was rude," I whispered to Alex as I bowed and shook his hand at the end of class. "I'm dealing with some personal things and took it out on you guys. You didn't deserve that."

He shifted uncomfortably. "Well . . . then . . . don't be mad at me; be mad at whoever is causing problems in your personal life," he replied. It so much reminded me of the type of black-and-white response my brother might give that I couldn't help but chuckle. I nodded, grinned, and collected my sparring gear. I pressed a towel against my red, sweating face and sipped water until the next class began.

I felt more relaxed and comfortable in the next class, which was advanced technique for red and black belts. Still, that little peek into my own darkness kept nagging at me. I felt like such a fraud! Who cared if I knew all the forms or if my roundhouse kick was high and pretty or if I could teach a second-grader how to do self-defense techniques? If I couldn't put what I'd learned into practice and adequately defend myself in a fight, had I really learned anything at all? Was I all talk and no action? Did I deserve to test for black belt that coming fall? Did I even deserve to be a "high-ranking" student?

The only other time I'd gotten that upset in a sparring class was when I was a child attending taekwondo classes as a green belt back in my hometown of Snyder. Sparring was immensely stressful; I would always freeze and panic during the matches. One night I made the classic rookie mistake of hitting myself in the nose as I was attempting to block a blow from my sparring partner. I did block the kick, but my hand bounced squarely back into my face. It surprised me much more than it actually hurt.

Furious over my mistake, I'd gone after the other kid in a blind rage, breathing fire and kicking viciously until my gentle-hearted teacher, Master Weber, pulled me aside and talked me down from the ledge. I was never really angry at the other kid, other than that he unwittingly exposed what I deemed to be an unforgivable flaw in myself: imperfection. I was mortified that I'd made what I deemed an unforgiveable mistake. There I was, Dorky Weird Quiet Talentless Melanie, making a mess out of yet another thing.

My heated reaction as a child was just a symptom of a much more serious problem. Even at a young age, I was deeply embarrassed by anything I deemed to be a sign of weakness, a proverbial stumble, a cause for people to laugh at me, or a reminder of how much I hated myself. Despite getting good grades and demonstrating artistic prowess, I believed I couldn't do anything right, and that attitude would haunt me well into adolescence and adulthood. My parents praised my achievements, but that wasn't good enough for me. Shame, humiliation, and feelings of unworthiness were ingrained in me so deeply and from so early on that to this day I am still digging out the shrapnel.

I've since mellowed out when it comes to making mistakes and getting hurt in taekwondo. As an adult advanced student, I have punched myself in the jaw by accident, nearly bloodied my nose during a roll on the ground, fallen flat on my behind countless times, and been kicked in the face more than once. The one time I did make the similar blocking mistake I'd made as a child (not during the sparring class where I was all bitchy at the beginning of this chapter), I didn't get angry or embarrassed as I would have as a severely insecure and self-loathing ten-year-old. Instead I pulled Chief Instructor Alex and another student aside, showed them the purple bruise my glove left on my lip, and cackled, "Look, I bitch-slapped myself!" before we all burst into hysterics.

These days when I think about that childhood incident, I'm not at all embarrassed about hitting myself in the nose. Rather, I'm much more embarrassed at how I reacted as that angry little green belt, just as I was (and still am) embarrassed for how I lashed out that night in February as an adult red belt / black tip. It seemed like I wasn't quite finished sparring with my demons yet.

CHAPTER 26

Adult Class

My gray, wintry mood was temporarily lifted by a romantic Valentine's Day weekend visit from Ricardo. It was his first visit back to Texas after moving back East. We put the endless discussions of the fate of our relationship on hold and instead enjoyed every moment we spent together cuddling at home, shopping, and catching up with friends.

To add to my lifted demeanor, the following Friday at the dojang, we held our very first adults-only taekwondo class following the regular six o'clock class. Taekwondo tends to attract the kiddie set, and my school was very small, so students of all ages attended class together. Sometimes it could be frustrating when we had to slow things down for the little ones, so I was very excited about taking a more challenging class designed just for teens and adults.

In our first adults-only class, there were seven students, ranging from an orange belt in his mid-twenties to Mr. Derrick, the black belt in his late sixties. As usual I was the token girl. I wasn't bone tired and brain-fried after the earlier Friday class, as I would be after Wednesday night sparring. Fridays tended to be more low-key and focused on the details of technique (forms, self-defense) rather than aerobic conditioning or speed.

First we warmed up with some light cardio and then moved on to jumps. As Chief Instructor Alex counted, we hopped into the air from a fighting stance and switched our feet with each landing. This drill was meant to simulate how we were to turn our hips in midair during jumping kicks. Red and panting hard, we all looked at each other and grinned.

"You can invoke the Over Thirty Rule when you need to," Alex reminded us. The Over Thirty Rule meant the adults could take a break when our bodies were urging us to stop. We adults tended to push ourselves harder than the children did anyway, so having that built-in safety feature kept us from getting injured or too worn out to continue with class.

We then did some work on the barre. With partners, we stretched our legs straight into the air, mindful to keep our shoulders and hips square to the wall as we grasped the barre behind us. Then we moved on to an exercise that hit a few techniques: facing the barre at a 45-degree angle, we flung our outward-stretched legs straight up behind us, heels jutting out and torsos dipping toward the ground. This was a great stretch that warmed up the hips and got the body used to being tipped over for side kicks. Alex bemoaned the fact that he didn't have a camera to snap a photo of all of us mid-swing.

"Now we'll do Melanie's favorite warm-up," Alex announced, catching my eye as I smiled and clapped my hands.

"This is for spin kick. I know when we first teach spin kick, you use a straight leg, but the more advanced version is when you whip your leg around in a hook." To demonstrate, he spun around and hooked his kicking leg in the air as if he were popping someone in the jaw. He gave me a nod and continued. "I showed Melanie this a few months ago, and now she has a nice, pretty hook with her spin kick."

Standing parallel to the wall, we reached across the front of our bodies with our left hands and grasped the barre. Then we began to spin around clockwise, leaning down toward our left shoulders and flinging our right legs out to simulate the pop of a spinning hook kick while we lightly held on to the barre for balance. I was feeling so confident about my spin kick that I thought I'd use it to break a board at my upcoming bo dan test.

Then we moved on to hand-to-hand drills. We began with what I can't describe any other way than "the blocking game." I have dense, bony little forearms that hurt like the dickens when they're slammed against somebody else's arm, so Alex took one for the team (i.e., he partnered with me) and let me bash his forearms as a demonstration for the other students.

This drill is great practice for sparring, when the student must move quickly and doesn't have time to execute full blocks. Facing each other with our left knees bent and both of our right legs straight back in a shortened front stance or walking stance, Alex and I raised our left arms with fists held tight. We flung our arms toward our knees and smacked our wrists together in a dual low block. Then we crossed our arms the other way and did low blocks again. Still using our left arms and rechambering with each block, we flicked our forearms up to chest level and smacked them together to simulate an inside-to-outside middle block. Finally, we both slung our bent left arms up to our foreheads and smacked our forearms against each other in high blocks. Low block, low block, inside-to-outside, high block. One, two, three, four. Then Alex stepped back with his left foot, and I stepped forward with my right foot. We repeated the process as we slid across the floor in a sort of synchronous violent tango.

If you're playing along at home, repeat the same thing on the right side, and keep moving forward (or backward if you are in the Ginger Rogers role). Alex and I had done this together several times before, so we got into a good groove fairly quickly. Pretty soon we were sliding back and forth, breathing rapidly and lulled into the rhythm of our smacking arms. We glanced up to realize the other students hadn't made much progress. Alex wandered off to help my classmates, and I admired the red welts forming on my forearms.

Then we practiced some reaction drills during which we quickly blocked random punches from our partners. We explored issues that couldn't be delved into as much when the kids were around—gauging correct distance, positioning ourselves based on our size, making sure we were grounded enough that we wouldn't inadvertently lose balance as we threw our opponents to the ground.

We finished with some target practice on the bags, again practicing distance and precision. Slamming your foot into a dense bag is a much different sensation than slicing it through the air. We took turns improvising different techniques—a roundhouse here, a ridge hand there (a more difficult technique using the meaty part of the hand near the forefinger and thumb as the striking surface), a sliding side kick followed by a spin kick. Once in a while we'd giggle self-consciously, but we were having fun and experimenting.

The most impressive move of the night was by the giant orange belt, a lanky fellow well over six feet tall who always made the little kids' jaws drop when he would wander into class with his motorcycle helmet tucked under his arm. He lurched toward the bag and whirled into a heavy-footed 360 roundhouse, bashing the bag with a sickening thud. Three hundred sixty roundhouse is also known as a tornado kick. It's a complicated kick, and in fact, as I was writing this section, I had to wander away from my computer into the living room several times and walk through it so I could properly describe it.

Here's one way to do a 360 roundhouse, and there are several variations: Start in back stance (think of a typical fighting stance in boxing or mixed martial arts, although the taekwondo people reading this probably just got offended. Sorry). Just for fun, start with your right foot in front and your left foot in back. Step forward with your left foot and start to pivot clockwise. As you're circling (360, get it?) on your left foot, lift your right knee to help you get some power to jump off with the left foot. Now, once you've done that 360 turn, jump up from the left standing leg and do a roundhouse kick in midair with the left foot before you land back onto your right foot. It's a fun way to chase someone down during sparring, and it looks really cool when breaking a board with it. The orange belt's kick wasn't the most precise or graceful 360 roundhouse I'd seen, but I certainly didn't want to be on the receiving end of it. You can also do the kick without the extra step at the beginning. Go ahead and try. I'll wait. . . .

The best part actually happened as I was driving home (listening to rap music, naturally). Something inside me shifted, and I realized I didn't even care if I got a black belt. That wasn't what was driving me anymore. I just wanted to keep learning and improving my skills and sharing it with the people around me. I just wanted to be in the dojang. I felt like I was finally home.

Since that first adult class, we expanded our repertoire to include complicated throws, defense against weapons, and cardiac conditioning. At least once during each class, we'd all dissolve into laughter and start one-upping each other as we compared injuries and pain in our backs and joints. Unfortunately, that first adult class in February 2015 wasn't enough to keep me from sinking into a deep depression.

CHAPTER 27

Vices

Late February and early March ushered in a slew of ice storms that shut down the roads and kept me home from work for several days. Now, before you start scoffing at Texans for running inside with our cowboy hats tucked between our legs at the sight of a few snowflakes, let me tell you about winter in the Dallas–Fort Worth Metroplex. Other than the Western Panhandle area, Texas doesn't get much snow, but North Texas gets *ice*. Ice, nasty sleet, and freezing rain can happen so fast the Texas Department of Transportation can barely keep up with sanding the roads. Even if there's barely a dusting of snow, the roads could be covered in several inches of slick, deadly, black ice.

It's too costly to keep the same type of weather equipment on hand that one might see farther north, so when there's an Icepocalypse, Texans just have to react with whatever we have on hand. Sometimes that means giving up and staying indoors.

During those bleak winter weeks of early 2015, the sky was perpetually gray, and the dreary weather and isolation started to get to me.

I became more and more dependent on alcohol to get through the dark, lonely days and the stress of what was now a strained long-distance relationship with no resolution in sight. During the days I was trapped at home by ice, it wasn't unusual for me to start drinking at eleven or even ten thirty in the morning. Even though I was staying fit through taekwondo and fairly healthy eating, I never could quite shake my love for the numbing, buzzy effect of alcohol, despite its risks to my health. I began drinking to numb my feelings and quiet the worrisome thoughts racing through my head. Sometimes I would drink half a bottle of wine in the evening. Some nights I would down the whole bottle. Often, with purple teeth and blurry eyes, I'd fall into bed wondering where my evening went.

The depression I was experiencing came to a head one Sunday in late March, two weeks before I was to test for bo dan, the last rank before black belt.

That day I had decided to skip a noon yoga class and stay home. The ice had melted by then, but it was still chilly and gray outside. I was lonely and agitated, which had become my normal state of mind during the past few weeks. I knew I was too uneasy and distraught to patiently spend time on my yoga mat. I consoled myself with homemade chicken cacciatore the way my half-Italian mother had taught me to make it: I sautéed onion and bell peppers in olive oil, added cubed chicken, and simmered the food in watered down tomato sauce before I served it over whole-wheat spaghetti. There—a healthy, wholesome, homemade meal. Surely that would calm my nerves. I hastily washed it down with half a bottle of wine. Thirty minutes later I was still feeling cranky and self-destructive. I needed something—a drug, another drink, anything to mute my mind and dull my senses.

"Fuck it," I muttered and drove a few blocks from my home to a nearby convenience store. I fidgeted in the aisles and finally made my way to the check-out line with a stash of sweets, my choice of secret indulgence. The man in front of me plunked two forty-ounce beers down on the counter. The cashier smiled sweetly at him as she rang up his order and then moved on to me: drunk, disheveled, and clawing at my purchases, which were a box of Pop Tarts, Reese's Peanut Butter Cups, a Snickers bar, and a pack of chocolate cupcakes. The man behind me asked for a pack of Marlboro 100s and a five dollar scratch-off lottery ticket. Everybody had their vices. After I got home, I wished I'd bought cigarettes and a lottery ticket too.

I spent the rest of the afternoon lying on my side on the couch and staring glassy-eyed at the TV as I gulped down the rest of the bottle of wine and forced myself to eat as many of the sweets as I could stomach. I could barely taste them. I was already full from my lunch; at this point it was just self-inflicted punishment, a sudden relapse of my long-buried binge-eating disorder. My brain was muted mush, and my defeated heart was desperate for a long rest.

It wasn't just missing Ricardo so astutely and feeling so uncertain about our future that got to me. It was everything: my listlessness and lack of motivation at work, regret that I hadn't formed a more solid network of friends and acquaintances to reach out to in my moments of stress and sadness, my own stubborn reluctance to reach out to the few friends I did have, loneliness from being iced into my home for days on end, and frustration that I didn't feel like I was making much progress in taekwondo. I didn't know what to do. I was in a vicious cycle of depression that I "treated" with alcohol and junk food, which made me even more depressed.

I finished the candy and was about to polish off a second chocolate cupcake when something deep and quiet inside me became suddenly loud and commanding.

Stop.

I rolled my bloodshot eyes toward my coffee table, which was littered with a shameful pile of junk food wrappers and napkins smeared with chocolatey fingerprints and maroon drops of wine. I scooped up the papers and stuffed them into the trash can along with the uneaten cupcake and picked-at box of Pop Tarts. I washed my sticky hands and took stock of myself.

I felt nauseated from the food I had eaten, deeply sad that I had relapsed into a decades-old and dangerous habit, and yet also oddly relieved. I was mentally and physically exhausted, and now my body and mind were demanding rest. If this was rock bottom, then it wasn't too bad. At least I had a comfortable home where I could care for my tired and abused carcass. As I shifted uncomfortably on the couch, the alcohol and sugar making me feel sluggish and jumpy at the same time, I considered letting this round of depression just run its course.

Sometimes I welcomed a wave of depression because it slowed me down and gave me an excuse to take a break from my normally busy (and anxiety-ridden) pace. I wanted to feel happy again, like I did when I was feeling productive and creative at work and making strides in taekwondo, but I wasn't sure how and didn't feel like putting forth the effort to figure it out.

For the next few days, I treated myself very delicately, as if I were recuperating from something debilitating and taxing. After my binge, my bloated body deflated quickly with my regular diet of brown rice, vegetables, boiled eggs, and fruit. After that fateful Sunday I decided to stop drinking all forms of alcohol. No beer, no whiskey, no delicious and dangerous wine. I couldn't depend on my stressful relationship to make me happy any more than I could the damaging substances I was forcing into my body. Ricardo couldn't save me, and neither could a bottle of Malbec. I had to be strong enough to carry myself across the finish line of the black belt test in October.

I vowed not to touch another drop of alcohol until the test, when I would pop open a bottle of Veuve Clicquot champagne I'd been saving for over a year. I would not buy any more alcohol, I would not drink it at restaurants or family gatherings, and my small wine collection would gather dust in the liquor cabinet. With my newfound determination, giving up the bottle was much easier to do than I'd expected.

Although I wanted so badly to love myself, I had no guidebook and little practice. The only thing I knew how to do to help myself feel better was to practice taekwondo and lose myself in its raw beauty and graceful power . . . plus, when someone is trying to kick me, it's really hard to think about anything else.

CHAPTER 28

Black Belt Candidate

Taekwondo proved to be a welcome respite from the weeks of sleet, gray clouds, cold weather, and especially my recent bout with depression, binge drinking, and binge eating. The first week of April, when the sun was finally starting to shine again, I went to the dojang for extra practice, since I would be testing for bo dan at the end of the week.

I had missed about a week of taekwondo classes due to a quick trip east to visit Ricardo in late March, right after I had my last hurrah with alcohol. My visit was like most of our other interactions as of late: picky arguments, worrying about the fate of our relationship, and fluctuations between affection and quiet resentment. By the time my long weekend came to an end, I was more than ready to be back in Texas.

I was a little worried about how I would hold up in taekwondo class, since I'd been absent, but I was thankful that I had something positive to occupy my mind. It was white belt class night, so I stayed in the back of the room to help two other lower-ranking students, who were also testing that Friday, while Chief Instructor Alex worked with the beginner students. Teaching and coaching took me out of my own head and forced me to focus entirely on someone else's needs. I had the same experience in my day job as an organizational development consultant. When I was facilitating a workshop or a team-building event or when I was coaching an individual, I was suddenly switched on with energy, even if I'd been dreading the event all the way up to when it started. Once I was in facilitator/coach mode I wasn't worried about how I looked or what I was saying. My only wish was to help the other people learn and grow.

Focusing on another person's needs helped me be present, which I longed to do but struggled to make happen. I always seemed to be ruminating on the past or fretting about the future. It was so easy for me to fall down the rabbit holes in my own mind. Approaching our interactions with a sense of caring and curiosity can pull us out of our own self-centered tunnel vision, if only for a few moments.

One of the testing students was a young yellow belt / green tip boy whose black belt grandfather, Mr. Derrick, came to our Wednesday night advanced class. The other student was the tall, lanky twenty-something orange belt who had impressed everyone with his strong 360 roundhouse kick in our inaugural adults-only class. He was being skipped two levels to green belt, similar to how I'd been skipped from white belt to green belt at the beginning of my training.

I felt a mix of empathy for the stress he was under and admiration for his capability to advance quickly. I remembered when I was a white belt, less than two months into my taekwondo training, when Grandmaster Kim told me he wanted me to skip the orange and yellow belt levels and test for green belt. I had been pleased that he recognized my innate skill, even as a beginner, but I was also terrified. Change can be a scary thing, even if it provides new and exciting opportunities and challenges. I wanted to give this young man the same encouragement I received from Grandmaster and other senior students.

The first thing I did was run them through Palgwe Yi Jang, the form used to test from yellow belt / green tip to green belt. I did the form with them to make sure they were comfortable with the sequence of strikes, kicks, and blocks. Then I watched them do it on their own. I reflected on the feedback my instructors had given me and tried to emulate them when I coached the students: Make sure the front snap kicks rechamber before you land. Breathe with every movement. Maintain a steady focus with the eyes. Put power into the blocks as if a real opponent were in front of you. Suddenly my problems with alcohol, food, and Ricardo seemed very distant and unimportant.

Mr. Derrick's grandson made the typical mistakes young children do: rushing through the form without breathing, loose fists, weak front stances. The adult orange belt looked pretty darn good—his breath was controlled and purposeful, he landed his stances before performing a strike or block, his eyes were focused, and his posture was strong. I reminded him to make his front stances lower and more solid and helped him correct a front snap kick that was flopping forward rather than being snapped back and landing correctly. I could tell his mind was getting wrapped up in all the things he had to do at once, which is overwhelming to a beginner. If he was making any particular mistake, it was what all adult students do fairly often (yours truly included)—thinking too much!

I got a taste of my own medicine when Grandmaster pulled me away from the other students and meticulously walked me through my own form, Palgwe Pal Jang, which is the eighth and final of the color belt forms. He picked apart each movement until I did it to his satisfaction. He watched me intently while reminding me to tighten up my timing, add more power to my blocks and strikes, and make everything look strong, not sloppy.

"You need to fix your side kick," he said with a withering look.

"Yes, sir." I nodded weakly and hurriedly tried the kick again. When I performed the form the final time, I tried to be mindful of the feedback I had given the other students—breath control, strong striking while staying loose and relaxed, proper foot placement, and of course, locking and then properly pulling back that damned side kick before landing. And to think, side kick had been my favorite kick when I was a child. *Ugh!*

Grandmaster trotted away to make some calls in his office, leaving me to continue my bo dan test preparation of jumping kicks and self-defense. I ended my workout by practicing my breaking technique with Chief Instructor Alex and two classmates, who held thick square pads to simulate boards. I started with an elbow break, one of my favorite hand techniques, and then followed it with a jumping front snap kick with my left foot. My finale was a spin kick, my old nemesis. I remembered watching with awe as a big teenage boy broke a board with a spin kick at my first belt test, and it seemed fitting to round out my color belt training with this particular kick. It felt cathartic to not only smack the crap out of a practice pad after my last few miserable weeks but also prove to myself that I could do something that once seemed impossible.

"Do the spin kick again," Alex said. "Make it more powerful."

Oh, you want power? I'll give you power! Watch how powerful I can—

Splat!

Somehow, in the course of two seconds, I had ended up flat on my back and staring up into the startled face of my classmate. On the plus side, I had knocked the pad out of his hands with a hard smack before I hit the ground.

"Did you see?" I squealed to Alex excitedly as I craned my neck and grinned maniacally at him. "I fell correctly! I kept my head up and protected it the whole time! I didn't even know I was going to fall! I just did it by instinct!" He stared at me, open-mouthed and silent. Nobody even laughed; we were all too stunned. I thought it was pretty funny but hoped it wouldn't happen during the test, or I'd never hear the end of it. After I'd blinked the stars from my eyes, I reset the pad, turned slowly, glared at my target, and kicked it with a satisfying *pop*. I threw my arms straight into the air like goal posts and did a victory dance to the side of the room.

"You're a good student. You have the taekwondo spirit," Grandmaster said to me after class. I was mopping my face with a towel and silently thanking God he hadn't seen me eat the floor during my botched spin kick.

Was it true? Did I really show the signs and spirit of a true taekwondo practitioner? The five tenets of taekwondo philosophy are courtesy, integrity, perseverance, self-control, and indomitable spirit. Grandmaster must have seen something in me that I didn't yet recognize. Although at times I still couldn't shake the ghosts of addiction and mental illness, I had grown so much emotionally since I joined the dojang. I had developed a new tenacity and courage that surprised me. There was a new fire inside me that hadn't been present before. Spin kick pratfalls be damned—I was beginning to believe I had that indomitable taekwondo spirit.

"Do you want to be an instructor?" Grandmaster asked, looking me in the eye.

"Yes, sir, I do." I suddenly felt very shy. I was reminded of when I turned in my testing application for red belt nearly a year ago, and he had reminded me of the importance and responsibility that came with that rank. The red belt test and my very first test from white belt to green belt were both important milestones in my taekwondo journey. Friday's test for bo dan would be one of the most significant tests of all. It would mark both the end of color belt training (ranks from white to red with two black tips) and the beginning of the next phase of my journey: training and testing for first degree black belt. The weight of it settled onto my shoulders but not in an oppressive way. It was a firm but gentle pressure, an invisible voice whispering, "You can do this."

Maybe this week of classes was some kind of spring awakening after a long mental hibernation. Maybe these last few weeks in March were a deliberate and needed period of suffering to fight through some old habits, resistance, and mental blocks. Either way, it was nice to feel happy and confident again.

—~—

The next day was a whirlwind of meetings and projects at work, which made the hours fly by and kept my mind off the test. Once I arrived home, I shed my dress and heels just as I had for my very first day of class as a white belt almost exactly two years earlier. I washed off my makeup, slicked back my hair into a ponytail, donned a pair of workout pants, and slipped on a faded black tank top, my lucky testing shirt.

I still had a quiet half hour at home before I had to leave for the dojang, so I drank a cold glass of ginger ale to settle my stomach and cool down my core. For good measure, I shoved a soft cloth ice pack down the front of my sports bra, hoping the chill would keep both my body and mind cool and calm. I kept the ice pack pressed to my chest while I splashed rosewater onto my face, meticulously groomed my eyebrows, and just for fun, reapplied some liquid liner into a neat cat's eye. I did a few stretches to ease the stiffness in my back from sitting at a desk for most of the day, threw my duffel bag in the car, and drove to the dojang.

Although I was usually very nervous during taekwondo belt tests I'd taken for lower ranks, this time I remained surprisingly calm. Maybe it was because I trusted my body to do what I had been practicing so diligently for months. Maybe it was because I was at my old familiar school with all the familiar faces, unlike some other testing students who came from branch schools. The main reason I stayed calm, though, was because at the beginning of the test, I told myself to enjoy this moment and make memories. Today's bo dan test would be my final color belt test. Like a final theater performance in high school or the last day of a job, this test was a send-off to a period of my life that I had savored but was ready to let go in order to make room for becoming a black belt.

I was sure I would attend more color belt tests in the future as a black belt, but never again would I be a testing color belt student. I let that thought sink in as I settled onto the floor by the wall. I smiled at the white belts throwing their blocks and punches with the mix of zeal and terror only a beginner could have. I sent silent thoughts of encouragement to the trembling orange belts and yellow belts, including the students I had coached earlier in the week. I mentally went through the self-defense techniques and forms with the green and blue belts. At times I would close my eyes and take a deep breath as my time to perform got closer and closer.

Finally, after several lower-ranking students had gone through their testing requirements, it was my turn.

After I had done a series of jumping kicks, my form, and self-defense techniques, I stood quietly facing the judges' table while other students finished their sets. At that moment a flush of blood, lymphatic fluid, and whatever else was sloshing around in my body suddenly felt like it was coursing through me like cars on a racetrack. I clasped my hands together and gazed at the floor as my face grew red with blood. Sweat poured thickly down my back. It was as if my mind and body were finally free to grasp the gravity of the moment. The last color belt test. The last step toward black belt. Savor this moment.

During sparring, I fought a teenage girl from a branch school where one of our masters taught. I finally understood what Ricardo had meant when he preached the benefits of competing or any opportunity to fight someone new. While this wasn't a competition, she was a completely new partner for me, so I only had seconds to figure out what to do in the ring. She put up a good fight that left me with a deep ache on my shin, but I got in some good hits as well.

For the final part of the test, board breaking, I ended up being the last one in line, which for a moment made me panic and wonder if I'd repeat the glorious fall from the night before. The diva in me took over and was determined to make myself the grand finale.

When it was my turn, I quietly directed Chief Instructor Alex, one of the masters, and Grandmaster, who were holding boards for me, into place. I slowly practiced my aim and placement for the elbow strike, the jumping snap kick, and the ever-troublesome spin kick. When I turned slowly to measure my distance for my spin kick, Grandmaster jerked his board out of the way and flashed a grin at me as if to say, *Quit messing around and get on with it!*

Go time. I slammed my elbow into the board with a shriek, turned and smacked the next board with the jumping snap kick, and whirled around to face the last board.

Pop! A piece of wood flew toward the mirror (and a class-mate's head) after I smashed through the board with a spin kick. Everyone cheered and started laughing. I flashed a silly, apologetic smile at the classmate who had narrowly dodged the flying shards and then bowed to my instructors as they grinned and handed me my broken pieces. Grandmaster shook my hand heartily and ceremoniously added a second piece of black tape to my belt to signify my new rank as bo dan.

"Bye, Melanie!" one of my younger classmates called to me as I walked to my car after I had changed back into my street clothes and said goodbye to my instructors.

"We're bo dans!" she screamed and threw her arms into the air. In the sky was a brilliant full moon shrouded by a pink halo. I smiled, basking in its otherworldly glow and feeling a deep appre-ciation of that evening's test and all it meant to me. All was right with the world.

Part Six:

BO DAN TO
BLACK BELT

CHAPTER 29

Sucker Punched

"I think we should go our separate ways," Ricardo blurted out, jerking his head to the side and raising his hands in supplication. We were chatting over our laptops using Skype, an internet service that allowed us to see and hear each other through our screens. He had now been living in DC for four months, and we were still figuring out how to manage our long-distance relationship. His pixelated image gazed at me from my computer screen and blinked.

It was a week after my successful bo dan test in early April 2015. I was still riding high from my new rank and very excited about testing for first degree black belt that October. I'd been dreaming about the black belt test for months, and I hoped Ricardo would be there to support me just as he had when I tested from white to green belt.

During our Skype video session, I had been excitedly chattering about what we could do during his next visit to Texas. Perhaps, I was telling him, we could go to an upcoming arts gala or to a nearby state park to see preserved dinosaur footprints, when he cut me off with what had become his favorite catchphrase when he was stressed out:

"We should go our separate ways."

No! Not this *again*. The back and forth, the good with the bad, the cycle of breaking up and making up . . . I couldn't take it anymore! After two real breakups and countless other incidents of him suggesting we "go our separate ways," I was tired of fretting and crying and panicking that he would leave me. While I had the same familiar drop in the pit of my stomach I'd felt during our other breakups or threats to break up, this time I felt a new emotion: fury. I bunched up my lips and flared my nostrils. This time I was going to call his bluff.

"Well, here we go again," I snapped. "Any time you don't get your way, you threaten to break up. You're in a bad mood, and suddenly you want us to 'go our separate ways.'" I rolled my eyes and waved my hands in mockery. "I swear this is the . . ." I started counting on my fingers. "It's about the seventh time you've pulled this breakup stunt. At least that's what I can remember."

"I don't want a long-distance relationship anymore," Ricardo protested as he tilted his face downward and clasped his hands together. "I don't see an end in sight . . . and . . . this is draining me. You asked me *three times* when I could visit. Come on, admit that it was too much. You do agree with me that you asked too many times, right?"

"Ooooh, *three times!*" I snarled as my pulse quickened. "You pester me nonstop to throw away my life here and move up to DC, but if I *dare* say I want you to visit a few times, suddenly it's too much. And in case you forgot, *you're* the one who *put* us in a long-distance relationship!"

"I *had* to go! I couldn't find a job in Texas!"

"Bullshit! You didn't even try!"

"Well, I had to go. I had to take care of my responsibilities," he blustered.

"Oh, that's right." I blinked dramatically. "You were thinking about your responsibilities when you were sitting on your ass in my condo not looking for a job!"

"Mel, you know that's not true. I tried to find a job. I just don't fit in down there. And you won't give me an answer about coming up here—"

"Why are we having this argument again? You've only been in DC for four months. We don't even know if your new job is going to work out. I don't think you care or respect the fact that I *own a home* and have a good job here in Fort Worth. I've lived in this area for nearly twenty years. I'm not going to just up and move like you without a good plan!" As I spat out the last sentence, my light Texas drawl suddenly sounded harsh and twangy.

"Baby, I *do* care," he pleaded. "I *had* to move. I wasn't finding work down there. I was trying so hard. I was living completely in your world. I sold off nearly everything I had to try and stay with you. Mel, we weren't working as a team. I tried and tried to get you to talk and to help me figure out a solution, and you just shut down all the time. You never gave me any feedback. That's why I wasn't motivated to look for a job."

Sometimes I felt like the roles in our relationship were reversed: I would stonewall like a man and refuse to talk while he, like a typical woman, would beg me to express my feelings and communicate. He would get angry at my sins of omission—not being able to anticipate his thoughts or feelings, not giving feedback, not asking the right questions, not showing enough concern. The more he pushed me, begged me, and scolded me, the further I withdrew into myself.

"How was that my fault? Whenever I did ask about your job search, you'd bite my head off! And it wouldn't have made a difference anyway if I'd begged you to stay. You would have just shrugged your shoulders and given me that smug, self-righteous look of yours and said, 'That's the way it is.'" My lips curled into a slight smirk.

By this time I was actually starting to enjoy myself. All the bitterness and spitefulness I'd been holding back for so many months came rushing forward with a vengeance. I wanted to be petty and mean. I wanted to cut deep and hurt him so it would overpower my own pain. My inner Medusa was ready to rumble.

Ricardo frowned and leaned back in his chair. "This . . . this is just too hard for me," he said quietly. "I'm under so much pressure with my job here. I want you by my side, but you won't move. This isn't working. And besides, you said you don't want to have a baby with me."

I couldn't believe he was bringing up the baby topic again. I still didn't understand how he would want me to have "his" baby when we were separated by over a thousand miles, he was still getting a footing with his job, and he was living with his parents in their cramped townhouse. How would this hypothetical baby solve our problems?

I lowered my face and looked him dead in the eye, well, as much as one could at an image on a computer screen. "Do you know what getting pregnant would do to me? My depression would nosedive. You don't care that if I get pregnant, I'll have to go off my medication that keeps me from *killing myself.* Don't think I won't be suicidal during pregnancy or after the birth. And how will you treat me if I put on baby weight? You think I've forgotten you said you liked me better skinnier?" I glared at him menacingly until he looked away.

"That's not the point, Mel." Ricardo rested his drooping chin on his palms.

"No, it isn't," I snapped, smiling with cold eyes. "The point is you keep changing your mind, and I'm not taking it anymore. You want to get married, and then you don't. You want to live in Texas, and then you don't. You say it's okay if I don't want to have a baby, and then you change your mind.

"You said you wanted to stay together forever, and now you want us to 'go our separate ways.' You've pulled this break-up-slash-make-up crap too many times. I am tired of you jerking me around. I love you, but I can't take this anymore. Don't ask for something you don't really want. Do you want to be with me or not?"

"I want to go our separate ways," Ricardo said hollowly, repeating his initial bombshell.

"Are you one hundred percent sure?" I curled my tongue carefully around my words, knowing they'd be my last. I was scared, but I knew if I was going to stand up for myself, which I had failed to do in the past, now was the time to do it. "You're saying you don't want to be in a relationship with me anymore? You're saying you want to break up?"

"Yes."

"Fine. *We're done!*" I bared my teeth and widened my stony Medusa eyes before slamming down the lid of my laptop. I immediately popped out of my chair, clapped a hand over my mouth, and stomped around my condo. I felt an odd mixture of relief and being absolutely drained. The indignity of being dumped over the internet by a man who had reeled me in with promises of love overshadowed the fact that I had finally stood up for myself. The control had gone on for so long that I didn't initially recognize I was free.

After a few minutes of pacing figure eights around the living room, I shuffled into the spare bedroom and stood for a long time in what had been Ricardo's closet. I grabbed a handful of his shirts, their wire hangers poking out of the necks, and tossed them flat onto the ground. I made sure the shirts didn't ball up or rumple. I didn't want to destroy any of his things; I just needed some kind of physical release. I poked my head out of the closet and eyed the storage boxes he had stacked neatly on a rickety shelf. I calmly grasped a box with both hands and dumped the contents onto the middle of the closet floor. As with the shirts, I took care not to damage any of the items. I just wanted to throw him away as I felt he was throwing me away. Even though in my heart I knew this breakup was long overdue, I was crushed by how casual and callous he seemed about it.

For the rest of the evening, I repeated the process: slowly grabbing a handful of shirts or a box, dumping the items carefully onto the floor, and pausing for a moment to admire my work. I continued until the closet racks and shelves were bare. Strangely satisfied, I eyed the piles of his things and closed the door to the spare room with a resounding *click*.

I was proud of one thing I did differently with this breakup than I had with others. While I did greedily pop a crumbling quarter of a Klonopin pill, the final dregs of my supply, I didn't once consider suicide, nor did I consider drowning my sorrow in wine. I was determined to stay true to my promise not to touch a drop of alcohol until after my black belt test. At the end of the night, I giggled darkly when I thought about this small victory and covered myself with a thin blanket on the couch.

Although ultimately it was a relief to end the relationship, since it had become so rocky, I was still in shock when it fell apart for the last time. After two years of a serious partnership, I was now a single woman again. After having a lifeline to another person who (supposedly) loved me, I was now alone. I would have to prove to myself, for the first time in my life, that I could be self-sufficient and confident without the approval or even the presence of a man. Like performing the new form I was learning for my bo dan rank, I would need to tap into my inner shrewdness and strength to get through the last leg of my journey to black belt on my own.

CHAPTER 30

Aftermath

Jay-Z's "99 Problems" blasted through my car radio speakers as I pulled off the highway on my way to taekwondo class. It was Monday, two days after the breakup with Ricardo, and I had finally peeled myself off the couch. I thought about the words of encouragement my parents had given me that night: stay true to myself, stay strong, and use this as an opportunity to get my life back. I narrowed my eyes to slits, gripped the steering wheel tighter, and willed myself to have a good time in class.

I entered the dojang to find it buzzing with energy. Two adult white belts were near the wall as they faced each other and slowly, tentatively practiced a front snap kick. Chief Instructor Alex was at the front leading other white belts through exercises, and one of my adult compatriots, a green belt / blue tip, was standing to the side coaching some yellow belt students on their blocks. Grandmaster was working with the remaining students on punches. I introduced myself to the two adult white belts after I changed into my uniform.

"She's getting her black belt in October," said Grandmaster, pointing at me and beaming. I blushed with a smile and joined my classmates for the beginning of our workout.

"Hmm, we haven't done this in a while," said Chief Instructor Alex with a wicked smile after we'd stretched. "Go get the four stand-up kicking bags," he said to two tall teenage boys. "Put them in a line in the middle of the room." The four heavy kicking bags were what you might see hanging from a chain in a boxing gym, but instead they were attached to sturdy circular stands so we could push them around the room. Once the bags were in place, we formed a line and began taking turns doing one roundhouse kick per bag at a time. Easy. A turn of the hip, a sling of the leg, a smack with the top of the foot; I've got this. Then we added two kicks per bag, then three, and finally worked our way up to doing ten roundhouse kicks on each of the four bags. Not so easy.

The more tired I became, the louder I yelled, as if the sheer force of my voice could knit my crumbling bones, unraveling muscles, and broken heart back together. By my calculations we each did 220 roundhouse kicks. We all ended up lying in a heap on the floor as we panted with exhaustion. I hoped the endorphins surging through my body would last me through the rest of the night.

They didn't.

When I returned home, reality came crashing down again. Reminders of my dead relationship wrapped their hands around my throat and sent a chill into my bones. It looked like it would be another sleepless night of stress, sobs, and a sore back from curling up on the couch. I had cried a lot, but I hadn't had the tsunami of tears that inevitably struck whenever I'd gone through a traumatic experience in the past. Those crying jags were the kind that had me doubled over and barely able to make a sound while slimy tears ran down my face, the kind that paralyzed me and made me think that things would never get better, that all hope was lost and my heart would never be whole again. Those were the times when the thoughts of suicide were most seductive. I was genuinely curious as to whether it would happen after this breakup of what had been my most significant relationship to date.

Funny, the great tsunami of unshakable despair never came after Ricardo and I split. Hopefully, that showed some emotional fortitude on my part, or maybe I was just relieved I had escaped the roller coaster in one piece. But I was still deeply heartbroken. Whenever I arrived home to my dark condo after a long day, I longed to go to sleep and make everything go away. I knew even after good days at work or good nights at taekwondo practice, I'd have to come back home to the low-hanging storm clouds waiting for me.

I was also a little fascinated by it all. Why had things happened this way? Was I meant to be on my own near the end of my trek to black belt? I thought about how my yoga teacher always shouted, "Stand in your power! You're powerful yogis! How you show up on the mat is how you show up in life!" when we would crouch into the deep lunge of the Warrior II pose during class.

I wondered if I *really* "stood in my power." My approach to life hadn't always been as positive, eager, and strong as it had been since I returned to taekwondo. It had been fraught with self-doubt, apologies, pleading, and paranoia. My confidence had been shaky for much of my life, and my emotional and mental stability threatened to crumble underneath me. It was hard to stand in my power during all those years when I hated myself and didn't believe I deserved happiness. Now, in the aftermath of being unceremoniously dumped by a man who had dangled threats and criticism over my head for nearly two years, the shaky confidence I had built up was starting to come loose at the hinges.

Where was my taekwondo confidence when I needed it?

To add to my anxiety and frustration, something else very important was missing besides my confidence: my period. It usually came like clockwork, but during this tumultuous April it seemed to have passed me by. Could I be pregnant? Was this some kind of cosmic joke? Some kind of cheesy ironic twist to the inevitable romantic comedy I seemed to be trapped in? I must have gotten pregnant while I was visiting Ricardo in DC in late March. Oh no!

Great, Ricardo and I break up, and then I find out I'm having a baby, which will force us to get back together, and I'll have to abandon the good life I've built for myself in Texas. Ha ha, Universe, very funny!

Would I have to sell my home and move to be with Ricardo and end up with a screaming baby in a tiny, overpriced apartment in a city where I knew no one? Or would Ricardo return to Texas and resent me for it? Would he marry me out of grudging obligation and then decide on a whim that once again we should "go our separate ways"? Then I'd just be another ex-wife, another mother waiting for his child support checks, and I would probably have lost everything I cared about in the process, including taekwondo.

No. *NoNoNoNoNo*, this could *not* be happening. It must be some kind of fluke. It had to be.

That week I bought four pregnancy tests. I nervously went through the dreaded pee-on-the-stick ritual, lined them up on the edge of my bathtub, and waited for the results as my heart pounded: negative. All negative. I eyed them warily and left them untouched in my bathroom for a few days in case by some force of black magic the results changed. I wouldn't let myself off the hook until I got my period and was absolved. I was guilty until proven innocent.

I spent the next two weeks buzzing in limbo, wondering if I was pregnant and just not showing any symptoms yet. I hoped taekwondo could keep my mind off this problem.

CHAPTER 31

I Hate Taekwondo . . .

for a Day or So

When you do something over and over, you either become stronger or you break. One night in early May, we had an unusually small class for Monday night, which was typically dominated by cardio conditioning and kicking drills, so one of the masters worked with me and another bo dan on our form. We walked through it piece by piece, performing each move over and over as we made tiny corrections each time.

"Come over to the wall; let's work on your side kicks," the master said, since apparently our kicks weren't quite up to scratch. Side kick is deceptively simple. It's one of the kicks we learn early in our training but is one of the most difficult to master. First, the student must hike up the kicking leg with a bent knee and flexed foot while keeping it close to the knee of the standing leg. Then, in a swift display of physics, the student must turn the hip of the kicking leg downward while shooting out the flexed foot, heel first. Meanwhile, the student is leaning slightly with fists held in protectively, as if making a set of perpendicular lines: the torso and kicking leg are the horizontal axis, and the solid supporting leg is the vertical axis. Then the student should quickly retract the kicking leg and gently release the foot onto the floor. Oh, and that all needs to happen within a matter of about two seconds.

Many students tend to shortchange the side kick by not pulling the kicking leg back once it's executed (i.e., rechambering) and instead let it halfheartedly fall forward before regaining balance. Another common problem is not fully extending the leg and locking out the kick, which diminishes its power. According to the master working with me, I wasn't fully extending my leg when I executed the kick, nor was I fully pulling back in my kicking leg and landing properly into a back stance. Hooray, I was a master of both mistakes! For the next half hour, I deconstructed and reconstructed my side kick, first holding the barre for support, then stepping away and doing "free range" kicks, and then finally hitting bags.

"Go slowly. Speed will come over time," the master said. "Get it right first." He left me by the mirror and wandered away to coach another student.

I did the side kick so many times I actually got worse before I got better. Doing side kicks over and over had that same unnerving feeling of staring at a word or picture for so long your brain disconnects from the meaning of it. The word begins to seem nonsensical, and the picture becomes dissonant shapes. My mind and senses started swimming, and my eyes blurred with sweat. At one point I became so tired and sloppy I accidentally punched myself hard in the jaw as I shifted my upper body downward while at the same time shooting out my leg to kick. Like my pratfall while doing a spin kick right before my bo dan test, it was a hilarious moment that I couldn't re-create if I tried. I was thankful the master (or worse, Grandmaster) didn't see it happen, but on the bright side, I learned firsthand how much pain my bony little fist could elicit.

Still, I refused to admit I was tired. When tears threatened to well up during the frustration of continuing to fail at executing a proper side kick, I focused on the pain in my muscles, tendons, and joints, a pain that was hewn from growth and triumph. It distracted me from the pain in my heart, a pain sprouting from profound grief and frustration and loss.

But the truth was I was really burned out.

I had been living and breathing taekwondo for the last several weeks, especially the weeks leading up to my bo dan test. My emotions were frayed with my recent breakup and terror over whether I was pregnant. It was hard to leave that stress and heartache at the door when I entered the dojang.

Just as I seemed to get worse with my side kicks on Monday, my sparring was abysmal that following Wednesday. I just couldn't move. I was so unmotivated. My brain understood everything I was supposed to be doing, but my body shut down. That old black magic of self-scrutiny, judgment, and criticism began to rage full force. I started thinking about how ridiculous I probably looked and how poorly I was performing. I was so frustrated with myself that I froze completely as my unfairly matched partner (a very tall and solidly built man) smashed kicks into my side and left ugly bruises on my elbows.

When my sparring deteriorates, the healthy aggression I feel toward my opponent turns inward to a more sinister, poisonous self-directed aggression. Here's a rough transcript of the ticker tape that started flowing across my brain during that particular sparring class: *Failure. Fraud. Liar. I look like a white belt. I'm embarrassing myself. I should walk out of the class and never come back!*

To add to my stress, Chief Instructor Alex was swarming around me again, shouting instructions I couldn't seem to follow. I wished he and my overly zealous sparring partner would leave me the hell alone.

"I know, I know! I'm not doing it right!" I finally snapped out loud through my mouth guard as I threw my hands up in disgust and turned away from my partner. When the fight ended, Chief Instructor Alex planted himself squarely in front of me and glared with angry blue eyes.

"First of all, don't talk while you're sparring," he said in a low whisper. "Second, if he's coming at you with those big kicks, you have to *move* out of the way. You can't just stand there and take the hit. You know what? Just go—go fight someone else. I'm tired of seeing this." He threw up his hands in frustration and stomped away.

In that moment I hated Alex, my sparring partner, Ricardo, and everyone else in my life who seemed to be oblivious to my private pain. Couldn't they see how overcome I was with anxiety and depression? Couldn't they see how desperately I needed help but how much I was stuck in my own isolated misery? Couldn't they tell I was crumbling under stress, including a not-yet-resolved pregnancy scare? It was the first time I truly considered quitting taekwondo.

After I got home from class, I closed my front door, rested my head against it for a moment, and exhaled softly. While my terrible performance had upset me, I felt a nagging unease about the underlying cause. I was still a self-loathing perfectionist, and it was eating me away from the inside. I was tired of having to be "on" all the time—the responsible employee, the sweet and long-suffering girlfriend, the hardworking taekwondo student.

I didn't want to keep getting up and facing the day as if nothing was wrong. I was tired of being a high-functioning crazy who never let myself truly hit rock bottom or let someone else take care of me. The realization of my swirling anger and self-doubt was tough to accept after all the hard work I'd done in therapy and the emotional growth I'd experienced over the past few years. Apparently, I still had a lot of work to do.

My heart broke that the last solid thing I was able to cling to—taekwondo—was now bringing out the worst in me. I had begun to dread it rather than dream of it. I wondered if I had begun to put too much emotional weight into taekwondo, like holding up the impossibly high expectation of a love interest to magically make me happy or hoping more money would solve all my problems. It doesn't work that way. Nothing external can live up to that expectation. Not even taekwondo.

After thirty-five years of ruling myself with an iron fist, I realized I could no longer remain sane while measuring my self-worth by my relationship status or by what I looked like or even how well I did in sparring class. It was killing me. I wanted to say, *Fuck it all!* and fade to black.

To top it off, my period had still not arrived. The next day I rushed to the drug store after work and bought four more tests. They were negative, but I still didn't feel satisfied. I skipped taekwondo class on Friday and spent the evening on the couch, mindlessly watching movies and twisting a blanket in my white-knuckled hands.

CHAPTER 32

And Then We Had Cake

"Mom, I'm pregnant," I blurted out. My mother was sitting next to me in my bedroom, her hands occupied by a knitting project. One of her legs was tucked under her while the other dangled off the side of the bed.

"What? How could this happen?" Mom gasped as she dropped her knitting needles in surprise.

Suddenly my vision went black, and then dozens of pink plus signs, the most unholy of crosses, floated into my line of sight. Each time one of them hit me in the face, a little bell would chime, as if I were in a video game: *Ping! Ping! Ping, ping! Ping!*

And then I woke up. *Ping!* My phone chimed with a text message.

The text from Chief Instructor Alex read: *We're celebrating Grandmaster's seventy-fifth birthday tonight. Please make plans to be there.*

I was still trembling from my unsettling dream. I must have dozed off when I got home from work. It was six o'clock on a Wednesday evening in mid-May 2015, and I was still on a hiatus from taekwondo after that stressful and humiliating sparring class.

Dang it, I really didn't want to have to go out and socialize and pretend to be okay. I sighed and put the book I had shoved under my pillow on my nightstand.

There was no question of whether I'd go to Grandmaster's birthday party. Loyalty to one of the few people I really cared about prevailed. I jumped out of bed and stuffed a clean uniform into my duffel bag. I stumbled into the bathroom one more time to eye the additional four pregnancy tests I had taken, just to make sure my little nightmare hadn't somehow changed the negative results. They were placed neatly in line next to the original four tests I had taken two weeks earlier. I couldn't throw them out until I knew I was free and clear. I scurried to my car.

"Were you on vacation?" Grandmaster asked brightly when I walked into the dojang. I smiled shyly, shook my head, and muttered something about having a bad week. He slung his arm around my neck in a half hug and then pushed me out onto the mat to warm up for an abbreviated class before the birthday party. I was quiet at first, keeping my distance from my classmates as I twisted my body and slung my limbs around to loosen up my muscles and joints.

Since we were using most of the evening time for the birthday party, Chief Instructor Alex wore us out with a fifteen-minute intense workout. I was dreading the thought of jumping, spinning, and kicking with sluggish legs, clogged sinuses, and a depressed mind, but I held up surprisingly well. Suddenly I had lots of energy, ki-yahping loudly, jumping as high as I could, and kicking with vigor. The air conditioning in the building was broken, but instead of complaining, I welcomed the heat. I felt like the last few weeks of stress and sadness were being squeezed out through the sweat pouring down my face and back.

We dispersed for the birthday party to set up folding chairs and a table with cake and plates. While we waited for everyone to take their seats, I had a riveting discussion with an eight-year-old about the refined motor skills one must use to open the complex and sublime Capri Sun, which was far superior to the crude juice box. I conspired with him not to tell his mom if he had a can of soda.

I've never considered myself a "kid person," but in the dojang I felt much more comfortable hanging out with the children. Still wondering if I might be pregnant, I felt some reassurance that perhaps I could pull this mom thing off after all. I was never one for baby talk, so sometimes I would forget I was speaking with grade-schoolers. We'd carry on a normal conversation as if we were coworkers chatting over coffee in the break room instead of a grown woman and a child young enough to be my own. Maybe it was practice for parenting the mini martial artist who was potentially growing inside me.

After we set up for our little party, one of the masters had us all—students, parents, friends, and children—stand and bow to Grandmaster. Grandmaster blushed and waved his hand in protest at us. The master cracked a few jokes and then said something that would stay with me long after the cake was gone: "This is a family. Grandmaster has been our father for all these years. For those of you who are new, welcome to our taekwondo family."

I've never taken the word "family" lightly. I'd never found a tight-knit group of friends that I'd consider "the family you choose," where we haphazardly make Thanksgiving dinner together and spill wine on the coffee table while we swap stories about our dysfunctional childhoods. Even though I spent most of my waking hours laughing, creating, and commiserating with my coworkers, I was hesitant to consider them a de facto "family." I was (and still am) very reluctant to share my heart with just anyone. I wondered in that moment at Grandmaster's birthday party if I had finally found my second family.

The room fell silent except for the rustling of the breeze in the window blinds and the plods and plops of a tiny child lost in her own innocent daydream as she played quietly on the mats.

We all had our own backstories and diverse winding paths that had somehow landed us in a little dojang in Texas on a breezy Wednesday night. We were all there because of him. We were all united as a family.

And then we had cake. And then, finally, my worried mind went quiet.

Even in light of my breakup, pregnancy scare, taekwondo frustrations, brief bout with alcoholism, and lingering anxiety and depression, I was holding up pretty damn well compared to how I might have reacted in the past. For that, I felt proud.

CHAPTER 33

Don't Let It Escalate

"Don't let it escalate," Chief Instructor Alex offered as a final tip for the evening. We had been abandoned by the other students after a late May Friday evening class, so we hung around the dojang for a little while to practice some advanced self-defense techniques. I was a little disappointed when he said that. I'll admit that I've fantasized about snapping the elbow and repeatedly stomping on the face of some nameless groping man, perhaps a drunk at a bar or a cocky frat boy trying to show off for his friends, while screaming, "Women aren't squeeze toys! If you do this to me or any woman again, I'll hunt you down and gut you like a fucking fish! You're *my* bitch now! Apologize to me before I knock all your teeth out!"

Turns out that's not really what martial arts is about.

"It's kind of like when you're in an argument," Alex continued. "You don't want to start yelling and letting things get out of control." I was envious that this guy, twelve years my junior, had already figured out the benefits of remaining calm and clearheaded. Meanwhile, it had taken me many years of humiliating blow-ups, breakups, breakdowns, and *teaching this communication crap at work* for the concept to start sinking in. Alex's taekwondo practice had obviously given him much more than just the ability to do an impressive jump spinning hook kick.

"Don't let it escalate" became one of our catchphrases and a silent mantra for me whenever I faced professional or personal stressors. At that point I was still dealing with the little post-breakup Mount Vesuvius in my head. It was spouting smoke and rumbling with fury, so Alex's piece of advice couldn't have been more timely.

When I returned home from our one-on-one practice session, I thought about the anger that was still simmering in my personal life. It had been a month since my breakup with Ricardo, and while I was feeling better in the dojang, I still had private moments of frustration and anger at home.

My anger would reach a boiling point and then fade until the next mental trigger was pulled. As angry as I was with Ricardo, even more so I hated his ex-girlfriend, the one in DC, the one with whom he'd had a long-term relationship before me. She had frequently texted and e-mailed him while we were together, and it never quite seemed like she was out of the picture.

He may not have had a physical affair with her while we were still together, but it seemed to me he never told her to back off for good. After we broke up, Ricardo admitted he had taunted me with the threat of her pursuing him as a means to persuade me to hurry up and leave Texas to join him in DC. He described it as "dangling her" in front of me. She was, according to him, "waiting in the wings."

At the time, it seemed logical to blame her, and I nearly wrecked myself emotionally from stewing over it. I couldn't see past my lingering, ill-placed, codependent love for Ricardo to recognize his (or my) part in the demise of our relationship. No, let's take the easy way out. Let's direct all the hatred toward this unknown person. She existed only as an idea, an effigy, a target on which I could pin all my frustrations and blame. It was easier to hate her instead of placing the blame where it sorely belonged. I also wasn't ready to admit my role in the deterioration of our relationship. I was so wrapped up in my vicious anger and lacked the clarity that could only come from time and hindsight. I was still too close to the action.

I continued to simmer with rage and self-pity. What if Ricardo had just been temporarily playing house with me until he could go back to his casual, noncommittal ways? I had always blamed his ex-wife and ex-girlfriend for his flakiness about marriage and his cycle of breakups and makeups. Never mind the fact that Ricardo must have left a door open if the ex-girlfriend kept buzzing around for opportunities to talk to him during the time he was with me. Who knows, perhaps he was dangling me in front of her too.

Still, the hatred I felt for her (and to a lesser extent, Ricardo) felt good, like a hit of a dangerous drug. I knew it was self-destructive jealousy festering from my own insecurity, but I wasn't ready to let it go. I fantasized about slamming my fist into her face while Ricardo watched helplessly. So much for not letting things escalate.

Uncontrolled anger will turn itself back on the one expressing that emotion, just as blind rage can cause a martial artist in a real-life confrontation to make a fatal mistake. It was a case of the tired but truthful adage of swallowing poison and hoping the other person dies. What they don't tell you about the poison of hatred is that at first it tastes like soda, candy, and cupcakes. When you discover how disgusting it really is, it's too late.

Don't let it escalate.

With time I slowly began to gain closure and do whatever forgiving I was capable of doing with Ricardo and the ex-girlfriend I had never met. Ricardo was long gone. I couldn't blame that woman, and at this point I'm ashamed I even directed my fury toward her. Our relationship had begun its demise long before he moved to DC. It wasn't like I wanted to get back together with him, even though the first time I referred to him as "my ex," the words tasted so salty

and waxy and foreign I never said them again. I'd refused to recon-
cile when we briefly spoke during the aftermath. I had gotten my
revenge by closing the door on us. So what was the point of fuming
with hatred anymore? I needed to release both of us.

I've often thought about the question Ricardo asked me on our
first date: "Would you rather know or not know?"

Here's my answer: at this point, several years later, I don't
know. At a certain point after a breakup—and this has happened
with every relationship—I stop caring. It's not a feeling of dislike;
it's a feeling of nothingness, as if it never happened. The details
fade, and any importance or value I'd placed on the person and the
relationship becomes rusty and flimsy. Maybe my subconscious
does this as a protective mechanism and blurs out memories I have
of relationships because I've allowed myself to feel too much and
hurt too deeply.

I'm not magnanimous enough to wish my forgotten exes well,
but I don't wish them ill either. They, including Ricardo, simply
don't exist in my worldview anymore. Unfortunately, this non-
plussed feeling, or lack of feeling, never takes hold until after I've
gone through months of grief over the loss of a relationship.

Ricardo, like the others I claimed to have loved or at least liked a
lot, has faded to nothingness. In retrospect it's hard to claim whether
or not I really loved him. The feelings we had over those two years
we spent together were intense, but I don't know if it was love. I was
attached to him because what I truly "loved" was the idea of being
in a relationship, being wanted, being *validated*. I'm not sure after
reflecting on my failed relationships that I can claim to know what
real, healthy, trusting, and mutually respectful love is. My therapist,
Ramona, once asked me to define love. I couldn't give her an answer.

At the time of the breakup with Ricardo, however, my answer
to his question would have been: I would rather not know. Had I

known it would end in tears and bitterness, I would have been even more anxious and fearful than I had been for the entirety of our relationship, and there were truly happy moments I wouldn't have been able to fully enjoy. It wasn't all bad any more than it was all good. I needed to go through that relationship to learn that I could be without a relationship. I needed to learn the hard way what I should and shouldn't tolerate and what I could realistically ask of another person. Only after he was gone did I learn that I could find joy and fulfillment in my own life and in my own activities.

I can't paint Ricardo as a one-dimensional antagonist. He was complex, flawed, and determined to survive, just like I was. I took for granted that he was willingly at my side at all times while he was living with me. Truth be told, I never did ask him what those long days of unemployment were like. I was in deep denial about it and was solely focused on keeping him in Texas for my sake. How did it feel to see his bank account rapidly dwindling? How did it feel to only see his children once or twice a year? How did it feel to be cooped up in a home where he was both a resident and a stranger? How did it feel to wake up to a day of disappointments? It's much too late to ask those questions.

Ricardo and I loved each other as much as two self-centered, depressed people could, and when the hurt began to outweigh the love, the relationship naturally imploded. We simply could not continue to go on side by side, so we had to go our separate ways, as Ricardo so aptly put it. Love was the only constant in an otherwise volatile, codependent relationship built on insecurity and desperation for companionship.

At the beginning and at the very end of our relationship, Ricardo declared that one doesn't grow in isolation. While I am grateful for all the growth I did experience in our relationship, I disagree that we can *only* grow under the shade of influence and experience with other people. People grow with each other, and then they outgrow each other so they can grow individually. Although I despised Ricardo in that fateful moment when he suggested we "go our separate ways," perhaps subconsciously we both knew that we had, in fact, outgrown each other. I do not regret the two years we spent together. Over the next few months as a single woman and black belt candidate, I would feel an independence, freedom, and self-reliance I'd never experienced before and would have never recognized without first living through its opposite.

Fittingly, when I began to let go of my anger and sadness about my relationship, my taekwondo performance improved dramatically. I'd finally gotten over my plateau. I brought a new ease and joyful aggression to sparring. I began to teach and coach younger students more frequently and with increasing confidence. My movements became stronger, crisper, and more precise. Whatever was blocking me from moving on and enjoying my life had finally been released.

And finally, at the very end of May, right when I was starting to get used to the idea that I might be pregnant, I got my period. It was almost exactly two years after Ricardo and I had first fallen head over heels for each other, and now the relationship was officially over, with nothing to keep us connected. Along with the flood of relief came a surprising, albeit very brief, twinge of sadness. Ricardo had clung to the notion that a baby would link us together forever, and as much as I scoffed at the idea, there was a little part of me that believed it too. Now, however, it was time to turn all my attention toward testing for my black belt.

The final link was broken, and taekwondo, my *true* love, was waiting for me.

CHAPTER 34

Pain in the Ass

W hile my heart and mind were changing, becoming stronger, and sorting through the last dregs of sticky anxiousness and sadness over the demise of my relationship, physically I ran into a brick wall. It all began deep in my right hip socket.

The first day of July, I felt it. Early that morning after I arrived at work, I strolled down the galley of cubicles to get a cup of tea in the break room. As I was walking, I had the uncomfortable sensation of an air bubble in my right hip, right where the femur connected to the socket. Strange. I hadn't noticed any extraordinary pain or discomfort during taekwondo class the night before; plus, I thought I had popped all the kinks out with a 5:00 a.m. swim.

Crap. It was back.

When I was in my late twenties, I had debilitating pain in the front of my right hip stemming from a misalignment problem with the right sacroiliac joint, one of those two little bumps on the left and right sides of the back of the pelvis. Driving was excruciating; after any car ride that was more than about ten miles, I would have to limp around in the parking lot once I stepped out of the car while my hip ironed itself out. Having a sedentary office job didn't help matters, since sitting in a cramped position made the pain and stiffness worse. I would squirm around for hours at work as I tried to ease the discomfort.

Thankfully, I was led to a very skilled physical therapist named Cody who helped me go from doubling over in pain every time I stood up to running half marathons. Ever since then, though, my right hip had been a bit of an adversary, an enemy I kept my eye on in case it went rogue again. After seven years of silence, it was ready to brawl.

By the end of the day, I noticed that the familiar old hip pain had morphed into what I called the "ring of fire," a burning sensation that encircled my entire hip from front to back and made me want to snap off my leg at the socket like a broken Barbie doll. My right sacroiliac joint was wiggling and popping like packing bubbles. Burning shivers shot from the inner meat and bones of my hip socket down the back of my leg. During my commute home, I was nearly in tears from the pain, but I did what I had done in the past when my bum hip flared up: I powered through it. My black belt test was inching closer and closer, and I couldn't afford to lose any training time.

For the next two weeks, my hip burned and ached, and the discomfort eventually switched from the usual spot on the front of the hip around to my backside at the very top of the hamstring, where I felt an achy tightness and sharp, shooting pain whenever I did a front snap kick in taekwondo class. The only relief I could get was when I would flick my leg at a funny angle and get a nice loud pop. If the pain was mostly on my backside, perhaps my old hip creakiness had died down, and I was just experiencing a muscle pull in my hamstring.

Then I wondered if it was tendonitis in my hamstring, which is a painful but not uncommon ailment of athletes. Someone suffering from "high hamstring tendonitis," as it's sometimes called, would feel tenderness just under the buttocks. I wouldn't know for sure until I saw a doctor, but I was still in some sort of jock *machisma* denial, so I put off making an appointment and soldiered on through taekwondo classes. I feared a doctor would order me to stop training altogether. There was no way I was going to let a little soreness deter me from training for my black belt test.

I spent the rest of August sitting on ice packs each night after taekwondo class. Sometimes the pain would leak down into the lower part of my hamstring, but most of the time, it would spread out at the very top of my hamstring and higher into my right buttock. I still didn't know if it was a muscle tear or a tendon problem, but what I did know was that taekwondo was becoming a royal pain in the ass. If I kicked any higher than my waist, I would feel a sharp blast of pain across the back of my thigh as I involuntarily gasped and winced. I began to feel more and more discouraged as my pain continued to increase. When my adrenaline was especially high, such as in sparring class, I didn't feel any discomfort, so I convinced myself I was getting better . . . until I was weeping in agony during my relatively short drive home from the dojang. This was getting ridiculous. I had to do something.

Luckily, Cody had taken a job at a sports medicine clinic in a hospital very close to my home, so we'd stayed in touch over the years. When my hamstring pain became unbearable, I sent Cody an e-mail, and by that night I had a response and a referral to a doctor who would be our formal go-between until he could start working on me again. It was time to stop being stubborn and get my ass in gear . . . or . . . well, at least heal my ass or something like that.

On a sunny afternoon in late August, I drove to Keller, a small community north of Fort Worth, to see an orthopedic doctor. Before the doctor entered the exam room, I was whisked to the back of the clinic for an X-ray.

Maybe I'm weird, but there's something deeply relaxing about getting an X-ray. The first time I had an X-ray was seven years prior for my original hip problem. The room had been dark and quiet, and as I lay on the flat suspended table, the X-ray tech gently rocked me back and forth to get me positioned just right. This time at the orthopedic clinic, I had to stifle a grin as I nestled myself on the table and eagerly waited for the tech to nudge me into position.

When I was a baby, my mother always held me in a rocking chair, a large old-fashioned blond-wood chair that still resides in my parents' home. Perhaps that's why I felt so safe and relaxed as I was rocked back and forth on the X-ray table. I was disappointed that the whole event only took about three minutes, and before I knew it, I was back in the bright exam room. I would have withstood more radiation, deep-fried ovaries and all, if I could have been rocked on that flat, hovering table in that dark little room all afternoon.

Dr. Boland was soft-spoken and tall, with hazel eyes that gazed intently as he shook my hand. He instructed me to lie on my stomach, then on my left and right sides, and finally on my back while he twisted my legs this way and that. When I told him I felt a pinch on the front of my right hip when my leg was bent, he raised his dark eyebrows and nodded. He looked thoughtfully into the air and then narrowed his eyes with suspicion at his laptop, which showed the X-ray that had just been taken of my hip.

"You see this white scrape on your acetabulum, uh, I mean, your hip socket? It's whiter than the rest of the pelvis? See?" He ran his finger along the picture of my pelvis on the screen.

I could tell he was trying not to use too much medical jargon. I refrained from telling him I had spent nearly seven years researching medical literature as a hospital librarian, and I wasn't scared of an acetabulum or two. I simply nodded and leaned in to look at the black-and-white image.

"That's calcification. It means there's a calcium buildup, and your femur and hip socket don't quite fit together," Doctor Boland explained, making a fist with his left hand and covering it with his right hand, as if his fist were the head of the femur fitting snugly into the hip socket. He moved his fist back and forth smoothly and then slightly tilted it off kilter to illustrate how my bones weren't quite fitting together right. He gazed off into space and started muttering under his breath.

"Hmm, I'm not sure if it's cam or pincer . . . maybe not, I don't see any bony spurs, which is good . . . hmm, pincer . . . no, maybe cam. . . ." He was referring to the different types of calcification that could occur, but there wasn't quite enough evidence on the X-ray to point to one specifically.

I watched him patiently until he made eye contact with me again.

"I'm not convinced of a labral tear; you'd have to get an MRI for that," continued the doctor. "But I strongly suspect femoroacetab—I mean, hip impingement syndrome. That's what's causing the pain on the front of your hip when your leg is bent." He was referencing the labrum, the ring of cartilage that follows the outside rim of the hip socket and separates the pelvis from the femur. Hip impingement syndrome inhibits the range of motion at the top of the leg and can cause a sharp pinching sensation when the affected leg is bent. It can also cause the leg to overcompensate in other areas, which manifests in pain in other places . . . such as in the top part of the hamstring.

Well, well, well. My years-old hip pain had officially come back with a vengeance and was literally trying to kick my ass. Looks like we both had scores to settle. Six days later, on the second of September, I was off to my first physical therapy appointment.

CHAPTER 35

Baby Got Piriformis

It felt appropriate that Sir Mix-a-Lot's song "Baby Got Back," which celebrates the glory of women's backsides, was playing as I drove to my first physical therapy session. After all, most of the pain I'd been experiencing for the last two months had been radiating out of my not-so-glorious ass. I was excited and a little nervous. While I was ready to put my full effort into healing, I wondered if I'd have to go through even more pain and discomfort to get there, and I also wondered how much I would have to modify my taekwondo practice.

The sports medicine clinic looked like a masochistic jock's dream: Exam tables lined the outer edges of the room, where smiling therapists massaged the limbs and backs of their patients. Elliptical machines and bikes anchored the area near the front desk, and the middle of the room was filled with exercise equipment you'd find at any gym: kettle bells, different-sized boxes for patients to step or jump onto, resistance bands, and Swiss balls. There was even a small basketball court in the center of the clinic. Cool.

As I waited for my appointment, I filled out forms with my insurance information. I drew little circles on an outline of a bald, sexless human figure to indicate where I was hurting. I looked around at the other patients and tried to figure out what their ailments were: The husky guy doing a slow baseball pitch might have had a rotator cuff tear. The young man slowly spinning the pedals of a bicycle while his crutches were perched against the wall was likely recovering from surgery. The tall, thin girl stumping around with an ice pack tightly taped to her knee was probably a high school volleyball star. Finally Cody, my therapist from seven years prior and now assigned (at my request) to my case, appeared around the corner, and I jumped up from my seat.

"I'm back!" I cackled and grabbed him in a back-slapping hug. Cody had a lean runner's build, a wry sense of humor, and most importantly, the magic touch for healing my pain. I knew if anyone could fix my broken body, it was Cody.

We were joined in the exam room by a shy, red-haired physical therapy college student who was shadowing Cody for the day. Cody got right down to business and did the same exam he'd done on me nearly a decade earlier. He sat on a stool and had me turn away from him. He gently tucked my shirt up into the bottom of my sports bra and pressed his thumbs into my sacroiliac joints.

"Roll down for me," he ordered cheerily. I bent over, exhaling as if I were doing a forward fold in yoga class—which put my bottom directly in Cody's face. Things were going to get intimate very quickly. (I was wearing pants! Don't get weird!)

"Hmm, okay, now march in place, knees nice and high," Cody continued in his soothing sing-song voice as he kept his thumbs planted squarely on the back of my pelvis. Once I stopped marching, he began running his fingers up and down my spine and poking the muscles encasing the vertebrae. He hummed the names of the muscles and tendons as if he were reciting a prayer.

"Go ahead and lie on your back for me."

I scooted onto the exam table. Cody raised my bent right leg and began twisting it around, just as Doctor Boland had, to check the alignment and see where the impingement was starting to really hurt in the right hip. When he turned my right knee in toward my groin, my eyes bugged, and I let out a squeak.

"Ah, there it is!" he exclaimed. "Let's take some time out to work on this before we do any exercises. Go ahead and lie on your left side for me." Physical therapy involves more than doing leg lifts or pulling on stretchy green rubber exercise bands. It also includes, at least in Cody's world, musculoskeletal adjustments and deep tissue massage, which meant that on most visits, my therapist would be cracking the hell out of my back and hip and kneading my muscles like my mother's homemade pizza dough.

Cody leaned over me as he circled his arms around my bent right knee and upper back, and then in a flash, he snapped my body together so quickly it knocked the wind out of me. I felt a satisfying crackle run through my spine. I turned over to my right side, and he crunched my spine again. He then had me grab the top of the table while he gave each ankle a hard yank, popping anything that was left to pop in my hips and spine.

"Everything's connected," Cody explained. "If I loosen up the back, it will help release the muscles in the hip. Then you'll be more efficient at your exercises." I raised my eyebrows in silent appreciation.

"Now I'm going to work on the psoas muscle," he said calmly as he eyed the timid student, who was standing stock still in the corner of the exam room. Cody was referring to the large powerful muscle in the hip that flexes the torso and legs together. The psoas major attaches on the lower spine and connects again at the top of the femur. When someone is referring to the "hip flexor," which is actually a group of muscles, they're most often referring to the psoas major.

"The art of therapy is knowing when to pause and work on something that's calling to you," Cody began as he perched on the table with one bent knee and one foot on the floor. He motioned for me to lie on my back, keeping my left leg straight as he rested my bent right knee across his own.

"As a student you might tend to compartmentalize—first take the history, then the objectives," he continued. "No, there needs to be a flow to it." He sank his fingers deep into the side of my right hip, which made me wince and inhale sharply. I felt shocked, curious, and a little disgusted at the same time. When he did a little fishhook move with his finger toward the ilium (the big bone in the front of the pelvis), I felt like he could have disemboweled me. The ancient Greeks referred to the psoas muscle as the window to the soul. It felt more like the gateway to hell.

"Just keep breathing," Cody said soothingly as he continued to do what I imagined a colon resectioning must feel like without anesthesia. I stared up at the ceiling and breathed slowly through pursed lips. Thankfully it was over in a minute or two, and he twisted my legs around again. As if by magic, the pinching in the front of my right hip was less severe.

I ended up on my stomach while Cody continued his lesson.

"See? Here's the piriformis," Cody said to the student as he poked the left side of my bottom. (You guys, it's fine! I was still wearing pants!) "It's a *lot* stronger on this leg, one of the strongest I've ever seen. There's a big difference between the left and the right."

Hmm, interesting. I knew I was getting more junk in my trunk throughout my training, especially in the more recent months. Skirts clung tighter, and my little T-Rex legs were pumping like pistons, but apparently my caboose was lopsided. Not sure if Sir Mix-a-Lot would approve.

"Wait a minute!" I said, my voice half-muffled by the pillow. "How can that be? I'm so right-leg dominant! I'm right-handed. My kicks are better on the right. I thought I was stronger on my right leg."

"You *kick* a lot with your right leg," Cody answered, "but you're *standing* on your left leg while you're doing all of that. If you favor kicking on your right, then that builds up your standing leg, giving you a really strong foundation. Your right leg is a lot weaker—maybe because you're overcompensating with the left leg for the longtime hip pain in the right—so you have nothing to hold you up when you kick with the left leg."

"Oh . . . so *that's* why my left-leg kicks suck so much," I mused, resting the side of my face back down on the pillow. Then I twisted my head around to face the student, who by this time looked a little green.

"I'm glad you're here," I chirped. "He's explaining everything, and you're asking all the questions I don't know how to ask. We're learning at the same time!" The student nodded his head politely and looked like he was trying not to think too hard about the fact that for the past twenty minutes he had been staring directly at my derriere while Cody poked and prodded me.

I was then assigned what would come to be called my "active hip warm-up." I marched the length of the clinic, lifting my knees as high as possible, and then switched the motion by trying to kick myself in the butt as I walked forward. Then I bent my knees and slung my feet up into the air one at a time as I slapped my foot with the opposite hand. I called these "Michael Jacksons," since they looked like the funny little leg flick the late King of Pop would do so often. Thankfully for everyone at the clinic, I did not incorporate a crotch grab or a scream into my active hip warm-up.

Since this was my first therapy session, and much of it had been taken up by assessment and some spinal manipulation and adjustments (and that gross psoas "massage"), we kept the actual exercises to a minimum. After completing my active hip warm-up, I did a series of leg lifts and squats to work on my strength and balance. I returned to the exam room so Cody could get a feel for how my body responded to the exercises. Once again I was on my back with his fingers jammed into my hip socket.

"Ewww, I feel like your finger is going to go through to the table," I mewled, trying not to let myself be overcome by nausea or, worse, a hysterical fit of laughter if I dared let myself think about how much it tickled.

"It might go through all the way to the floor," Cody murmured quietly and dug his fingers in even deeper.

I went to sparring class later that evening and got the green light from Grandmaster and Chief Instructor Alex to hang back and just serve as a referee for the matches. My hip and hamstring already ached from the fast-paced warm-ups we did at the beginning, so I knew I'd better take seriously Doctor Boland's and my physical therapist Cody's warnings to back off. I focused more on coaching than fighting, although I did chase around a few of the kids and let them punch me in the stomach. I was happy to shift gears. Coaching gave me that nurturing fix I needed; plus, it always helped me improve my own taekwondo skills by giving me a different and more intellectual perspective of the sport.

"You don't have the body you had at eighteen anymore," one of the masters teased me after class, reminding me that I needed to go slowly for a while and care for my injury.

"But in my head I do!" I joked before stumbling out into the parking lot. It was so hard and frustrating to hold back when I'd been so active my entire adult life. I was determined not to quit taekwondo, even if all I could do was hobble along the sidelines and smack the kids with focus pads when they didn't move fast enough.

So that's how my life would be for the next two months: a balancing act between staying active and playing it safe. My yoga teacher always said smart yogis modify; they listen carefully to their bodies. I'd like to think that's what smart black belt candidates do too, so I resigned myself to finding the right balance between pushing myself and trying to heal. I hoped I would be able to stave off the pain at least until after my test was over. I wasn't too worried, though. Every good sports story needs some kind of setback near the climax, right?

CHAPTER 36

Growth Spurt

"So how many months is it between red belt and black tip?" asked Sophia, a young blonde student, tilting her head and narrowing her hazel-flecked eyes at me. It was a Monday night in late September 2015, and I was stretching out my tender hamstring. Sophia was sporting a brand-new red belt, still stiff and shiny and creased from her Friday night color belt promotion.

"Four," I said absentmindedly, grabbing my foot and bending my leg at the knee for a quadriceps stretch. Once a student hit red belt, the rate of promotion to black tip and later bo dan slowed to four-month intervals, and then six months between bo dan and black belt. During this time, the student would be learning skills that were more advanced and intricate than what was demanded of them at lower color belt ranks. Even though black belt might be a year and a half to two years away, a red belt student already needs to be thinking of black belt as the next goal.

"Four months. It's four, four, six!" piped up Thomas, an adult blue belt at the back of the room.

"See, he knows too," I said, nodding at Thomas. I wanted to tell the little red belt not to get too wrapped up in rushing from one test to the next. There was a lot to enjoy in simply being a red belt . . . and black tip . . . and bo dan. I hoped she would slow down and savor the moments and the little joys I'd had since I donned a red belt over a year ago . . . but sometimes people need to figure things out on their own.

It started to really hit me that I would be testing for black belt in a month. I hadn't even been thinking about getting a black belt when I first reentered the taekwondo world. At that point I had just needed to get away from myself and my little Fortress of Solitude and Whiskey. Finally, after years of searching, I'd found something that quieted and focused my mind and opened my heart. I became more nurturing and loving with the people around me in the dojang than I ever had during halfhearted friendships that died out or sporadic attempts at joining social groups. My connections to those people had long since fizzled. Meanwhile, through taekwondo I found acceptance, friendships, and a new-found confidence in myself that I'd never had before. As long as I could find a place to practice martial arts with other like-minded people, I knew I'd be happy. A black belt was just gravy.

First degree black belt is by no means the pinnacle of the taekwondo student's journey. It just means you've completed basic training, and your instructor trusts you not to kill the little kids in sparring class. You keep growing and changing and uncovering more and more layers as the years go by. You get to see taekwondo through the fresh eyes of new white belts and learn nuances you would have never discovered on your own without the guidance of more seasoned black belts. You get back what you invested in it a hundredfold.

"Do you *want* to be a black belt?" I asked Sophia, raising my eyebrow. She nodded emphatically.

"Then you'll have to work hard. Do you remember your form?" I asked, leaning down to look her in the eye.

"Yes, but it's confusing," she said, miming some of the motions of Palgwe Chil Jang, the red belt form.

"Okay, we'll work on that after the white belt class is finished. We have to be quiet until then."

She gazed at the white belts and mused, "I like watching them sometimes."

"You can learn how to teach by watching a white belt class," I whispered. "You have to know how to do all that *and* be able to teach all that to be a black belt." She nodded again and started mumbling under her breath the techniques white belts had to learn: stretch kicks, front snap kick, low block. . . .

Although I felt discouraged by my lingering injury, I was energized during that night's class. It had lots of variety to keep us on our toes, and the enthusiasm was infectious. Being around people I cared about definitely helped lift my spirits. It seemed my overflow of love for taekwondo and my fellow students didn't quite shine through as much as I thought it did. I was bustling quickly toward the door after class when Chief Instructor Alex popped up behind me and asked nonchalantly, "Did I hold you over?"

"No, why do you ask?"

"Well," he continued as he straightened chairs, "I see you rushing out most nights, and you don't talk to anyone. Sometimes it comes across as standoffish." His tone was matter-of-fact rather than sounding offended or accusatory, which was usually the way other people have acted when they've addressed my introverted nature.

I was crestfallen but not surprised. I've always had a quiet, serious expression and am hesitant to enter conversations. Some would say I have Resting Bitch Face. I just call it my Blank Not-Giving-a-Shit Introvert face. Arched eyebrows and slightly upturned eyes don't help my attempts to look like a nice person. Some people have wondered if I'm about to cry, whether I'm angry, or if I'm just a snob. Those assumptions have all been true at one time or another, but for the most part, I'm simply in my own little world and am not concerned with what's going on around me. Maybe it's just a case of the world thinking a pretty woman owes it a constant smile.

I can be very nurturing and caring, but some days . . . I just can't engage. I don't care. I'm not interested. I've chosen to live my personal life in an isolated way, somewhat by habit and somewhat by default, so it's a bit jarring when other people want me to spend time with them. It's not social anxiety. I simply don't need the same level of interaction that others do. I really and truly don't care if another human being even looks at me all day.

It was hard for me to fathom that others could feel differently. Sometimes I felt—and still feel—like I had to "fake it" as a normal human to function in our society. I've forced myself to smile at babies when I'd rather ignore them. I've joked around with people in line at the grocery store but only if they initiated the exchange. I've become adept at small talk in social or work situations, but inwardly I feel exhausted and disgusted with myself for having to put on a mask. I'm always polite. I'm just not always engaging.

And then I thought about something my yoga teacher had mentioned in a class a few days earlier: coachability. Being coachable is having the ability (and willingness) to accept feedback and try something new or make a change. I had always brushed off suggestions from people to be more personable because I figured they were just more sensitive to whether people paid attention to them. That was their problem, not mine. I put up my tough-girl walls and claimed I didn't need or want people in my life. However, I had received some very valuable feedback from my taekwondo instructor. It was up to me whether I was going to accept and use it.

"Okay, I'll be more involved," I said, smiling as I rested my hands on a chair.

"Good, because, well . . ." Alex began shyly, not meeting my eyes, "I'm grooming you to be my assistant instructor . . . um, one of them anyway."

"Of course, I'll stick around. Whatever you need!" I said quickly. I was experiencing something I hadn't felt very often in the past: a rushing sense of loyalty. As much as I'm a serial monogamist in romantic relationships, I'm very much a commitment-phobe with friends or groups of people. The thought of getting together with a throng of people and, ugh, spending time with them made me want to lock my door and bury myself in books. But in the dojang? That was a different story. My instructors and classmates were my second family. I would do anything for them, and to this day I still can't quite figure out why or how they made it past my massive walls. I didn't have to make a conscious effort to be more nurturing or loving or positive with them. I just was.

From then on, I made the point of socializing a little more before and after class, and eventually it felt natural.

Perhaps I could pull this being human thing off after all.

While I was becoming more outgoing in the dojang, my growing confidence continued to seep into my persona elsewhere. Sure, my relationship had crashed and burned, but elsewhere it seemed that things were looking up, especially in the workplace. I was a few years into my role as an organizational development consultant on a team with men who had decades more experience than I did, and I was finally feeling comfortable and secure with my place on the team.

My boss continued to praise my "intense and intentional" approach to my work, and my male colleagues frequently asked for my advice and told me how much they respected my perspective. I often voiced my opinion in meetings and carried on friendly and respectful debates with my team members. And I was finally getting to do with clients what I loved doing in the dojang: coaching. (Except I couldn't yell at my business coaching clients to do push-ups.) I had done a complete one-eighty from where I'd been a few years earlier. I wasn't the shy, scared, sad little girl I'd been since childhood.

As for dating, I was completely turned off by the idea of getting back on the scene. It had only been a few months since

Ricardo and I split, but I felt something beyond that—a type of unfamiliar but very comfortable detachment. It wasn't a version of Single Melanie I'd ever experienced before: I didn't resent Ricardo (at least not any longer) or men in general. I didn't feel sorry for myself, and I found myself enjoying my solitude more than ever. When my work friend Madeline asked me about "the elephant in the room" over lunch, I had no idea that she was referring to the fact that I was single. My relationship status didn't even occur to me.

I no longer believed I was a helpless victim being rejected by a conspiracy of men. I was too busy training for my black belt test, leading meetings in the boardroom, rounding out my fitness training with swimming and yoga, keeping up my blog, and, well, writing this book. I didn't long for companionship or attention from a man. I simply didn't care anymore. I'd never felt so free. I was free from my own judgmental clutches and the misery I had inflicted upon myself in the past when I found myself without a relationship.

Although I was happier and more confident, I had not entirely snuffed out the flame of depression and anxiety. I learned, however, to deal with it in a healthier way. My moods continued to cycle, and my anxiety would whisper incessantly in my ear, but it was more muted than it had been in the past. At times I found myself searching for things—regrets, worries, anything—to ruminate over just to kill time, as if my brain couldn't stand any empty space, but I didn't sense the emotions overpowering and tormenting me as they had in the past. There was a part of me that didn't (and still doesn't) want to let the mental health problems go. I like the manic buzz and the creativity that flows from it, and I like the quiet moments of hibernation that depression has allowed me. My mental illness would sometimes get the better of me, but rather than break down, I paused and listened. Why did it need my attention? What was it trying to tell me?

It was surprisingly easy to avoid alcohol during the last months of training for my black belt. Alcohol, specifically wine, had once accompanied my surges of anxiety and depression, not to mention being my sidekick whenever I brewed a fresh batch of marinara as I watched mafia movies. I hadn't had a drop since that gray gloomy Sunday in late March and did not miss the fuzzy, numbing effects of alcohol as much as I thought I would. When I had a scratchy throat from summer allergies, I longed for a splash of whiskey in honeyed tea, but otherwise alcohol no longer crossed my mind. The mild rosacea that left tiny bumps and flushes of red across my nose and cheeks lessened, and my blood pressure dropped by a few points. More importantly, my depression loosened its grip on me after I stopped drinking.

I still planned to start imbibing again after the black belt test in October, beginning with that bottle of Veuve Clicquot I'd stashed away. I love wine, and not just for the slow-building heady buzz. I love the texture, the taste, the complexity of smell and flavor, the beautiful color of it, how it can complement anything from filet mignon to peanut butter crackers (cabernet sauvignon and a really dry cheddary chardonnay, respectively, in case you're wondering).

The difference would be that once my self-imposed oenophilic exile was over, I would truly be able to enjoy wine without being weighed down with the anxious expectation for it to save me from my worries or give me a false sense of cheer and peace . . . at least that's what I chanted to myself as my lonely wine collection waited for my return. For now, though, I had a black belt test to prepare for.

CHAPTER 37

Exorcism

About two weeks before my black belt test in late October, I went to sparring class, which I had been avoiding, since it had caused the most pain and irritation in my right hamstring. The sudden, explosive movements of fighting usually resulted in a deep burning in my leg afterward and lingering discomfort as I tried to go to sleep. I knew that while my leg was improving, it wasn't completely healed, so I was taking a risk by going to class, especially when my test was so close. I didn't care, though. I was beginning to feel more daring and determined. Fighting, pain or not, was helping my heart and mind heal . . . even though it was a pain in the ass.

Ever since my bo dan test in April and my traumatic breakup shortly thereafter, I felt like the transformation I'd been going through thanks to taekwondo was accelerating. I made it through the emotional pain of splitting from Ricardo and embraced life as an unattached woman. I attacked my physical pain head-on (well, after sitting on it for a month, but you know, better late than never).

I pushed myself hard that night in sparring class. I wanted to feel everything, emotionally, mentally, and physically, even when my leg burned with pain or my mind squirmed with bitter memories. I wanted a release. I wanted my body to wring out the toxic buildup my mental illnesses had created for so long. I wanted my broken-but-still-standing heart to furiously pump blood. I wanted to celebrate the strength and resilience of my injured body. And for a thirty-six-year-old woman with a bum leg, I did a fine job of kicking some ass after a month's absence in sparring class.

I paid for my enthusiasm the next day. As predicted, a night of sparring got the tendons and muscles in the back of my right leg riled up again. I had a physical therapy session that day, so Cody, accompanied by the shy student who had joined us for my first session, got right to work on my angry hamstring. I lay on my stomach while Cody began poking around my leg and bottom to find the source of the irritation.

"Ugh, right there. That's where it hurts," I said with a grimace. Cody's hand stopped at the center of the top of my thigh, where it rounded into my right butt cheek.

"Where are you?" asked the student.

"The ischial tuberosity just above the gluteal fold," Cody answered, as if my ass were a stretch of highway and my ischial tuberosity were a mile marker.

"Am I in the neighborhood?" he asked, gingerly pressing his finger into the crease between my buttock and hamstring.

"What? Oh, uh, yeah," I answered.

"Yup, I can feel it."

"Ew, you can tell? Wow."

"Let's try and isolate that glute," Cody said, poking his finger into the piriformis, the muscle that sticks out of the side of the bottom, and lifting my foot into the air as I bent my knee.

"Okay, press against me, and fire up that glute! Come on, squeeze, squeeze, squeeeeeeeze!" he shouted. I clenched my teeth, exhaled sharply, smashed my forehead into the pillow, and pushed against him with all my might . . . and my sad, underdeveloped right-side butt cheek barely tightened at all. Cody let down my leg gently and looked at me with mock disappointment.

"*Really?* Man, that side can't do anything!"

"I can't even feel it," I said, just as disappointed. I could make the left side of my butt, especially my overdeveloped piriformis, dance on command. But the right side? *Nothing.*

During our previous exchanges, we had never really addressed what was staring everyone in the face: my ass. Now, Cody has been familiar with my lower half from the very beginning when he worked on my hip in 2008, long before I rejoined the taekwondo ranks. (Yes, I wore pants every time.) He was an absolute professional and a skilled clinician, and I had unshakable trust in both his propriety and his ability to get in there and treat the problem, intimate area or not. But still, when it came to matters of actually talking about it, we were quite Victorian. We danced around it with euphemisms, calling each side a "glute" with a gruff jockiness in our voices or referring to my butt cheeks as "them," never referring to what *they* actually were. I figured we needed some levity, and now was as good a time as any.

"Now I can really say that I'm half-assing it!" I whispered giddily. Cody wheezed out a laugh and doubled over. We both stifled our giggles and got back to work. Now we were going to engage both "glutes" and see if they could work as a team.

"Squeeze them both; let's see how strong you are," Cody said, keeping one finger jammed in the side of the right buttock to continue pinpointing the source of the pain. I squeezed as hard as I could, but I was still misfiring.

"Pretend you have a million-dollar bill between them, and you don't want to lose it!" he said encouragingly. "Don't let it go!"

I began shaking and screeching with laughter. "I'm going to suffocate from laughing so much!" I shouted, my face still half-buried in the pillow. Finally I got control of my snickers and squeezed in earnest. Cody shoved two pillows under my stomach.

"Try pulling in your core at the same time you're squeezing," Cody instructed, drawing in two fingers on my lower back, indicating how he wanted me to pull in my abdominal muscles. "This will isolate that glute." He turned his gaze to the red-haired student. Once in a while when the student didn't have much to do, Cody would command him to try out something a patient was doing so he could feel it firsthand. The student scrambled to attention and looked at him expectantly.

"You try it too. Do an anterior tilt with your pelvis and squeeze back your bent leg. Feel it? If there's a posterior tilt, it won't work as well." The student looked a little baffled, but he did as he was told. From the corner of my eye, I watched him suck in his stomach and kick his leg behind him trying to simulate the same butt cheek squeeze that I was doing.

"Okay, you can get up. I'll show you one more thing to help that right-side glute fire," Cody said, tapping my back and then slapping the side of the table. He grasped the table with his right hand as he leaned back into his bent right leg. He lifted his left foot slightly off the ground as he did a squat on his right leg. I grasped the corner of the table and followed suit.

"Really sit back. That's why you're grabbing the table, so you can go pretty far down without falling." I scrunched down toward the floor and continued trying to squeeze my right butt cheek and not let my back or other big leg muscles try to take over.

"Really appreeeeeeciate the feeling," Cody said, doing a slow squat to illustrate his drawn-out words. "Then come back up. Appreeeeeeciate, then back up."

"Appreeeeeeciate," I mused, rolling the word around in my mouth. "There's something poetic about that."

"Just do your squats." Cody smirked and walked away to check on a patient who was resting her injured back on a heating pad. After I finished appreciating the burning sensation from those one-legged squats, I returned to the exam room so Cody could take a final assessment of my ever-irritated left psoas muscle. While my first experience with the joys of psoas massage was on the right side, which had presented the hip impingement, we discovered over the next several weeks that my left hip was tightening up significantly.

Although my strength was improving in my right leg, my left leg continued to compensate by working harder. As the stronger standing leg, the left leg had been bearing the brunt of the labor for years, and it wasn't about to shirk its duties now. My balance was vastly better on the left leg, as was my strength and stability, which was evident during the squats, leg lifts, and other therapeutic exercises I was assigned. It was only natural, then, for the muscles in that leg to thicken and tighten with the burden of doing the work for both hips. Nearly every week, Cody had to dig his fingers into my left psoas muscle to relieve the tightness and irritation, and more often than not, I experienced a pain I had not fathomed before.

"I'm feeling pretty good. I think those exercises loosened me up," I said excitedly to Cody as he dug his thumbs into the sacroiliac joints on the back of my pelvis and drummed my vertebrae with his fingers. I hoped my positive outlook would somehow lessen the inevitable pain I knew was soon to come.

"Mmm-hmm, we'll see about that. Bend down for me," Cody instructed, pinpointing the pelvic joints with his hands as I rolled over to touch my toes and slowly stood back up as I breathed deeply. I assumed my position lying on the table and bent my right leg.

"Hey . . . this side feels really good!" I said as he thoughtfully pressed his fingers into my right psoas muscle. He dug around some more and then bent my leg in farther to see if it still pinched in the front, indicating the hip impingement syndrome. It did tingle, but it wasn't nearly as painful as it was when I had first seen the orthopedic doctor.

"Which means the left side might be really bad!" we said in unison and widened our eyes at each other. I sighed as if heading toward the gallows, bent my left leg as Cody walked around the side of the table, and prayed for the best. I thought about how interesting it was that Cody could use his hands as his second set of eyes, tiny cameras that could sink through layers of clothing, skin, fat, and connective tissue to help him identify every muscle, joint, tendon, and bone. It was like he was reading my body by Braille.

"I think it's amazing how you can just tell by feel which muscle is which. It must have taken you a long time to—oh!" I was silenced by an angry, burning sensation deep in my left hip, right near the socket itself.

I have never experienced pain like this in my life. It's not that I have an unusually high tolerance for pain, but most of the time, I'm a trooper about enduring it. This "massage" was pushing my limits, though. When I began to feel searing pain shooting from Cody's fingertips, I nearly slapped his hands away in a primal instinct to protect myself. Instead I gasped and clenched my fists into angry white balls and breathed sharply through gritted teeth, even though his fingers sank deeper into my hip socket with every exhale, and the white-hot pain burned brighter. I shoved my fists into my eyes, which I had screwed shut as a way to calm my panicking lizard brain. Sweat began to break out on my forehead, and tears sprang to my eyes. My inhales became shakier as I sipped in air and tried to mentally escape the present situation. I imagined myself in a new dobok, with the telltale black lapels of an instructor. A shining, perfect black belt encircled my wai—

"*Ouch*!!"

"You're doing great; just breathe," Cody murmured gently. "Back to what you were saying—yes, I've been doing this long enough that I can feel what's going on. The students . . . well, I think they get a little scared. They'll get their hands into the muscle, but if the patient flinches, they immediately back off. They have to power through it and . . . stay there."

As if to emphasize his point, he kept his hands pressed firmly and deeply into my hip even as I was gulping for air and turning red. He dug deeper and deeper until his fingers no longer felt human and were instead piping hot daggers burning into my flesh. I rolled my tear-filled eyes into the back of my head and hoped at some point I would go numb.

"*Whoo!*" I laughed weakly with relief when he finally removed his hands. "I almost cried!"

"You *were* crying," Cody replied dryly. "I think I just did an exorcism."

Later that night I discovered a pink bruise on my hip. That must have been where the demon pain exited. It *had been* an exorcism.

CHAPTER 38

Final Exam

S peaking of exorcisms, late October 2015 was marked by flooding of Biblical proportions. Fall in North Texas can be quite pleasant—it's mild and breezy like spring but without tornadoes and hailstorms. Unfortunately, Texas weather is quite temperamental, so sometimes fall can also be a dangerous time of heavy rain and flash flooding. The days leading up to my black belt test made me consider trading in my Honda sedan for an ark. Rain burst from the bloated sky, and water gushed furiously down Fort Worth's streets, washing away cars and scattering debris in its wake. I wondered if this was some sort of final cosmic test of my will before I could earn my black belt.

Although I had long anticipated my black belt test, I savored the last few weeks leading up to it. I was alert, but I wasn't anxious. During the month of October, something inside me had shifted. It wasn't that my energy was low. It was just a different energy. I felt calmer, more careful, and more calculating. During each class, I wanted to practice the calm I'd hoped to feel during my test, when I knew my adrenaline would be pumping, and my nerves would be dancing furiously. I wanted to be able to control my breathing, my heart rate, and most importantly, my thinking while I was performing kicks, sparring with a partner, or breaking a board with my fist. Surprisingly, I didn't feel very nervous during those last few weeks, torrential rainfall and all, and I'd stopped having anxious taekwondo-related dreams about forgetting forms . . . and in one instance forgetting my pants.

I was quieter during the final classes leading up to my test. I still smiled a lot and joked around with my instructors and other students, but I was more subdued. There was no point in trying to cram or make any major changes to the way I did things. I had learned everything I needed to learn up to this point, so now what I needed to focus on was minor fine-tuning and making sure I was comfortable with what I needed to do. I was down to a lean 115 pounds, and my hamstring pain had lessened considerably. My instructors often teased me that I was a black belt already thanks to my dedication and hard work, but I would just shake my head and say softly, "No. Not yet. Let me earn it."

The day of the test was a family affair. My parents, grandparents, cousin, and my cousin's girlfriend had traveled from Tulsa and braved the Texas floods to be with me on my special day. The last time my extended family had gathered together just for me was at my graduation for my master's degree in library science twelve years prior. Graduation is different from a black belt test, though, because when I received my diplomas, I was severing my ties with my universities. I was so sick of exams, classes, paperwork, and projects. By the time I donned a cap and gown, I couldn't wait to get away from my respective schools.

When I got my MBA in 2012, I skipped graduation altogether, instead choosing to spend the weekend in Tulsa with my parents, where I celebrated in a much more understated way by sipping wine and smoking a cigar in the backyard with my dad. No crowds, no boring speeches, no fuss, and I had a nice little buzz going. I didn't even have to wear shoes.

Unlike a college graduation, my black belt test was an event that further solidified my commitment to my dojang. It was more like when I went through the sacrament of Confirmation at my Catholic church in Snyder. Catholics don't get much of a choice about whether to be baptized or not, since it usually happens shortly after birth, so Confirmation is a chance to circle back with the young Catholic and ask, "Are you sure you want to do this?"

The Confirmation ceremony marks the moment young people take responsibility for nurturing their faith and to state, "Yep, I'm in it for the long haul." A black belt test holds the same significance: the student makes a commitment to stick it out and go through the tough stuff in order to reap great spiritual and emotional rewards. Whether it's Confirmation or a black belt test, your grandma is there, your forehead gets greasy, and if you're lucky, there's cake afterward. Yep, I was in this taekwondo thing for the long haul . . . and for cake.

On October 24, 2015, the day of my black belt test, I wondered if I would still have that sense of calm and ease that had guided me through the last few weeks and days of training or if my anxiety was going to rear up with a vengeance. Even though I always felt well-prepared and confident during my color belt tests, something, whether it was my subconscious or sympathetic nervous system, dialed up my anxiety. A few minutes into a color belt test would leave me feeling stiff, shaky, sweaty, and breathing shallowly.

As luck would have it (sort of), over the final days leading up to the test, I was so distracted by caring for my aching right hamstring, staving off some threatening lower back pain, and making sure I arrived home safely after driving through the treacherous North Texas rain that I seemed to have used up any remaining anxiety. I spent the morning of the test going through my usual ritual: stretching and sipping ginger ale with a soft ice pack stuffed into my sports bra under my lucky black testing tank shirt. I used an electronic back massager to warm up my hamstring, which was still behaving itself for the most part. After my family and I arrived at the dojang, I changed into my uniform, greeted my instructors and fellow testing students, and began to warm up. I wondered when my heart would start to flutter. So far, so good.

Testing for first degree black belt is a little bit like what I imagine freshman hazing to be: everyone is yelling at you, you jump on command, and you feel like an idiot. They could yell at me all they wanted. At this point all I cared about was (1) remembering my right from my left foot during the flying kick portion, (2) nailing my board-breaking sequence, and (3) not throwing my back out or ripping my hamstring.

A black belt test, at least for first degree, is basically a blown-up version of a color belt test in terms of structure. After formally lining up and bowing to Grandmaster, students sat on the side of the room until they were called up by Grandmaster, one of the masters who flanked him on either side, or by Chief Instructor Alex, who was responsible for giving all the commands during the test. Just like a color belt test, there are kicking requirements, forms, self-defense, free sparring, and board breaking. I decided to psych myself out and pretend I was just attending an extra-long class in my old familiar dojang with the instructors and classmates I had grown so close to over the past few years. Nervous yet? Nah.

Testing for first degree black belt is essentially demonstrating that the student has mastered all color belt techniques, or what we consider basic training. We began by doing every kick and kicking combination we had learned up until this point: snap kicks, roundhouse kicks, side kicks, back kicks, spin kicks, combinations of multiple kicks, and every sliding, jumping, and flying version of the basic kicks. This added up to thirty kicking requirements, performed on both the right and left sides. We had done mock tests a few times, so I knew what to expect and paced myself as I had when I ran half marathons. I conserved my energy, controlled my breathing, and concentrated on execution and form. Was I sweaty, red, and disgusting by the end of this section? Most certainly. Was I nervous? Nope.

Forms and self-defense went well following the kicking portion, although I had a momentary blip of forgetfulness. We did several different forms, and during the simplest form's simplest movement (stepping forward and punching), I froze and felt as if I had suddenly awoken from a dream. *Where am I? Who are all these people? Why am I dressed like this? Oh shit, I forgot everything . . . oh wait, step forward and punch! Whew!* Was I nervous after that minor flake-out? Honestly . . . no.

Even though sparring was probably my weakest taekwondo skill, I always felt the most relaxed during the sparring portion of belt tests. Sparring forces me to be present and single-minded. Being distracted even for a second can lead to getting bashed in the stomach (or the face). Students testing at the black belt level did not wear pads. The purpose was not so much to make hard contact but to demonstrate speed, accuracy, skill, variety of technique, and most importantly, control. When sparring without pads, my classmates and I inevitably made light contact when blocking kicks or punches (besides, two people kicking at the air look stupid after a while), but we avoided hard blows to the body and head.

For one of my fights, I was paired with a tall teenage girl who had trained at a different school with one of the masters. She was prim and soft-spoken, and although she was skilled, when she had attended training sessions with us, she seemed aloof and disinterested. Our sparring match started without fanfare, and at one point, frankly, I got bored. She seemed to be walking through the motions, and I was there to have fun, so I amped up the energy level (and moved the violence dial up just a smidge). Even though I genuinely like everyone I've fought with, I always add in the tiniest dash of crazy to keep it interesting. Swiping a hook kick at someone's face keeps them at bay for a moment, and it makes a petite little flower like me look like a bloodthirsty psycho, which is exactly what I wanted them to think. I suppose this next part was a bit immature, but I said I was sometimes the villain, remember? I skirted around my opponent, moving in on her aggressively and throwing kicks at her furiously. I was just getting into a nice vicious groove when Grandmaster spoke up.

"Miss *Gibson*," he said pointedly, smirking slightly and motioning his palms downward as a silent gesture for me to back off.

"Yes, sir," I said sweetly, smiling brightly and trying to stifle a giggle. My grandmother later told me how surprised and impressed she was that a delicate little woman like me could put up such a fight against this girl and against two other bigger teenage boys. Bingo! Who doesn't like showing off for their grandparents? And you may be wondering, was I nervous throughout this portion of the test? You should know the answer to that by now.

The board-breaking portion was especially meaningful. Not only did it mark the end of an incredible and hard-won journey, but it brought me full circle to my childhood taekwondo days in Snyder. Master Weber, now a seventh degree black belt who still operated his branch school in my West Texas hometown, had traveled to Fort Worth to attend the test. He had known me as a shy, sensitive ten-year-old and was reintroduced to a shrieking, sweating, slightly less shy thirty-six-year-old woman. Not only was he watching me complete my testing requirements, but he was also in on the action and served as one of my board holders for my breaking portion. I was called to the floor, bowed to Grandmaster, and was asked what techniques I would be using.

"I will start with a jump roundhouse kick with the right foot, then do a spinning back fist with the right hand, and I will end with a flying snap kick on the left foot," I said confidently in my best facilitator voice. Master Weber held the board for the jump roundhouse kick, Chief Instructor Alex and another black belt stood next to him ready for the back fist, and one of the masters stood a few feet away holding a board above his head for my finale, a flying snap kick.

After I carefully placed my holders just so, I paused and let out a deep exhale. Go time. I bounced into the air and bashed the first board with the jump roundhouse kick. *Pop!* Then I turned around and slammed my knuckles into two boards with the spinning back fist. *Crack!* I turned toward my final holder, ran a few paces, and leapt into the air, scissoring and extending my legs like a dancer as the top of my left foot crashed up through the final board. *Smash!* The room broke into applause.

Nervous? Not in a million years.

We lined up to bow to the flags and to our superiors. After dismissal, the masters made their way down the line of students, bowing and shaking hands with each person.

"*Told you it was easy,*" whispered Chief Instructor Alex as he grasped my hand. My parents and grandparents rushed out of their chairs to embrace me.

"That was really good! It was fun to watch!" Mom exclaimed.

"Good job, pumpkin!" Dad chimed in.

"I think I need a grandparents sandwich," I said, sliding in between Grandma and Grandpa as they hugged me from either side. After chatting with Grandmaster, Master Weber, Chief Instructor Alex, and the other masters, my family trekked back to my condo. Another cousin from Dallas, her brother, husband, and two little girls were already en route. Once everyone arrived, we popped open the bottle of Veuve Clicquot champagne I'd been saving. And just like after my Confirmation Mass twenty-three years earlier, we had cake. All was right with the world again.

A few days later Grandmaster awarded us our black belts. There was no special ceremony, no decorated judges' table, no fanfare. During a regular class night, we were instructed to sit down while Grandmaster, with Chief Instructor Alex's help, handed out stiff, plain black belts to my classmates and me. Our official black belts, which would be embroidered with our names and rank, would arrive in the mail a few weeks later, so we made do with our temporary belts. We eagerly wrapped our belts, still heavily creased from being wrapped tightly with rubber bands, around our waists and took a few photos. After the hours-long test and fun family gathering, it felt very understated, which in an odd way seemed appropriate. This wasn't the end of my journey. It was simply a step along the way.

EPILOGUE

The Beginning

I n early November, two weeks after I was awarded my black belt,
Grandmaster received the shipment we'd been eagerly awaiting:
new doboks and official belts for the newly promoted students. Our
new belts had our full names and the school's name embroidered in
bright yellow in both English and Korean. I had already changed
into my faded white uniform and plain temporary black belt when
Grandmaster motioned for me to come into his office.

"Look, the new doboks are here! Go change. I want to see."
He held out a plastic package with a crisp uniform folded neatly
inside. Black belt uniforms are typically better quality than stan-
dard plain white uniforms and are most noticeably distinguished
by black lapels. I examined the labeling and frowned.

"But it says size four on the package. I wear size three—"

"It's a three. I already checked it. Go change!" Grandmaster
smacked my shoulder with the package and shoved it into my
hand.

I nodded sheepishly and trotted to the back of the dojang to
change uniforms in the women's restroom.

Wearing my new, stiff, glowing-white dobok with black lapels, I gazed at my reflection in the square restroom mirror. I hadn't yet become accustomed to the stark black around my waist, since I'd been so used to seeing a pop of red for nearly two years. I rested my left hand on the knot in the center of my belt while I ran my right hand along the thick, ribbed black cloth. My fingers traced my name along one end of the belt. At the bottom of the other end of the belt was a single embroidered yellow stripe: first degree black belt. It was a signifier of both a great accomplishment and the many years of training (and stripes) I had ahead of me.

There's a pervasive misconception that a black belt marks the end of one's taekwondo training. While my comrades in martial arts know that couldn't be further from the truth, it seemed like everyone I spoke to outside of that realm (other than my parents, who knew damn well I wasn't leaving the dojang) thought I had reached the peak of my martial arts proficiency. Right after I tested for black belt, several friends and coworkers asked, "Now what?" as if I'd gone as far as I could, and it was now time to go do something else. Even Chief Instructor Alex seemed surprised when I showed up to class the Monday after the test wearing the same eager, goofy grin as always. I didn't want to "reward" myself with a day off. I was too excited about learning something new.

Some people also assumed that as a first degree black belt, I was suddenly the most deadly, lethal creature in the world. If I had a nickel for every dumb joke someone made along the lines of "Oh, I'd better not make you mad!" or "Do you have to register your hands with the police now?" I'd be able to buy a different dobok for every day of the week.

The reality was: I was back at the beginning. In fact, the little mnemonic we had around the dojang was that *jyo kyo neem*, a Korean term that roughly translates to "assistant instructor," the label designated for first degree black belts, means you're a "joke," because you're at the bottom again.

I might have become a first degree black belt, but in terms of taekwondo expertise, I was still a novice. I was like a rambunctious toddler who had become very good at running around, screaming, and breaking stuff but was still stumped by situations that required more refined motor skills and intellectual capability, such as buttoning a shirt. I still had so much to learn.

By the time I reached my black belt, I had only just recently begun to break some bad sparring habits. I'd also only had a few opportunities to try out defense against weapons, during which I'd spent my time flapping my hands, giggling, and getting "killed" because I couldn't think or move quickly enough when my opponent slashed at me with a rubber knife. I still couldn't quite remember all of the color belt one-step sparring (self-defense) techniques. And my jumping spin kick? If that's all I could use to defend myself, I'd better just go full Texan and buy a gun.

I'm not discounting the skills I learned in lower ranks. Color belt training, from white belt all the way to bo dan, provided me with a strong foundation to build upon for the decades I have ahead of me as a black belt. I knew that remaining static in my practice and assuming I'd learned all there was to learn would not get me to the next level.

Being a newbie again was actually refreshing. It would keep my mind active and my body on high alert. One of my favorite songs by rapper Jay-Z is "My First Song," which is about treating each project as if it were his first song, no matter how rich and famous he became. The best part is the introduction, an interview with the late rapper The Notorious B.I.G. Biggie gives some sound advice on how to approach one's passions: stay humble, work hard, and act as if you were an intern on the first day of a job. That's how I wanted to approach taekwondo: a black belt maturity on the outside with white belt curiosity and humility on the inside. I was a veritable martial arts Oreo.

Taekwondo would hopefully be a lifelong and ever-evolving practice. The fact that there was so much to learn and master at every black belt level gave me hope that I would never become jaded and complacent. My instructors and classmates are stuck with me as long as I can tie a belt around my waist and jump around with them in class.

~~~

Still in the women's restroom, I straightened my black lapels and hooked my thumbs into my new belt as I took stock of the changes that had occurred in me in the last three years.

My face was less gaunt than it had been before I returned to taekwondo, as I was no longer subsisting on whiskey and sleeping pills for my nightly meal. My shoulders and biceps were rounded from countless punches and push-ups, and my thighs had grown thick and defined from repetitive kicking and jumping. My right hamstring still ached with the lingering pain I'd been experiencing for the last four months, and the rest of my joints and muscles creaked and sighed with the memories of old injuries and strains. My forearms were dotted with bruises from the grips and blows of opponents. A single tiny gray hair had sprouted at the left corner of my forehead. Beyond the black belt, the sturdy legs, the aches and pains, and even the new gray hair was the largest and most welcome change of all: the self-reliance and steady confidence that now emanated from my heart.

I was still eager to please and liked to put smiles on people's faces, but I no longer worried whether people liked me. I still enjoyed and appreciated compliments, but they paled in comparison to how I now felt about myself. I finally recognized that I was a good person and accepted myself for who I was. I stopped second-guessing myself and apologizing for my existence. I knew I could kick ass in other parts of my life as much as I could in a sparring match.

One of the most profound changes in me was my newfound freedom from the "need" to be in a relationship in order to be happy. I had wrapped up much of my self-worth in what men thought of me. Since my late teens, I'd thought I needed a man's love, or at the very least, a man's attention, to feel happy and whole. I had wasted years chasing men who would never love, respect, or even acknowledge me. The more I pursued the love I was incapable of providing myself, the emptier I felt inside. By practicing taekwondo, I learned how to respect and love myself more than a man ever could.

As for Ricardo, I think we both needed each other as support systems until we were able to function independently on our own. Our independence took us in separate and irreconcilable directions. It was comforting to have someone who cared about me at my early color belt tests, but by the time we split, I knew I was strong enough to continue the journey to black belt by myself. My family, the people who truly loved me and accepted me for who I was, were at the test that mattered the most. I doubt I would have had the eerie sense of calm I experienced the day of my black belt test had I been worrying about the fate of my relationship.

Although my story began as a reluctant romantic comedy, this is not a memoir that ends with an eleventh-hour love story. I didn't catch the eye of a hunky transfer student from another taekwondo school, and I didn't reopen my online dating profile, which is how I'd met Ricardo. Unlike my reactions to previous breakups, I chose not to pursue dating after Ricardo and I ended our relationship. I wanted to allow myself ample time to grieve what I had lost and be grateful for what I had gained. I had never appreciated being single before. I'd always resented the lonely nights and silent weekends as I spent my time agonizing over unrequited love or desperation for someone new. Now, for the first time in my life, I felt grateful and content to be on my own. I was excited about exploring all the possibilities for adventure that I had brushed aside in my vain pursuits of relationships. Gratitude, joy, and self-respect had replaced the tears, neediness, and bitterness.

While taekwondo helped me find myself, it also helped me find my people. Although I've always been and will always be a lone wolf, I'd been searching for a community where I felt complete acceptance. I knew I needed to connect with others, if only to get out of my house once in a while, and more importantly, out of my churning, depressed mind. Nothing stuck—not the Bible study groups, running clubs, swing dance and tango enthusiasts, or fair-weather friends—until I rejoined the taekwondo ranks after a twenty-two-year absence. I had found my second home and my second family at the dojang.

Taekwondo drew me out of my hardened shell as I interacted with my classmates and instructors. I felt so much joy in my practice that I couldn't wait to share it with others through teaching and coaching. I was able to give of myself freely without feeling the need to be guarded or evasive. In taekwondo class I could be a better version of myself. I could be a doting, compassionate mother, a role I will never want in "real life"; a leader that I'll never strive to be in my professional life; and a funny, outgoing, loyal friend, which I haven't been capable of being to people who've known me outside of taekwondo.

I wondered how different I might have been had I stayed with taekwondo as a child. It would have given me purpose, focus, and discipline and, more importantly, calmed me the hell down. Perhaps I could have avoided the crushing disappointments of my dating misadventures, the unnecessary worry over getting through school and finding jobs, and the haunting torment of my depression and anxiety. Maybe there wouldn't have been so many nights spent sobbing on the floor, wailing in frustration, and resenting the agony of being stuck in the suicidal limbo of not wanting to live but also being too afraid to die.

On the other hand, perhaps it was just as well that my family and I stopped training in 1991 when I was twelve. If I had earned my black belt as a teenager, I might have simply turned my interests toward other activities, which is what I've seen happen to some of the younger students at my dojang. I certainly wouldn't have appreciated the emotional and mental journey of earning my black belt if I'd gone through the process as a child. Had I made it to black belt back then, taekwondo might have fizzled into the blurred memories of my youth and would have never demanded a resurrection the way it did when I was thirty-three.

Maybe I had to go through all that unpleasantness—the breakups, the panic attacks, the crying jags, the death wishes, the anxiety—to become who I am today. Had I not gotten to the brink of total mental self-destruction, I would not have been motivated to change. I would not have gained the exponential growth I'd experienced through taekwondo. No, I wouldn't change a thing.

My therapist, Ramona, once remarked that I seemed to be "becoming more real," not too dissimilar from the comment my boss had made about my blossoming personality. I had been hiding my pain and anxiety behind a mask of superficial accomplishments for so long that I didn't know how to truly be myself. Once I began to accept and appreciate who I was through the strides I made in counseling and the leaps I made in taekwondo, the protective façade began to crumble. I thought about Ramona's comment as I stood in front of the restroom mirror at the dojang, looking into my staring blue eyes and gazing at my black belt, the symbolic manifestation of who I had become and who I really was.

I came back to taekwondo when my mind and heart were finally tired of fighting. Oddly enough, kicking and screaming in taekwondo class finally quieted the kicking and screaming inside my soul and mind. It forced me to grow up. I became more optimistic and laughed a lot more. I stepped up to challenges and no longer felt threatened or intimidated by the people around me. Now that I knew how to fight, I no longer went looking for a fight. I took charge of my life and refused to allow myself to continue playing the helpless (and blameless) victim. I found a strength in myself that had been silent for too long.

A rap at the door pulled me out of my daydream.

"Melanie, are you ready? We're about to start class!" a fellow black belt called through the closed door. I blinked and took a deep breath.

"Yes, I'll be right there!" I straightened my black lapels one last time, pulled the ends of my new black belt taut, and smiled. I narrowed my eyes at my reflection as I straightened my shoulders. Not bad for a cubicle dweller who's pushing forty. Not bad at all.

I pranced onto the training floor, my heavy new uniform rustling like a giant Chinese paper lantern. I twirled around, and my classmates smiled admiringly and congratulated me on my promotion. Chief Instructor Alex rolled his eyes and smiled.

"Get in line, Black Belt."

I giggled and ran to the front of the room, eager to begin my new journey.

Acknowledgments

J ust as when I trained for and earned my black belt, I have been supported and guided by several kind and talented people as I brought this book into existence. Many thanks to Brooke Warner, Samantha Strom, Jennifer Caven, Julie Metz, and the team at She Writes Press for taking a chance on my book and guiding me through this exciting process. My thanks also goes to Linda Joy Myers for her coaching during the class she co-taught with Brooke Warner, "Write Your Memoir in Six Months." What began as a whim and a few words on a computer screen has become a dream realized.

A bow and a gamsahamneda to all my taekwondo instructors and fellow black belts for their knowledge, patience, and partnership: Greg and Donna Gafford, AJ Wall IV, Christina Compton, Won Chik Park, Terry Avery, Riad Nusrallah, Jim Long, Nate Hernandez, Talia Hernandez, Erin Fry, James Kang, Danny Hendrix, Adriana Gonzalez, Jake Castillo, Shawn Huynh, Vivian Weinman, Elizabeth Perez Azerad, Liam McCracken, Diego Ruiz, Austin Mar, Zachary Dilling, Sarah Ziehme, and others. I also offer a bow to my long-term students and now fellow black belts Mackinley, Quinn, Brenna, and Emry Fesmire. I will still yell at you to keep your hands up no matter how old we all get.

Big hugs to Margaret Blakely and Meredith Oney for coaching me through the rough parts, celebrating the good parts, and telling me the things I didn't want to hear when they were what I needed most.

A blinking page in cyberspace connected me to martial arts devotees across the world. Thank you to my Little Black Belt blog readers. You've helped bring my words to life.

My fellow authors (and Texans) Sophornia Davis and Troy Bernhardt inspired me to chase my writing dreams early in my memoir journey. Thank you.

I am indebted to Robert Knight and Scott Bowersox for putting me back together on numerous occasions.

Thank you to my brother, Michael, and sister-in-law, Stephanie, for their support and encouragement of my taekwondo and writing pursuits (and a bonus to Michael for being my very first sparring partner).

Finally, my gratitude and love go to my parents, John and Denise Gibson, for introducing me to taekwondo, loving me, and listening to me through every step of my journey to black belt and beyond.

About the Author

Melanie Gibson was raised in Snyder, Texas, where she began taekwondo training at age ten. She has a bachelor's degree in English from Texas Woman's University, a master's in library science from the University of North Texas, and an MBA from the University of Texas at Arlington. Melanie has worked in the healthcare industry since 2004, with roles as a hospital librarian, corporate trainer, and learning designer. Melanie continues to pursue advanced taekwondo black belt degrees and writes about martial arts and life in general on her blog Little Black Belt (http://littleblackbelt.com). She lives in Fort Worth, Texas.

Author photo © Wesley Kirk of Vision & Verve

Selected Titles from She Writes Press

She Writes Press is an independent publishing company founded to serve women writers everywhere. Visit us at www.shewritespress.com.

Learning to Eat Along the Way by Margaret Bendet. $16.95, 978-1-63152-997-9. After interviewing an Indian holy man, newspaper reporter Margaret Bendet follows him in pursuit of enlightenment and ends up facing demons that were inside her all along.

A Different Kind of Same: A Memoir by Kelley Clink. $16.95, 978-1-63152-999-3. Several years before Kelley Clink's brother hanged himself, she attempted suicide by overdose. In the aftermath of his death, she traces the evolution of both their illnesses, and wonders: If he couldn't make it, what hope is there for her?

Broken Whole: A Memoir by Jane Binns. $16.95, 978-1-63152-433-2. At the age of thirty-five, desperate to salvage a self that has been suffocating for years, Jane Binns leaves her husband of twelve years. She has no plan or intention but to leave, however—and there begin the misadventures lying in wait for her.

Insatiable: A Memoir of Love Addiction by Shary Hauer. $16.95, 978-1-63152-982-5. An intimate and illuminating account of corporate executive—and secret love addict—Shary Hauer's migration from destructive to healthy love.

Manifesting Me: A Story of Rebellion and Redemption by Leah E. Reinhart. $16.95, 978-1-63152-383-0. When Leah Reinhart was six years old, her family joined a cult in Oakland, California—and she spent much of her life afterward trying to break free of the damaging patterns she was taught there.

Don't Leave Yet: How My Mother's Alzheimer's Opened My Heart by Constance Hanstedt. $16.95, 978-1-63152-952-8. The chronicle of Hanstedt's journey toward independence, self-assurance, and connectedness as she cares for her mother, who is rapidly losing her own identity to the early stage of Alzheimer's.